BOMBS IN THE CONSULTING ROOM

What does one do when a dangerous paedophile, nearly six feet seven inches in height, threatens to kill you? How does one manage when a brain-damaged, psychotic patient spits on the office floor two hundred times during the first consultation? And what does one say when one member of a warring couple reveals the most horrific acts of sexual cruelty?

In perhaps his most gripping book to date, Professor Brett Kahr offers colleagues a detailed glimpse into the challenge of working with highly distressed and disturbing individuals in long-term psychotherapy. Kahr explains the ways in which such deeply troubled people hurl "bombs" into the consulting room, leaving considerable "psychological shrapnel" in their wake.

The book contains five sensitively and compellingly written clinical chapters, followed by several historical chapters that explore the ways in which Donald Winnicott attempted to manage the bombs in his consulting room, often of his own making. Kahr then examines the pioneering contribution of Enid Eichholz (later Enid Balint) who, during the Second World War, created marital psychoanalysis as a means of dealing with couples ravaged by actual wartime bombs. The book concludes with an historico-clinical chapter on how thoughtful and sophisticated classical interpretation can reduce the impact of clinical bombs. Kahr even provides us with an examination of his favourite "top ten" interpretations in the history of psychoanalysis!

A unique and helpful volume, written by a practitioner steeped equally in psychoanalysis and history, *Bombs in the Consulting Room: Surviving Psychological Shrapnel* will be essential reading for anyone who has ever felt frightened while treating patients.

Professor Brett Kahr has worked in the mental health field for over forty years. He is Senior Fellow at the Tavistock Institute of Medical Psychology in London and Senior Clinical Research Fellow in Psychotherapy and Mental Health at the Centre for Child Mental Health in London. A Trustee of the Freud Museum London and of Freud Museum Publications, he has written or edited fourteen books, and he has served as series editor for more than fifty-five other titles. He is Consultant Psychotherapist at The Balint Consultancy and works full-time with individuals and couples in London.

Books by Brett Kahr

D.W. Winnicott: A Biographical Portrait (1996)

Forensic Psychotherapy and Psychopathology:
Winnicottian Perspectives, Editor (2001)

Exhibitionism (2001)

The Legacy of Winnicott:
Essays on Infant and Child Mental Health, Editor (2002)

Sex and the Psyche (2007)

Who's Been Sleeping in Your Head?
The Secret World of Sexual Fantasies (2008)

Life Lessons from Freud (2013)

Tea with Winnicott (2016)

Coffee with Freud (2017)

New Horizons in Forensic Psychotherapy:
Exploring the Work of Estela V. Welldon, Editor (2018)

How to Flourish as a Psychotherapist (2019)

Celebrity Mad:
Why Otherwise Intelligent People Worship Fame (2020)

On Practising Therapy at 1.45 A.M.:
Adventures of a Clinician (2020)

BOMBS IN THE CONSULTING ROOM

Surviving Psychological Shrapnel

Brett Kahr

Routledge
Taylor & Francis Group

LONDON AND NEW YORK

First published 2020
by Routledge
2 Park Square, Milton Park, Abingdon, Oxon OX14 4RN

and by Routledge
52 Vanderbilt Avenue, New York, NY 10017

Routledge is an imprint of the Taylor & Francis Group, an informa business

British Library Cataloguing-in-Publication Data
A catalogue record for this book is available from the British Library

Library of Congress Cataloging-in-Publication Data
A catalog record has been requested for this book

ISBN: 978–1–78220–660–6 (pbk)
ISBN: 978–0–429-43895–0 (ebk)

Edited, designed, and typeset in Palatino
by Communication Crafts, East Grinstead

To four truly awe-inspiring teachers:
Dr Bernard Barnett,
Dr Abrahão Brafman,
the late Dr Susanna Isaacs Elmhirst,
Dr Laura Etchegoyen.
These wonderful men and women have taught me so very much
about defusing bombs.
I thank them with my deepest gratitude.

"Wel may *þe* barn blesse *þat* hym to book sette."
[Well may the bairn bless whoever set him to books.]

William Langland, Will's Visions of Piers Plowman, Do-Well,
Do-Better and Do-Best, c. 1362–1399, B-Text, Passus XII, line 187
[Langland, c. 1362–1399, p. 476]

CONTENTS

PART **II**
Inflaming and defusing bombs

BOMBS IN THE CONSULTING ROOM

I am very sorry indeed that I had to miss your paper. A patient of mine blew up and had to be seen that evening.

Dr Donald Winnicott, Letter to Dr John Klauber, 9 November 1964
[Winnicott, 1964b]

Introduction

When you are among your olives, think occasionally of a panic-stricken and scribbling ghost, through whose phantasmal brain a million frenzies are forever pouring—in vain! in vain!

Giles Lytton Strachey, Letter to Virginia Stephen
(the future Virginia Woolf), 24 August 1908 [Strachey, 1908, p. 16]

During the 1940s, the bombs of the Nazi Luftwaffe had wreaked havoc on Londoners. Many people had lost their homes. Others had lost their limbs. And still others had lost their loved ones (Rudnytsky, 2000; Stansky, 2007; Kahr, 2017b). Some became so traumatised that they began to suffer from a new syndrome, which eventually became known as the "shelter neurosis" (Mackintosh, 1944, p. 29): a compulsive urge to seek refuge in underground bunkers, not only during air raids but, in fact, at every available opportunity.

Amid the carnage of the Second World War, an Englishwoman by the name of Mrs Enid Eichholz created a series of citizens' advice bureaux in London, designed to offer practical and emotional support to those devastated by these bombings. Fortunately, Enid Eichholz did not develop a "shelter neurosis"; by contrast she, like many of her fellow civilians, endured the attacks with calm and equilibrium. With characteristic British understatement, Eichholz (1944, p. 92) recalled, "When the flying bombs first began to fall most of us disliked them considerably."

These hugely deadly bombs caused damage of the most sadistic and disgusting variety and decimated untold numbers of lives. In fact, many of the children, grandchildren, and great-grandchildren of the victims of the 1940s air raids continue to experience the traumatic reverberations of such horrific experiences to this very day.

But bombs come in many shapes and sizes. And although one cannot compare an explosive bomb, replete with fuse, to bombs of a more metaphorical nature, every single practising mental health professional encounters "bombs" aplenty during the course of an ordinary working day in the consulting room.

Not long ago, one cold wintry morning, I unlocked the door to my office at 6.40 a.m., removed my overcoat, and then, seeing a flashing light on my telephone, I began to listen to the messages that had accumulated overnight on my answering machine. Before I could put down my briefcase, a crazed woman started to scream at me from the tiny electronic machine perched on my desk: "Brett Kahr, you fucking bastard . . . you don't know *me*, but I know *you* . . . I found your name on a website of therapists, and I need to see you. It's four in the morning, and I can't understand why you're not picking up the telephone. I need you. I need you *now*, you God-damned piece of shit. I hope you fuck off and die. I hope you die right now. I'm never calling you again. But please ring me back as soon as possible."

Although I have practised psychotherapy for well over thirty-five years, I had not received a telephone message of this nature before, nor have I since. I had never met this woman, and none of my colleagues had referred her to see me; and yet she found my number and left a most terror-inducing message on the machine—as though someone had thrown a bomb, or at least a grenade, into my office. In truth, I became rather shaky for a few brief moments and also rather concerned about my own physical safety. As the sole person in my office building at 6.40 a.m., I felt rather alone and even somewhat frightened.

As I collected my thoughts, I began to experience some compassion for this unknown woman, who had left no telephone number and who has not called again since. But I must confess I found her verbal attack extremely vicious and quite unsettling.

If the aforementioned Enid Eichholz had received a similar message on her telephone answering machine, I suspect that she would have tutted that she "disliked it considerably".

As psychotherapeutic and psychoanalytic practitioners, we must, of course, navigate many unpleasant situations. And although the vast majority of our patients will comport themselves with decency and with dignity, others do not.

I recently worked with a couple who had begged for assistance with their deeply anguished marriage. Both highly intelligent and accomplished professionals, they had come to hate one another with a sadistic passion. The wife would scream to me about her husband, seated only inches away, "He's a fucking piece of shit. I hope that he chokes on his own vomit. I hope that he dies, and that I'll get all of his money." The husband screamed back, "I can't stand that bitch. She's grown so old and fat. I find her body repellent. Just looking at her makes me want to become a homosexual."

Endeavouring to catch my breath and to collect my thoughts amid this salvo of verbal venom, I began to formulate an interpretation about the possible origins of such savagery, but before I could utter more than two or three words, this toxic couple then displaced their hatred onto me in the most tormenting fashion. The husband screamed, "Don't give us any of your Freudian shit. We've heard it all before. You're a fucking charlatan." The wife chimed in and declaimed, "And I can't believe the fees you charge. You're nothing but a greedy Jew."

Although I stood my ground and endeavoured to persevere with compassionate understanding and symbolic thinking, I did, at that moment, wish that I had never entered the mental health profession, lamenting to myself that I would have had a much calmer life had I studied accountancy!

Naturally, the "bombs" with which we have to contend—invariably expressions of unprocessed, undigested, and unneutralised infantile hostility—in no way compare to the bombs that Mrs Eichholz and her fellow Britons endured on the Home Front during the Second World War. But whether one experiences a physical bomb or a psychological one, the shrapnel can often sting, or even kill, and those of us who expose ourselves to such toxicity need a great deal of help and support.

Enid Eichholz worked very effectively with survivors of the London bombs, but she needed greater assistance, and so she eventually trained as a psychoanalyst and ultimately married a psychoanalyst, Dr Michael Balint, and became immortalised as Mrs Enid Balint.

In an attempt to engage with the question of psychological bombs and psychological shrapnel, I have assembled a series of essays in which I explore very different sorts of attacks in the consulting room. In Part I, I present five papers devoted to the theme of "engaging with bombs". In the first chapter I describe my work with a violent paedophile who threatened to kill me and who destroyed some of the furniture in my office. In the second chapter I offer an account of my efforts to treat an elderly woman who communicated entirely with spittle and drenched my office in saliva. In the third and fourth chapters I provide a glimpse into some horrific acts of cruelty perpetrated by marital couples, many of whom screamed so intensely and behaved so abominably towards one another—and, occasionally, towards me—that it became quite difficult to think during the course of psychoanalytic sessions. And in the fifth and final contribution to this section, I investigate the acts of cruelty perpetrated by otherwise peace-loving patients. In some cases, such acts of sadism had resulted unconsciously in one or more deaths prior to the commencement of treatment.

In Part II, I have included three quite different chapters, drawing upon my training and experience as an academic historian. These essays, on the general theme of "inflaming and defusing bombs", plumb the rich ancestry of psychoanalysis to explore how some of our leading forefathers and foremothers either ignited bombs in the consulting room through their own frailties or, by contrast, helped to defuse them through the application of sustained, sane labour.

Dr Donald Winnicott, one of the most potent figures in the history of world mental health, made so many contributions to our understanding of human psychology that he has spawned an entire library of grateful tributes (e.g., Kahr, 1996b, 2011b). But in spite of Winnicott's valiant work as an Air Raid Precautions warden in North London during the Second World War, and in spite of his capacity to survive deadly bombs on an all-too-frequent basis, Winnicott did, from time to time, propel some bombs of his own in the midst of his clinical work with highly challenging patients. In the first contribution to this section, I have examined how he sublimated his own hateful, bomb-like emotions into a brilliant theoretical and technical contribution—his classic paper on "Hate in the Counter-Transference" (Winnicott, 1949b). But, in spite of this remarkable achievement, Winnicott nevertheless also betrayed his classical psychoanalytic training and often became ensconced in some very dangerous bomb-like situations with some of his fragile patients.

In the second chapter in this section, I consider, by contrast, the majestic achievements of Winnicott's sometime analysand, Mrs Enid Balint (the former Mrs Enid Eichholz), who drew upon her deep resources of psychological sturdiness in order to defuse bombs aplenty by creating the field of marital psychoanalysis, helping untold numbers of couples in deep distress. During the Second World War both Donald Winnicott and Enid Eichholz Balint had to negotiate actual bombs falling from the sky, but Winnicott also unleashed some bombs of his own, while Balint contained quite a few. Thus, by turning to these archivally informed case histories, I believe that we might well enjoy the opportunity to learn from both the brilliance and from the disasters of our ancestors.

In the final offering in this section, I include a clinico-historical chapter about the role of the "interpretation" in psychological practice, underscoring how, in my estimation, this very classical but, nowadays, somewhat unfashionable method, pioneered by the early Freudians, still possesses the greatest ability to calm the troubled waters of the insane mind. I argue that the traditional interpretation, perhaps more than any other clinical intervention, helps psychoanalytic practitioners to defuse the bombs that we encounter so regularly in the consulting room.

I hope and trust that these eight chapters will provide young students and older colleagues alike with an immersion into some of the more unusual and painful moments of clinical practice both from a contemporary and also from an historical perspective. Although the consulting room will often be experienced by patient and analyst alike as a calm, thoughtful space in which horrible secrets may be revealed and explored, the office can also turn into a bomb site from time to time, especially when working with our more ill patients or with couples who bring the worst of themselves and of their marriages into our workplaces.

I earnestly hope that by sharing some of the uglier moments of clinical practice—the bombs and the shrapnel that follow—and by drawing upon instructive and inspiring episodes in our professional history, we can all learn some important object lessons that will help to fortify us in our future clinical struggles.

PART **I**

ENGAGING WITH BOMBS

The truth is, we like to talk over our disasters, because they are ours; and others like to listen, because they are not theirs.

"Comtesse de Soissons", in Anonymous [Letitia Elizabeth Landon],
Francesca Carrara: In Three Volumes. Vol. III, 1834.

CHAPTER ONE

The paedophile who threatened my life

The best chances of recovery in mental disease are obtained when a patient is treated early.

Dr Robert Henry Cole, *Mental Diseases: A Text-Book of Psychiatry for Medical Students and Practitioners*, 1913
[Cole, 1913, p. 291]

Many years ago, during a fifty-minute session in my consulting room, a teenage sex offender tried to kill me. Fortunately, I survived.

In the pages that follow, I provide some sense of my experience of working with this violent and troubled juvenile paedophile who threw bombs into the lives of several young people and who, in his psychotherapeutic sessions, also gave me a taste of that experience.

Clinical material

The case of Alfonso

The referral

I began to work with "Alfonso", a 16-year-old male sexual offender, in the latter months of 1996. Alfonso had committed several acts of sexual abuse, including not only undressing many prepubescent youngsters but also perpetrating full penetrative intercourse on three young girls, all aged 5 years.

Naturally, the local department of social services assigned to care for Alfonso had serious concerns about the aggressive behaviour of this young person. Alfonso had first come to the attention of the social services authority as a small boy: his mother had put him up for adoption during his eighth year, claiming that she could not care for him adequately; indeed, she feared that she might beat Alfonso physically if she had to continue living with him. During the previous year, Alfonso's father had died from a heart attack, and no doubt the sudden loss of his father proved highly unsettling, not only for Alfonso but also for his mother and his six siblings. Consequently, Alfonso then progressed from one foster care home to another, becoming increasingly violent towards both children and adults, hitting and screaming with great frequency.

At the age of 14, Alfonso attempted to strip a physically and intellectually disabled 10-year-old girl of her dress and brassiere; on another occasion, he had removed his own trousers and underpants in the presence of an 8-year-old girl in a toilet, urging her to take her clothing off as well. Later that year, he progressed to violent vaginal penetration with three different 5-year-old girls, whom he had abducted from a nearby playground. The local authorities became increasingly anxious that this troubled teenager posed a high level of risk to other young children; and a senior social worker referred the case to the Young Abusers Project: a pioneering collaboration among the Tavistock Clinic in London, the Department of Health, the National Society for the Prevention of Cruelty to Children, and the National Children's Home Action for Children.

The psychiatric assessment

Alfonso first presented to the Young Abusers Project in 1995, for both psychiatric and psychological assessments. His designated social worker requested an expert opinion on three particular issues and concerns:

1. a determination of the risk of significant harm that Alfonso posed to other people in the local community, especially young children, as a result of his physical violence and his sexually abusive behaviour;

2. a recommendation regarding the suitability of Alfonso's current foster care placement;
3. a recommendation for treatment options, should the Young Abusers Project be able to demonstrate that Alfonso did, indeed, suffer from a potentially treatable psychiatric condition.

In order to undertake a full evaluation of Alfonso's mental state, my colleagues at the Young Abusers Project drew upon a substantial amount of documentation from social services and the police, as well as reports by previous child psychiatrists and child psychologists who had evaluated this highly troubled person over the years. The Young Abusers Project also arranged for Alfonso to be assessed psychiatrically by a specialist child psychiatrist, and subsequently a clinical psychologist from the Young Abusers Project undertook an even more extensive psychological assessment of Alfonso's cognitive capacities.

Alfonso arrived at the offices of the Young Abusers Project near Christmas, 1995. The staff who had first evaluated him did not anticipate meeting such a tall, broad-shouldered teenager, of black African origin, standing more than six feet and six inches in height, and weighing roughly 250 pounds. Alfonso proved somewhat paranoid and uncooperative during the two formal psychiatric interviews, and he revealed evidence of his deeply entrenched sadistic tendencies during the very first encounter by throwing a chair across the room. In spite of Alfonso's violent outburst, the interviewers persevered with the psychiatric assessment, and they managed to ask Alfonso many pertinent questions about his abusive behaviour towards younger children.

Surprisingly, Alfonso spoke rather rapidly and freely about his capacity to become excited by prepubescent girls, and he described how he had inserted his "hard cock" into the "ginas" of the little children, and how this had aroused him. He also confessed for the first time that both he and a male school friend had targeted young girls together, and that on more than one occasion Alfonso and his chum had raped two different girls with great violence and that, in the midst of these sexual and physical assaults, Alfonso and his friend would switch positions, penetrating each youngster in turn. These particular disclosures of sexual abuse by Alfonso emerged for the first time during the course of the psychiatric assessment.

In the midst of undergoing these clinical interviews, Alfonso admitted that he wished to be helped by the Young Abusers Project, and that he spent much of his time worrying about being arrested by the police. Alfonso told my colleagues that he dreaded the prospect of imprisonment.

Shortly after this disclosure, Alfonso became extremely sullen and depressed, and he refused to lift his head. He thus revealed his capacity for feeling shameful affects that might ultimately be mobilised in psychotherapeutic treatment.

Later that month, Alfonso underwent a full battery of psychological testing. During the psychological assessment, Alfonso proved much less willing to engage, and he refused to produce any pictures for the Draw-A-Person Test or for the House–Tree–Person Test, even though the psychologist had asked him to do so. He did, however, respond grudgingly to some of the projective tests, notably the Thematic Apperception Test (TAT) cards, although he complained that he had difficulties concentrating, claiming that he needed to "clear my head". Towards the end of the testing situation, Alfonso became noticeably tearful. Overall, he performed rather poorly on the Wechsler Intelligence Scale for Children–Revised (WISC–R), receiving a full-scale intelligence quotient (IQ) score of 52, which placed him in the "moderate learning disability" range.

During the administration of the Comprehension Sub-Test of the WISC–R, the psychologist asked Alfonso what he would do if he happened to walk past a stamped envelope. Quite tellingly, Alfonso responded that he would "leave it on the floor, walk past it". This communication, in particular, seemed highly indicative of both his internal world and of the tremendous neglect and deprivation that Alfonso experienced throughout his childhood. I suspect that he very much identified with the "stamped" envelope lying on the floor, unposted, as this mirrored his earlier experiences of having been abandoned by his mother at a young age and then passed along from one foster home to another in succession, depriving him of any continuity or security during his crucial early developmental years.

After the completion of his assessment, the Consultant Child and Adolescent Psychiatrist at the Young Abusers Project formulated the following conclusions. On the basis of his sexually abusive behaviour, Alfonso displayed all the indications of the DSM–IV diagnosis for "Pedophilia" (302.20), but as he had not yet reached his sixteenth birthday at the time of the report, he could not be ascribed this diagnosis. However, it became quite clear that Alfonso did indeed fulfil the criteria for the DSM–IV category of "Conduct Disorder, Solitary

Aggressive Type" (312.00). He also fulfilled the DSM–IV category of "Mental Retardation" (318.00) (American Psychiatric Association, 1994). At the present time, it still remains unclear to what extent Alfonso's learning disabilities had resulted from a primary organic deficit or had emerged as a consequence of prolonged psychological traumatisation (e.g., Sinason, 1992). The final report summarised Alfonso's case thus:

> "Bringing these diagnostic features together, therefore, Alfonso could be described as a young man with a background of psychosocial deprivation and learning difficulty. His history of generally aggressive behaviour towards peers has now developed into a particular form, that of sexually abusive behaviour towards young females. This pattern is likely to persist and may develop into a permanent personality disorder, particularly if Alfonso's current and to some extent self-acknowledged difficulties are not addressed appropriately."

My colleagues concluded that Alfonso posed a serious risk to young children, especially young girls; and they also expressed concern about his capacity for angry or aggressive behaviour or ideation towards older women. My fellow staff members also commented upon Alfonso's substantial physical size of six feet and six inches, and his muscular capacity to perpetrate actual bodily harm against children as well as against adults.

In view of these serious matters, the Young Abusers Project recommended that Alfonso should never under any circumstances be left alone with children. Colleagues also expressed concern about the viability of Alfonso's current foster care placement, especially in view of the fact that his foster mother had a 5-year-old son of her own, and that this small boy would certainly be at risk of significant harm from Alfonso, given the patient's history of arousal in the presence of young children. The Young Abusers Project recommended that a supervised residential care facility would be more appropriate than a private foster care home in the community for such a disturbed and disturbing boy. Finally, the team recommended that psychotherapeutic treatment would be of great value to Alfonso, with the proviso that any such treatment might well cause him to become aware of deeper layers of aggressive affect, and that such a recognition might result in the stimulation of further aggression, which would require careful case management.

Alfonso's very committed local authority social worker discussed the implications of the psychiatric and psychological reports with senior staff at the social services department; all of them agreed that Alfonso did, indeed, pose a severe risk to children in the community; the local authority therefore agreed that the Young Abusers Project should provide psychotherapeutic treatment for him. The social worker then asked Alfonso for his views on the matter, whereupon he replied that he *did* wish to talk to somebody, but that he would prefer to speak to a black psychotherapist. At that time, the Young Abusers Project employed only three psychotherapists, including myself, all Caucasian; therefore, the services of a black clinician could not be offered.

The psychotherapy assessment

Alfonso had to wait approximately nine months until I could see him for our preliminary psychotherapy assessment sessions. The Young Abusers Project could not begin treatment until we had received assurances that the local social services department could provide funding for the work on an ongoing basis and, of equal importance, that a professional escort could be engaged to transport Alfonso to and from his psychotherapy sessions. We further insisted that an allocated social worker would continue to manage Alfonso's case and to support the treatment. It would not be feasible or helpful for Alfonso to travel to my office on his own, as the risk of acting out against children en route would be too great. My colleagues and I assumed that psychotherapeutic treatment would stir up many anxieties for this fragile young person, and that he would need a responsible parental figure to contain some of his fears both before and after sessions.

I had discussed the case at length with my team colleagues, and we all agreed that I would meet with Alfonso for two preliminary psychotherapy assessment sessions in order to determine his suitability for psychoanalytically informed work. In view of the great distance that Alfonso would have to travel, as he lived outside London, it would not be possible to offer more than one fifty-minute session per week.

Alfonso arrived on time for his first psychotherapy assessment session in the autumn of 1996, escorted by his social worker. I opened the door to my office at the appropriate time, and I introduced myself briefly to both Alfonso and to his social worker. I then invited Alfonso to enter the consulting room, and I asked the social worker to remain in the adjacent waiting area. The Young Abusers Project relies on such escorts not only for transportation purposes but also to provide an additional sense of security for both the patient and the psychotherapist. All of our patients know that their escorts will be waiting for them on the other side of the door, and I have come to appreciate the ways in which this knowledge reduces the temptation for patients to become more violent than necessary during treatment sessions.

I then closed the door to the consulting room and I sat in my chair behind the couch. With enthusiasm, Alfonso hopped into a chair on the other side of the room, directly across from my own seat. I now had an opportunity to observe his physical presence. He filled the leather chair fully with his large frame, and he splayed his legs wide open in a truculent and sexualised manner. I realised that I had never before worked with such a physically intimidating patient, and in my mind I became preoccupied with stereotypes of violent young black men. I remained silent, eager to learn how he would respond to this unusual yet long-awaited situation. Alfonso did not speak at all; instead, he began to look around the consulting room, his eyes soaking in every detail, and stared relentlessly at the couch, the bookshelves, the Persian carpet. After he had absorbed the room visually, Alfonso then turned his head towards the ceiling, and he peered first at the upper right-hand corner of the ceiling, and then at the upper left-hand corner. He continued to do so for many minutes, staring anxiously, as though searching for something. It suddenly occurred to me that during Alfonso's last visit to the Young Abusers Project he would have met with my psychiatric and probation service colleagues in a video suite, where he would have undergone a video-recorded psychiatric assessment as part of the project's ongoing research work.

Five minutes had elapsed, and neither of us had spoken out loud, but although Alfonso had not verbalised any anxieties at this point, he had certainly communicated extensive fears through his scoptophilic behaviour, thus prompting my first interpretation. I looked at Alfonso and told him that I could see how necessary it seemed for him to scan the room with his eyes, noting that he had never visited my office previously, nor had he ever met me before, and it would therefore be important for him to see what sort of a room he had entered and what sort of a person I might be. I then commented that he seemed particularly concerned with the corners of my ceiling, as though searching for a video camera. I suggested that Alfonso might be pleased that I had no such device in my room, but that he might also be worried, in case the presence of a video camera made him feel safer so that other grown-ups could see what he did at every moment. This intervention seemed to make some sense to Alfonso, and after I had mentioned the missing video camera, he smiled and began to talk to me.

Promptly, he told me that he did not want to speak, because he had very bad memories of my probation service colleague, Mr X, who had co-facilitated the initial psychiatric interview some months previously. Alfonso moaned that "Mr X treated me like some sort of an idiot. He made me show him what I did to those girls by using some dolls. He asked me if I knew the names of private parts, as though I didn't. He was a real jerk." I responded to this outburst of denigration by mentioning that I knew that several professional colleagues had diagnosed Alfonso as suffering from mental handicap and learning disabilities at various points during his life, and that perhaps he worried that I, too, would treat him as a stupid person who did not understand what grown-up people had to say. Alfonso smiled once again, as if to indicate that I had succeeded in alleviating at least a very small amount of his anxiety.

Alfonso then began to stare at a delicate nineteenth-century engraving that hung in a frame over my analytic couch. The engraving depicted a group of travellers heading on a journey. Alfonso continued to stare at the picture and then blurted out, "I bet that painting was done in 1980." I wondered why on earth Alfonso mistook this very old picture for a work of art from 1980. Concretely, I reasoned that even a person with absolutely no training in art history would be able to sense the value and age of this engraving. But I soon realised that 1980 represented, in fact, the very year of Alfonso's birth. I then shared this insight with him, and I commented, "I wonder whether you chose 1980 as the date because that is the year in which you were born. And this drawing hanging over the couch shows a group of travellers going on a journey. Perhaps you have a wish to go on a journey here with me, starting over at the very beginning. And you must be wondering what sort of journey it will be." The patient looked somewhat more mystified, but he responded by telling me that his father had once bought him a set of drums, and that he liked to play on these drums. I found myself wondering whether Alfonso's comment about the drum set represented some unconscious acknowledgment or validation of my interpretation about the nineteenth-century engraving, as though I had given him a small present of a kind in the form of rudimentary psychological understanding.

As the first assessment session drew to a close, I reminded Alfonso that he had come here in part because both his social worker and the staff at the Young Abusers Project had recommended that he do so but, also, in part because he himself had asked for help. My patient grunted, "Yeah, that's right."

I told him that I had learned of his request for a black psychotherapist, and that he may have felt disappointed to meet with a Caucasian man instead. He nodded his head in agreement, but then he told me that it did not matter. I explained to Alfonso that he and I had an important decision to make regarding whether he would come back to see me every week to discuss his problems and his difficulties. Unhesitatingly, he nodded that he very much wanted to return. I reminded the patient that he and I would meet at precisely the same time the following week, and that he might wish to use the intervening week to think carefully about what it might be like to see me on a regular basis.

The following week, Alfonso returned for the second of his psychotherapy assessment sessions, accompanied once again by his social worker. He spoke prosaically about his week, painting a rather gloomy picture of his desolate life. He explained how he would spend all day in bed, watching one television programme after another on his satellite system. He reeled off the names of each programme, their starting times, as well as the names of the central characters. Alfonso reported this information in a bleak telegraphic style, which communicated both the emptiness of his external world and the profound schizoid defences that he had erected against his overpoweringly violent internal world. I hypothesised that Alfonso had recited this list of television programmes for me in an effort to describe the empty nature of his life and that, in view of this, he wished perhaps to embark upon psychotherapy in the hope of obtaining some enlivenment. Alfonso smiled slightly, and he nodded in agreement.

Towards the end of the second psychotherapy assessment session I explained to Alfonso that I saw no reason why we could not work together, that I would agree to meet with him at a regular weekly time, and that this would be an ongoing arrangement. I also sketched out the clinical calendar, informing him that there would be regular breaks in the psychotherapy at Easter, during the summer, and at Christmas. Additionally, I clarified my relationship to the Young

Abusers Project, informing him that I work as a staff psychotherapist for the project, and that I would not be communicating directly with Alfonso's own social worker, but that the social worker from the Young Abusers Project might well do so, from time to time, especially if any of the grown-ups involved in Alfonso's care had significant worries about his safety, or about the safety of other children.

Just before the fifty-minute hour ended, Alfonso glanced at a very green leafy plant that sat on a table against the wall of my consulting room. This particular plant had blossomed very well over the years, and it had sprouted many different shoots, which trailed to the floor. Alfonso turned to me and asked, "Who waters that plant?" I did not respond directly, whereupon Alfonso remarked, "Plants should be watered five times a week." It struck me as rather extraordinary that a disabled and uneducated young person should, nevertheless, be able to have an intuitive sense that, in full psychoanalytic treatment, the patient attends five times per week. Although Alfonso knew little or nothing at all about the practice of psychotherapy, I suspect that he sensed that most working adults go to their offices from Monday to Friday inclusive, and, moreover, I suppose that Alfonso had begun to wonder why I could see him only one day of the week, instead of five. I interpreted this to him; he smirked and then admonished me in his Midlands hipster patois: "What you talking about, man? I speaking of your plants." Regardless of his denial of the wish to meet with me every day, I understood Alfonso's commentary about the frequency of watering as a very hopeful sign, suggesting that Alfonso possessed the capacity to internalise some good psychic nourishment.

We then embarked upon regular psychotherapy sessions.

The first term of treatment

Alfonso did not reveal an enormous amount of information about his violent tendencies or his abuse of small girls during the two psychotherapy assessment meetings. I suspect that he feared to do so in case I might refuse to offer him a treatment vacancy. However, once the psychotherapy had begun in earnest, Alfonso quickly unleashed a torrent of violence and abusiveness, providing me with a glimpse into his very tortured mind.

Alfonso spent the majority of his early sessions telling me that although I might imagine that he spent all day at home, he really enjoyed an "intergalactic" career as a World Federation boxer, and that after his sessions he would dash off to Gatwick Airport and begin

a week of gruelling training sessions and fights overseas. He boasted
that he had fought in Borneo, in Chicago, in New York, in Paris, and
in many other cities besides. Alfonso also claimed that Mike Tyson,
the famous boxer (and convicted rapist) had become his special mentor, and that Mr Tyson had arranged exciting fights in which Alfonso
could demonstrate his skills and techniques. It did not surprise me
that Alfonso, a young black sex offender, should identify with Mike
Tyson, an older black man who has had the perverse capacity to
transform his own aggressive libido into a career structure that has
brought him considerable fame and wealth. Above all, I regarded
Alfonso's deeply entrenched "intergalactic" fantasy world as a desperate attempt to fly from his extremely arid life in England, and as
a means of informing me of the extent of his violence.

Although Alfonso devoted most of his sessions to fantastic tales
of international boxing tournaments, he would often slide into a
more overtly infantile mode of communication; at times he would
pluck a book from my shelves, return to his chair, and curl up his
very large body into a little ball. He would then open one of my
clinical textbooks and pretend that he had taken a copy of *Goldilocks
and the Three Bears*, whereupon he would recite the story of "Goldilocks" in an extremely girlish, high-pitched voice, revealing a very
frightened and timid child within his large frame. The internal terror became extremely clear as Alfonso modified the story of "Goldilocks" to include a scene in which the three bears come home from
the forest and tear "Goldilocks" to shreds, using their sharp teeth
and claws. I often became confused as to whether I had a menacing late-adolescent boy with me in the room or, rather, a petrified
3-year-old child. In fact, both aspects of Alfonso's character structure appeared in the course of each session, though not in such a
structured manner that one would regard him as a case of dissociative identity disorder.

Alfonso did not speak either about his family of origin or about
his foster mother. I had the impression that he found it too dangerous to talk about real people while in the consulting room, and so he
focused his attention instead on fictional characters such as "Goldilocks", or on out-of-reach characters such as Mike Tyson. Alfonso
also regaled me with a series of credible imitations of personalities
from very unsophisticated television soap operas and films, and he
particularly enjoyed mimicking the comical American actor Jim Carrey in the film *The Mask*, in which Carrey repeats the words "Somebody stop me!" with a particular dramatic flourish. Alfonso would

often lapse into his Jim Carrey voice, shouting "Somebody stop me!" several times during the session. I interpreted that perhaps Alfonso hoped that I would be able to stop *him* from feeling so angry and so violent and so sad inside.

On another occasion Alfonso jumped up on the window-sill of my consulting room, which overlooks the main High Street. He managed to open the top of the window, and he shouted out in a very loud and pained voice, "Help! Help! Please help! This horrible man is keeping me here against my will! Help! Help!" Naturally, I felt very panicky at this point, and I became rather worried that some passer-by would telephone the police. But I then realised that Alfonso wanted me to feel as frightened as he had always felt. In a quiet voice I suggested that although Alfonso had shouted "Help!" out the window, he really wanted to ensure that I knew how much *he* wanted help from *me*, and that he must have wondered whether I would be able to assist him with his feelings. To my surprise and relief, this verbal intervention succeeded in calming Alfonso considerably; he then removed himself from the window-sill and sat down in the chair once again.

Towards the end of the first trimester of treatment, Alfonso's long-standing social worker retired; for three weeks, different untrained escorts had to bring him to his sessions, pending the appointment of a new social worker. Alfonso found this loss very difficult indeed, and his violent behaviour in the session increased dramatically through-out this time. Such data absolutely reinforces the necessity for a stable external environment during the community-based treatment of a forensic patient such as Alfonso. Eventually, a new social worker—a woman—began to escort Alfonso, and as the weeks wore on, the patient became somewhat more calm and contained. I spoke about the ways in which the change of social worker had mirrored the many different homes in which he had lived over the years, with a veritable succession of foster mothers. I also verbalised his anxiety about what sort of constant figure I would be, and whether he would arrive next week to find a different psychotherapist sitting in my chair. Alfonso simply sniggered with derision.

As our first break approached, Alfonso became increasingly anx-ious, and he devoted much of his session time to a detailed, yet ficti-tious, recitation of his airplane itinerary. He would brag, "Next week, I is goin' to the Bahamas to fight Big John Smith, and then I is goin' to board a plane to Florida to fight him again, and then I is goin' on a plane to Spain to fight El Caballero." I commented on Alfonso's frequent references to plane flights, and I wondered whether he had begun to have fantasies of whether *I* might be going on a plane over the forthcoming holiday break, and that perhaps he had also begun to have anxieties about whether I would return. Alfonso simply screamed at me and called me a "fucking fool"; he told me that I had lied to him and that, really, he knew that I had *never* actually boarded a plane in my life! He found the thought of me disappearing too unbearable—very reminiscent of the father who died suddenly from heart disease during Alfonso's latency years.

The second term of treatment

Alfonso did, in fact, survive the first break in treatment, and he returned promptly for the start of his second term of psychotherapy. But as the fourth, fifth, and sixth months of our psychotherapeutic encounter unfolded, Alfonso became increasingly violent, both verbally and physically, during his sessions. It may be that he now felt it safer to unmask the really treacherous areas of his mind, knowing that I still wanted to work with him, and that I did, in fact, bother to return after the first holiday period. He routinely scowled and sneered and smirked at virtually every comment that I would make, deriding all of my interpretations with considerable contempt. The psychotic and magical nature of his internal world became increasingly rich. Alfonso not only spoke about his special relationship with the aggressive black rapist Mike Tyson, but, in addition, he also claimed that he had begun to have secret meetings with yet another black hero, also accused of violent crimes—namely, the pop star Michael Jackson.

Alfonso told me that he had now given up his career as a World Federation boxing champion so that he could earn a huge salary as Head of Security for Michael Jackson. He provided me with untold details of Michael Jackson's putative timetable and, rather creatively, he informed me of all the secret measures that he would have to adopt in order to keep Mr Jackson safe at his many concert appearances. He then explained that he had employed a gang of security officers who had sworn complete and utter allegiance to him, and that these men would kill anybody who tried to hurt Michael Jackson or Alfonso himself.

This gang of security agents—albeit imaginary—became a particularly menacing contingency as the weeks unfolded. Alfonso frightened me when he explained that, on the previous evening, he and his gang of officers had loaded their silencer revolvers, and had gone cruising through the streets of London, looking for white men to abduct. They found one white man who wore glasses (as I do), and they tied him up and threw him into the boot of their car. Alfonso claimed that he and his men then drove the kidnap victim to an abandoned warehouse near a wharf, and systematically tortured him, blinding him with a knife, and carving lines on his chest until he bled to death. Afterwards, Alfonso claimed that he and the gang cut the white man up into a million pieces, and threw the remains of his body into the river Thames.

During our next session, Alfonso sat in quite a sullen and silent manner. But then, most unexpectedly, he stuck his hand into the pocket of his trousers very quickly, as though reaching for an object, and then removed his hand even more quickly, shaping his fingers like a pistol. In a flash, he aimed his long fingers at me and shouted "Pow", pretending to shoot me. Naturally, I did become very scared at this point, but I tried not to show it. Alfonso leered at me, and he told me that unless I played my cards right, I would also end up like the abducted white man, diced into many pieces and floating in the river. The "Goldilocks" voice of the first trimester had disappeared, and I now had an extremely good indication of the deeply disturbed violent nature of this young sex offender.

After pretending to shoot me with his fingers, Alfonso told me that his gang of security officers had instructions to pick him up at Heathrow Airport and to drive him in a limousine to Michael Jackson's mansion in London, prior to a concert performance at Wembley Arena. In recounting this fantasised story, Alfonso committed a very revealing parapraxis. Consciously, he had intended to say, "My men are gonna *meet* me at Heathrow, and drive me to Mr Jackson's mansion." But instead, he actually said, "My men are gonna *beat* me at Heathrow and drive me to Mr Jackson's mansion." Fortified by Professor Sigmund Freud's (1901a, 1901b, 1904a) observations that slips of the tongue often reveal unconscious wishes, I interpreted that although Alfonso enjoyed telling me about how he and his gang would spend their time killing people, his slip of the tongue indicated just how frightened he had become of this gang that he had created, and that perhaps he really worried whether his own aggressive wishes would result in somebody beating *him* up. I also wondered aloud whether he even feared that I, or a member of the Young Abusers Project staff, would *beat* him up as well.

This interchange between the two of us proved transformational. Alfonso now began to develop a deeper appreciation that his wish to terrorise resulted from his own fear and from his own experience of having been terrorised. I also became more secure in my work with this dangerous man once I realised that he found me more frightening than I found him. As soon as I made my intervention, Alfonso curled up into a big ball once again; he grabbed a box of tissues and then began to eat one of the tissues in a moment of acute anxiety. He subsequently placed two of the stark white tissues over his black face, which I understood as his wish to identify with me and with my whiteness, and as an expression of his deep desire for me to rescue him from inside the awfulness of his aggressive interior.

Tragically, Alfonso's new social worker resigned from her post at the end of the second trimester. She explained to the social worker at the Young Abusers Project that she had accepted an offer of employment elsewhere, protecting much younger children. Although the staff at the Young Abusers Project had made every effort in our initial negotiations with Alfonso's social services department to ensure continuity of escorting, this arrangement could not be honoured, and so his external world now matched his internal world, with extreme unreliability prevailing. At the end of every single meeting Alfonso began to ask me anxiously, "When's the next session?" I told him that our session would be held at the same time, next Tuesday, as always, but that in view of the change of social workers, perhaps he had begun to find it difficult to believe that his psychotherapist would actually show up for work.

Sadly, Alfonso did not attend for his last session before the next holiday break. I received a message late in the day from the manager of the local social services department, informing me that although she had tried valiantly to find a temporary escort, nothing could be arranged. Our social worker sent a stern letter of protest to the social services department, reminding them that they had a contractual obligation to provide a reliable escort for this disturbed patient. I myself sent a "holding" letter to Alfonso, expressing my regret that an escort could not be found to bring him to his last session before the break, and that I would, as agreed, plan to see him at the appointed time, three weeks hence, after the Easter pause.

The third term of treatment

Alfonso returned from his break looking very depressed and very forlorn. He told me that he wanted to jump off a cliff, then stab himself with a knife, then hang himself with a rope, and then swallow a whole bottle of poison. Never before, or since, have I heard a patient report such dramatic suicidal ideation. I linked this depressive outburst with the fact that he had not seen me before the Easter break, and that although he had received a letter from me, he must have felt very abandoned by all the adults looking after him. Strikingly, Alfonso then picked up a heavy clinical tome from my shelf and proffered the book to me, whispering, "With this book, I thee wed." I suggested that perhaps he had a wish to be married to me so that we would always be together, and he would therefore never have to experience any more of these painful separations. Alfonso's expression of homosexual transference had clearly unsettled him, and he instantly retorted, "You're crazy. I don't wanna marry you!" I suspect that Alfonso found his yearning for closeness far too dangerous.

In the following session, Alfonso entered the consulting room and asked me somewhat sheepishly whether these sessions would be "confisential"—his attempt to pronounce the word "confidential". I reminded him of our particular confidentiality policy at the Young Abusers Project, whereupon he whispered that he had something very important to tell me. Once, during Alfonso's seventh year, his mother and father had begun to fight rather violently. Indeed, his mother got so angry that she ran into the kitchen, pulled a large carving knife from the kitchen drawer, and wielded it menacingly over the father's head. Although she did not strike the father with the knife, the father became highly distressed, and he suffered a fatal heart attack right there on the spot.

Alfonso had never communicated this story to anybody before. All the social workers and probation officers knew that Alfonso's father had died from a heart attack, but nobody had heard about the specific moments that had preceded his cardiac arrest. The professionals had assumed that the father must simply have had a history of heart disease. Alfonso told me that he supposed his mother must have actually murdered his father—as indeed, she did, in a way. This important piece of biographical information helped me to gain a much better understanding of Alfonso's penchant for being threatening to others.

I now developed a greater comprehension of his fantasy of using a *knife* to carve up an anonymous white man and cut his body into a million pieces. I also began to formulate thoughts about the way in which Alfonso used his own penis as a cutting knife that penetrated the bodies of little girls, who may have come to represent his own teenage mother in fantasy, whom Alfonso wished to kill for depriving him of his father. The story of the death of Alfonso's father also shed more light on his wish to pursue a fighting career and to have a gang of security officers protecting him from violence.

Alfonso's capacity to speak about a real-life incident between his mother and his father represented a huge developmental advance. He no longer felt the urgency to fill the sessions with fantastic talk of Mike Tyson and Michael Jackson, but he had, at last, begun the long and painful process of speaking about real people from his actual biological family. Thereafter, he even began to talk about his index offences, although not in any great detail, whereas during the first two terms, he had refused to admit that he had ever raped little girls at all.

As the long summer break loomed, Alfonso began to look incredibly sad but less and less vicious. The quality and quantity of his language changed markedly, so that he spoke more about actual people and events, and he did not indulge in quite so much fantasy in the sessions. He became angrier as well, and on one occasion he ripped the dust jacket off of a book on my shelf. I told him that he must not do this, and that he no longer had my permission to touch my books, until I felt that he could manage better. This imposition of a helpful boundary seemed to contain him further, and he presented, thereafter, in a much more relieved way, knowing that at least one adult in his life would not permit him to become violent in action, only in words.

In the penultimate session before the end of the first year of treatment, Alfonso stuck a saliva-soaked piece of chewing gum on the wall of my consulting room. Although I felt quite angry initially, and also rather tempted to tell him to remove his chewing gum at once, I ultimately regained my own internal composure and interpreted Alfonso's chewing gum gesture as a deep-seated wish to be stuck to my wall over the break, so that he would not have to endure yet another long separation.

After one year of psychotherapy, Alfonso became much less violent towards the residential staff in his care facility, and he appeared to be much less depressed—so much so that the Young Abusers Project received a letter of thanks. It seems as though the psychotherapy had begun to work.

Regrettably, shortly thereafter, the local social services department withdrew its funding, not only for the psychotherapy sessions but also for the train travel and for the escort, and they informed us that Alfonso could no longer make the long journey to London every week. Horrified by this news, I offered to continue working with this young man without remuneration, but the social services department explained that they could not authorise such an arrangement. Heartbreakingly, the treatment had to end.

We insisted that Alfonso be permitted to return to London at least one more time in order to say goodbye, but on the day in question, the social worker became ill and had to cancel the appointment.

Such complex negotiations made me only too appreciative of the luxury of working with individuals who attend sessions without escorts and who have much greater control over their external life circumstances.

In the end, I had to write a letter to Alfonso, explaining that, in spite of our attempts to extend the length of his treatment, the social services department would not authorise this due to budget cuts, and that we would, alas, have to conclude our work. Naturally, I told him that I had appreciated having had the privilege of working with him, and I extended my very best wishes to him, hoping that he would be able to preserve some of the work that we had undertaken together.

Conclusion

This essay about one year of work with Alfonso, a young adolescent sex offender, represents only a fragment of a complex piece of forensic psychotherapy. It provides no more than a glimpse into a very emotionally charged clinical interaction.

Although we cannot, at this stage of the work, make any definite conclusions about the ultimate capacity of psychotherapy to transform the mind of a juvenile paedophile on a permanent basis, it pleases me to report that during the several years of my employment at the Young Abusers Project, not one single young person had re-offended sexually during the course of individual psychotherapy. Thus, although no assurances can yet be offered as to the ultimate efficacy of psychoanalytic psychotherapy for young sex offenders, such evidence suggests that psychotherapy may actually perform a very powerful containing and preventative function.

In view of the relative inefficacy and the arguably sadistic nature of castration and other somatic treatments for paedophiles (e.g., Freeman, 1979), we must begin to find a more humane way of understanding the origin and the maintenance of paedophile behaviours and fantasies. Although the outpatient treatment of forensic patients remains a relatively uncharted territory, as many psychotherapists still harbour fears—sometimes justifiably so—about working with aggressive patients (cf. Welldon, 1993, 1994; Kahr, 2018a), the field has become increasingly prominent in recent years, providing us with greater hope.

By working psychoanalytically with young children and adolescents, we have a rich opportunity to observe the development of paedophilia *in vivo*, before the personality structure becomes more ossified. In this way, we hope that a potentially valuable service can be provided to the community by intervening with young sex offenders—indeed, defusing their bombs—before these teenage criminals become intractable paedophiles whose sadistic enactments will cause great harm and devastation to the lives of many children and their families.

Note

A much abbreviated version of chapter 1 appeared in a collection of essays on *The Mind of the Paedophile: Psychoanalytic Perspectives*, edited by Professor Charles W. Socarides and Professor Loretta R. Loeb (Kahr, 2004).

CHAPTER TWO

From the treatment of a compulsive spitter: a psychoanalytic approach to profound disability

Let's purge this choler without letting blood.

"King Richard II", in William Shakespeare, *The Tragedie of King Richard II*, 1595, Act I, Scene i, 153

On patients who cannot speak

In 1895, Dr Josef Breuer, the noted Viennese physician, published his now classic case history of Fräulein Bertha Pappenheim, better known as "Anna O". In a work of deep originality, Breuer (1895, p. 23) demonstrated that through the art of conversation, which the patient herself referred to, in German, as the "Redecur" or, in English, as the "talking cure" (p. 23), Fräulein Pappenheim experienced a veritable "Kaminfegen" (p. 23) or "chimney-sweeping" (p. 23) of her cluttered mind. Josef Breuer's experiences with "Anna O" proved highly impactful, not least to the young Sigmund Freud, who, over the course of a lifetime, elaborated upon Breuer's work and thus developed the very foundations of the modern practice of psychotherapy.

For more than a century, the role of "talking" has maintained pride of place within the psychoanalytic treatment situation, and one might argue that virtually all accounts of such work underscore the importance of eradicating the resistances that inhibit the flow of verbal free associations. Through the facilitation of talking, psychoanalytic practitioners endeavour to minimise human sorrows. Indeed, speech occupies such a seminal position in psychoanalysis that when confronted with silent patients, clinicians strive to improve the capacity for verbalisation.

The many papers devoted to the treatment of the silent patient imply that, with enough time and trouble, our verbally inhibited patients will eventually learn how to talk (Fliess, 1949; Khan, 1963; Winnicott, 1963b). Dr Ernest Jones best encapsulated the psychoanalytic process as one devoted to the encouragement of speech when, in 1922, he wrote to Sigmund Freud about Mrs Joan Riviere: a woman who had undergone an analysis from each man in turn. As Jones (1922, p. 454) reported, "Her symptoms are much better (she can talk fluently at a meeting where she was once dumb from Angst) and she has a far-reaching insight."

Does, however, the capacity to verbalise constitute a *minimum* requirement for psychoanalytic work? Must every patient speak to us in *words*?

In the 1920s, Melanie Klein (1927a, 1927b) created quite a stir in psychoanalytic circles by attempting to work with extremely young children who had not yet developed full linguistic capacities; and she did so through the use of play techniques. Certainly, Klein's (1932) close observations of little girls and boys offered hope that patients might find a means of speaking, albeit not necessarily in traditional language.

But what about those patients who *never* develop a capacity to talk, in spite of having reached senescence?

Throughout the first half of the twentieth century, a small but sturdy band of psychoanalytic practitioners endeavoured to treat patients suffering from extreme neuropathology or from traumatisation, many of whom could not communicate in a traditional free-associative fashion and could not even engage in play therapy, as young children do. This pioneering group of clinicians defied Freud's (1904b, p. 550) recommendation that one requires "ein gewisses Maass natürlicher Intelligenz" ["a certain measure of natural intelligence" (Freud, 1904c, p. 254)] in order to undergo analysis (cf. Freud, 1906); and these forward-thinking clinicians attempted to work with severely and profoundly handicapped men, women, and children in psychodynamically orientated psychotherapy or psychoanalysis.

Dr Leon Pierce Clark, an early member of the New York Psychoanalytic Society, wrote a landmark book with colleagues on *The Nature and Treatment of Amentia: Psychoanalysis and Mental Arrest in Relation to the Science of Intelligence*, chronicling their efforts to offer psychotherapy to mentally handicapped individuals (Clark, Uniker, Cushing, Rourke, and Cairns, 1933). Others, such as Dr Leona Chidester and Dr Karl Menninger of the Menninger Clinic in Topeka, Kansas, undertook similar investigations (Chidester and Menninger, 1936). And in Great Britain, Dr Simon Lindsay even attempted to use the couch with severely "retarded" men and women (O'Driscoll, 1999, 2000, 2009; cf. Almásy, 1936).

Building upon these fledgling efforts, more contemporary practitioners such as Madame Maud Mannoni (1964, 1967, 1999) in France, and Dr Patricia Frankish (2016), Professor the Baroness Sheila Hollins (Hollins, 1990a, 1990b, 1997; Hollins and Sinason, 2000), Dr Valerie Sinason (1986, 1988, 1990, 1991a, 1991b, 1992, 1999, 2010), and many others in Great Britain have created a new profession of "disability psychotherapy" (Kahr, 2000b, 2000c, 2014a; Blackman, 2003; Wilson, 2003; Cottis, 2009a, 2009b; Corbett, 2014) in an effort to provide therapeutic opportunities for those non-verbal, brain-damaged, handicapped, behaviourally challenging individuals who might, traditionally, not qualify for treatment.

Fortified by the work of such inspiring colleagues, I had the privilege of joining the Tavistock Clinic's Mental Handicap Team and Mental Handicap Workshop nearly thirty years ago, where I had the opportunity to learn about how one might engage with patients struggling with significant disabilities. Nowadays, we refer to these men and women not as "retarded" or as "handicapped" but, rather, as "learning disabled" or as "intellectually disabled". Whatever terminology we may deploy for our own categorical purposes, these individuals, who cannot use our "talking cure" in quite the same way as more verbally fluent patients, even psychotic ones, might do, present huge challenges to psychotherapeutic workers.

In an effort to demonstrate something of the complexity of the clinical interchange with the severely and profoundly disabled or handicapped, I offer an account of my work with an elderly non-verbal, brain-damaged woman, to whom I refer as "Albertina". We met weekly over a period of eight years, during which time both she and I struggled and, I hope, sometimes succeeded, in communicating with one another, in spite of the fact that she talked not in *words* but, rather, in *spittle*.

Clinical material

The case of Albertina

Nearly three decades ago, while working in an outpatient mental health clinic, our team received a referral from a Consultant Psychiatrist, asking us to consider providing psychotherapy for a 63-year-old handicapped, brain-damaged woman who lived in a supervised hostel, and who had become increasingly "unruly", hitting other elderly residents with kitchen implements. This woman, "Albertina", had recently developed a penchant for creeping up behind some of her fellow patients and then thwacking them on the skull with a metal pan! To compound matters, Albertina had, for many years, spat compulsively, often as much as one thousand times per day.

When the director of the clinical service read out the psychiatric report, the entire team began to snigger in a most uncomfortable way. In spite of the fact that all of my colleagues had worked in the handicap field for many years, the prospect of treating a patient who spat so relentlessly produced notable waves of anxiety. When the director asked, "Who would like to see this woman for a consultation?", everyone shifted uncomfortably in their seats, and no one volunteered. Eventually, I—then the youngest and most inexperienced member of the team—agreed to offer an assessment. One of my colleagues immediately told me that I should purchase rubber sheeting for my consulting room; and another colleague insisted that I should speak to my general medical practitioner beforehand to enquire whether I should be inoculated against hepatitis. Clearly, the prospect of any contact with Albertina proved to be most distressing.

In keeping with the tradition of the clinic where I worked, those offering psychotherapy to the profoundly disabled or handicapped would often meet with relatives beforehand in an effort to learn as much about the family as possible; hence, prior to the first assessment, I arranged an appointment with Albertina's younger sister, who, it seemed, had urged the staff members of the care home to organise psychotherapy. The sister had undergone psychotherapy herself, and she knew that it could be a very helpful process.

Albertina's sister responded warmly to the invitation to attend for a preliminary conversation, and she arrived at my office carrying three heavy shopping bags in her left hand, and three heavy shopping bags in her right hand. As she placed these weighty parcels on the floor, she emitted a huge sigh and exclaimed, "I couldn't find a taxi anywhere, and so I had to lug these bags halfway across town. I'm exhausted." The sister, it seems, could not have found a more concrete or evocative way of conveying the sheer sense of burden that she experienced, caring for such a disabled, handicapped elder sibling.

The sister explained that Albertina had suffered from some sort of minor brain damage at birth, possibly from perinatal anoxia, but that she did not know the precise details. Although somewhat "slow" as a child, Albertina could, nevertheless, attend school like other children. But when she was 8 years of age, the gardener who tended the family's lawn may have sexually assaulted Albertina. Although the sister underscored that no one could prove the gardener's guilt with certainty, after this point in time Albertina never spoke again. Tragically, Albertina's father had endured a long struggle with alcoholism; during Albertina's adolescence he disappeared altogether and cut off all contact with his family. The mother became depressed and then, some years later, received a diagnosis of schizophrenia.

Albertina's sister also told me that the patient could emit sounds of anguish, "like the cries of a hyena". But on the whole she communicated predominantly through violent assaults with her fists and her feet, punching and kicking family members, staff members, and fellow residents in her care home. Above all, she drove everyone to a state of desperation through her constant expectoration, which left staff feeling sullied and hopeless. When particularly distraught, Albertina would even smear her vaginal secretions, as well as her faeces; and prior to the menopause, she also rubbed her menstrual blood onto her face and clothing.

During this preliminary consultation with Albertina's sister, I commented upon the heavy burden that she—the younger sibling— had to bear, and that I could understand why she had arrived at my office laden with a multitude of heavy parcels. I risked an interpretation to the sister, postulating that, perhaps, in spite of her inability to hail a taxicab, she still harboured a hope that she could find a "car", or indeed a "Kahr" (a pun on my surname), to help her and the staff members at the hostel to manage such a challenging person as Albertina. The sister laughed affectionately at my comment and sighed, "Yes, we are all rather hoping that you can do *something* with my sister. Anything would be helpful. *Anything* at all."

As Albertina would not be able to come to my consulting room by herself, she would require an escort. Due to staff shortages at Albertina's hostel, the sister very generously offered to pay for a private social care worker to fetch Albertina and transport her to see me weekly, and, crucially, to wait for Albertina in an adjoining room during the psychotherapy sessions. The sister thanked me for my offer of help, collected her six heavy bags, and set about arranging for Albertina and the escort to see me a few days hence.

The following week, Albertina arrived with her escort for her very first psychotherapeutic appointment. As one might imagine, I experienced considerable trepidation, uncertain how one might work with a woman who did not speak in words and who spat so compulsively. But at the designated time, I opened the door to my office and beheld both Albertina, an elderly woman with a terrified expression on her face, and also her escort, a motherly-looking woman of middle years whose punctual timekeeping and calm demeanour certainly inspired a sense of hopefulness. I introduced myself to both women simultaneously and invited Albertina to step into the consulting room, while the escort—a savvy and sensitive person—underscored that she would remain in the adjoining waiting room.

This troubled looking woman then followed me into my office, and I gestured to a chair and invited her to take a seat. Albertina, a diminutive woman with a head full of wild, unkempt grey hair, perched herself on the edge of the chair, and I sat in my seat some six feet away. Knowing that she rarely ever left her hostel and that she might be quite frightened at meeting a new person in unfamiliar surroundings, I thought it would be useful to introduce myself again, and so I explained, "Hello, my name is Brett Kahr, and as you know, your sister thought it might be helpful . . ."; but before I could continue my sentence, Albertina leapt out of her seat and began to walk around my consulting room in circles, touching the desk, the bookshelves, and various parts of the walls, rather like an animal marking her territory. She did not utter a sound. I remained silent, uncertain whether to allow her the space in which to familiarise herself with this new office, or whether I ought to say something. But, as I recall, in view of my relative inexperience, I found myself somewhat stunned, and I had nothing of value to say.

Albertina continued to circle the room, investigating each nook and cranny. She walked in a very unbalanced way, as though she had broken her ankle or as though she had drunk too much whisky! As she stumbled back and forth across the room, she reminded me of the psychogeriatric patients with whom I had worked years earlier on the back wards of an old-fashioned psychiatric hospital, many rocking all day long in catatonic states. After a short while, I made a tentative comment to Albertina, "It might be very strange for you to come to a new room, such as this one, and to meet someone that you have never met before." But my comment seemed to fall on deaf ears. Albertina had made no eye contact with me whatsoever—only with the walls and the furniture and the floor.

And then . . . she began to spit.

First, she emitted several mouthfuls of spittle onto the wall, and then, she smeared the liquid with her hands. Next, Albertina spat three or four times on the carpet at one particular spot, and then she walked around the room and spat several times more. Thereafter, to my surprise, she dribbled three or four mouthfuls of saliva onto the index finger of her right hand and subsequently plunged the digit harshly into her right ear, making a very audible squishing noise in the process. She rammed her finger in and out for about a minute or so, simulating the motions of sexual intercourse. Albertina then retracted her finger and began to lick it. Subsequently, she spat several times more on the floor.

Throughout this ordeal, I remained quite stupefied, unable to think intelligently or, indeed, creatively, and although I may have uttered a simple remark here or there, I believe that, for the most part, I remained staggeringly silent. In truth, I felt rather as though someone had exploded an extremely messy bomb in my otherwise tidy office space.

Having agreed to offer a consultation to a compulsive spitter and having discussed the case in advance with my team colleagues, I knew that Albertina might very well spit on *me*. But thus far, she had not done so.

The patient then turned towards me and began to walk in my direction, as I remained on the other side of the consulting room. My anxiety level rose considerably. Albertina saw my appointments diary, which I had left on a small table beside my chair, and she fixed her gaze upon it and began to fill her cheeks with spittle. I then rose from my chair in a flash and I seized my diary, removing it from view, perhaps as a desperate plea that she must not spit on me. Albertina seemed to tolerate my imposition of a spatial boundary and continued to walk round the room.

Albertina spat more and more, and I made occasional quiet remarks about how her expectoration masked her fright, verbalising that it might seem quite strange for her to come to an office such as mine and to meet a new person for the first time. Albertina stuck her finger into her mouth, and then quite quickly inserted it between her legs and began to masturbate. I suggested that it might be helpful if she could return to her chair at this point, but she refused to do so. I then interpreted that when I had taken my diary away from her, she may have felt that I did not want to have anything to do with her, and that she therefore had no other option but to masturbate herself in this solitary way.

To my surprise, this remark seemed to make sense, and, to my relief, Albertina removed her fingers from underneath her long skirt. She then resumed pacing the room and continued spitting on the floor. Her capacity to produce so much saliva quite amazed me, but she had no difficulty generating more and more spittle from her mouth, which she then projected, missile-like, onto the floor and the walls of the consulting room.

After having left her mark upon many surface areas in my office, Albertina then spied the entryphone, attached to the wall near the door. She lunged steadily towards this phone and lifted the receiver, examining every inch of the beige plastic with great care. Then she began churning her cheeks, manufacturing yet another puddle of spit, and within seconds she gobbed directly into the speaking part of the entryphone. I must confess that I felt quite defeated by this point, and I began to fantasise about how on earth I would begin to clean up all the fluids that Albertina had deposited throughout my room, and wondered *where* the caretaker in my building kept all his scouring supplies!

Albertina spat three or four times into the receiver of the telephone, so much so that I became worried that she would short-circuit the device itself. I became quite dumbstruck, uncertain whether to remove the telephone from her hands or attempt another futile interpretation, or simply to sit in resigned fashion, staring in amazement at this most challenging and unusual patient. Happily, my thoughts returned to me, and I eventually offered an interpretation: "As I have said, I know that you must be scared. You do not know whether I am a safe person or whether I will harm you in some way. And you are here in an unfamiliar room that you have never visited before, and you might be wondering why you have been brought here. I think that you are covering the entire room with spit to make it your own, so that it becomes a safe place. And I think that by spitting into the telephone, as you are doing now, you are trying to find a way to talk to me. I know that it is difficult for you to speak in words, as I am doing, so you are using your spit as a way of communicating with me."

I became immediately concerned that I may have talked far too much at this point, or, indeed, in too sophisticated a manner; but to my great relief, Albertina stopped expectorating, dropped the receiver of the entryphone and left it dangling by its cord, and then stumbled into the middle of the consulting room and slumped down on the floor in a heap, whereupon she began to cry. Albertina did not cry in an audible way; instead, she did so in complete silence, with tears streaming down her face, looking extremely sad. Suddenly, the emotional atmosphere in the room became transformed considerably, as both Albertina and I experienced some relief, I suspect, that the mad acting-out and dashing around could at last be calmed and contained, and that, perhaps, something could ultimately be understood.

I responded to Albertina's tears by commenting: "I can see how very unhappy you are. And I think there is a part of you that really does want to have some help. And you might be wondering whether I can help you, or whether your sister and the staff members at your hostel have sent you here as some sort of punishment." Albertina looked at me directly for the first time, stared into my eyes in a plaintive fashion, and then began to cry even more profusely. The liquid now began to trickle out of her lachrymal glands rather than out of her mouth: spittle had turned into tears. At that moment, Albertina began to move from a state of paranoid-schizoid persecution, in which she found the world a frightening place, to one of more depressive functioning, better able to recognise the sadness of her state of being (Klein, 1946). I took some comfort in remembering that many experienced clinicians from Melanie Klein onwards had come to regard the appearance of depressive position mentation as a sign of some hope (e.g., Hinshelwood, 1994; Anderson, 1997).

Eventually, Albertina ceased crying, and then, as though to regulate herself somehow, she extended one of her palms in front of her face and spat into it, albeit somewhat more slowly and gently than she had done previously. She then proceeded to rub the saliva into her scraggly grey hair, twirling the strands around in a repetitive fashion. I became instantly aware that this episode of spitting seemed to be different in quality from her previous spitting activities, and I began to wonder whether spitting could have many diverse meanings for this patient. Perhaps, at times, it provided Albertina with a weapon for launching aggressive attacks, or as an attempt to ward off fear and anxiety; and perhaps at other times she used spittle as some form of self-soothing or comfort. As a non-verbal patient, Albertina spoke not in words, but in spits; and it would befall to me as her new psychotherapist to begin to find a way to decipher the language of "spittingese".

After what seemed an interminable amount of time, the end of this extraordinary fifty-minute session began to loom, and, in a soft voice, I explained that we would soon have to pause for today, but that it might be helpful for us to consider whether Albertina might wish to return the following week for a second meeting. Naturally, I did not expect a straightforward verbal reply, nor did I receive one. Instead, Albertina sat down on the couch at this point—the first time that she had done so—and she removed her shoes and her socks, while I stared in amazement. I commented, "It is very striking that just as I have explained that we shall have to say goodbye in a few minutes, you have now taken *off* your shoes and socks, as though you are trying to settle in. Perhaps you are showing me the part of you that *does* wish to stay here." Albertina stared into space, rocking back and forth, seemingly oblivious to my remark. But she seemed quiet and more peaceful than at any point previously during this first consultation. She swayed on the couch and, thankfully, she refrained from any further spitting.

As the hour drew to a close, I told Albertina that it would be very helpful if she could put her shoes and socks back on in preparation for her departure. She then rose from the couch, picked up her foot-wear, and walked towards me, proffering the shoes and socks like a tiny child who wishes her parent to dress her. I remarked that having seen her remove her shoes and socks only minutes before, I knew that she could probably put them back on all by herself, but that perhaps she wanted reassurance that I might be someone who could help her. Silently, Albertina sat down on the floor, and in a slow, laborious manner, she spent the next three or four minutes pulling up her socks and tying her shoelaces.

I then explained that I would now open the door to the office so that she could be reunited with the escort who had brought her to see me. In Albertina's presence, I spoke to the escort and explained that I would be very happy to meet with Albertina the following week at the same time, and that Albertina could, over the next few days, think about our meeting. I explained that it would be helpful for Albertina and me to have another meeting, so that she could then have more time to decide whether she might wish to come to my consulting room on a regular weekly basis. The escort nodded silently and dip-lomatically, and with understanding; she then turned to Albertina, encouraging her, "Say goodbye to Brett." Albertina stared at me with forlorn eyes, looking very sad that our time for today had come to an end, and she mumbled, "Buh—Bweh", which I thought might mean "Bye, Brett". Once again, I bid both Albertina and her escort farewell, confirming that I would look forward to meeting again at this same time the following week.

After Albertina and the escort had departed, I breathed an enormous sigh of relief, and then I went in search of cleaning fluids and began to scrub the walls and carpet of my office. I estimated that Albertina had spat approximately two hundred times during the course of our first fifty-minute session.

Albertina did, indeed, return with her highly professional and reliable escort the following week. During this second consultation, she spat only half as frequently, perhaps no more than one hundred times; and although I still regarded these spitting episodes as signs of desperation and helplessness and fury, I took great comfort in the fact that between our first and second meetings the frequency of her "presenting symptom" had reduced by half. I wanted to believe that Albertina might have found our first meeting hopeful and comforting, and that the presence of an attentive and tolerant man might have helped to "contain" her need to spill the liquid inside her body onto my floor and walls.

At the end of the second session, I told Albertina that I thought it might be useful for her to meet with me on a regular weekly basis. I explained that both her sister and her staff members thought that this would be a good idea, but, above all, I wanted to know *her* thoughts about this possibility. Albertina stared at me intently, and she walked slowly to the entryphone attached to the wall, lifted the receiver— much as she had done the previous week—and spat into the little holes. I interpreted that perhaps she did want to find a way to talk to me. I then explained that I would be pleased to offer a weekly time, and I concluded the second meeting by speaking about the many practicalities that I would discuss with any psychotherapy patient: confirmation of the appointment time; a brief outline of the annual calendar (noting that we would have regular breaks at Christmastime, Easter-time, and during the summer); and so forth. I had no clear notion of whether Albertina understood my comments, but I felt that I had no recourse other than to assume some degree—if not quite a high degree—of understanding.

Little did I know that Albertina and I would ultimately meet on a weekly basis, without interruption, for the next eight years.

I regret that I cannot do justice to the intricacy and complexity of such a lengthy piece of psychotherapeutic work in the context of this chapter; I shall provide, instead, a brief survey of the way in which Albertina's distressing presenting symptom—namely, compulsive spitting—transmogrified over time.

I soon came to learn that her spitting behaviour served a multitude of purposes. For instance, on certain occasions, when expectorating into the telephone, Albertina wished to convey her desire to communicate, in spite of her lack of words. At other times, while ramming her fingers into her spittle-soaked ears with tremendous ferocity, Albertina evoked a suspicion of some early sexual trauma.

The ear-penetration symptom proved particularly distressing to watch, and in my view it really required some sort of strong and clear verbal interpretation. As Albertina invaded her eardrum with increasing speed and violence—drawing blood on one occasion—I hypothesised, "You are ramming your finger into your ear in a very hard way, and it looks as though you are hurting yourself quite painfully. I wonder whether you are trying to show me that perhaps somebody else had once put something hard and wet and hurting into a part of your body." Over the months, I had to repeat this interpretation, almost word for word, on many occasions. Sometimes my comment calmed Albertina and helped her to stop; at other times, the interpretation caused her to jam her finger into her eardrum again and again, at which point I surmised, "I know that you find it very hard to hear what I have just said, and you are blocking up your ear so that you cannot listen to me." This comment often proved effective and allowed her to remove her finger and then sit down calmly in the centre of the room.

Albertina used spitting as an indication of her wish to speak and, perhaps, as a means of communicating an early traumatic experience of sexual assault. But, additionally, she spat as a way of expressing her tremendous hatred, particularly at the end of the session. During the early months of psychotherapy, whenever the escort appeared at the door at the conclusion of each hour, Albertina spat on the floor by the exit in bullet-like fashion.

During the early months of treatment, I often experienced waves of nausea as a very powerful countertransference reaction. In her landmark studies on disability psychotherapy, Dr Valerie Sinason (1988, 1992, 2010) has observed that such responses will often emerge during work with severely and profoundly handicapped patients who subsequently confess to some experience of early sexual abuse. In view of what the sister had told me prior to the onset of treatment about the possibility that a man may have molested Albertina, one could not help but wonder about abuse when observing the patient's finger-jamming symptom and also her penchant for lying on the couch, face-down, bucking her hips, and also masturbating from time to time in the session in a most violent fashion. Whenever I interpreted that Albertina wished for me to know that many years ago someone might have hurt her body, the symptom often diminished, as did the countertransferential nausea.

Over time I came to realise that Albertina and I had become involved in a four-stage process. In the first stage of symptom-presentation, Albertina evoked a feeling of *stupefaction*, leaving me quite dumbstruck (rather like herself), as the sheer shock of her dramatic spitting attacked all possibilities of thinking. In the second stage, I began to experience *toleration*, in which I could use my infant-observation skills to watch, quite simply, her behaviour and communications, while endeavouring to formulate some working hypotheses as to their possible meanings. After navigating through stupefaction and toleration, I could then enter the third phase, that of *interpretation*, and then a fourth stage, namely, one of *resolution*, in which, as a result of surviving the stupefaction, tolerating the symptom, and then rendering a classical interpretation, the symptom would begin to reduce in intensity (Kahr, 1995a, 1997).

This model of stupefaction–toleration–interpretation–resolution proved most helpful to me in providing an anchor and a structure in what otherwise seemed to be a chaotic sea of spittle. Indeed, as I persevered in my efforts to understand the meaning of Albertina's behaviours and symptoms, and as I continued to offer tentative interpretations, the frequency of spitting continued to decrease, often rather markedly so. After the initial session, in which Albertina spat perhaps two hundred times, followed by a second session in which she did so approximately one hundred times, I would estimate that subsequently, during the first year of psychotherapy, she would spit on average between twenty and thirty times per session. However, during the second year of psychotherapy the rate of spitting reduced even more, to roughly fifteen spits in each fifty-minute session. The symptom became increasingly contained, and by the sixth year Albertina rarely spat more than once in each session—an enormous contrast to the bomb-like barrage of our first encounter. During the seventh year of psychotherapy, she ceased spitting entirely!

As Albertina began to communicate less and less frequently with saliva, she became more and more keen to draw pictures with crayons.

Her artwork often consisted of little more than rough lines or shaky circles, but she immersed herself in this process with gusto nonetheless. Albertina's relationship to the crayons themselves proved to be far more revealing than the actual contents of her primitive sketches. In the early days of the psychotherapy, she would often break off the pointy tips of the crayons and throw them across the room, prompting me to comment on her fear of long objects. Sometimes she would insert a crayon into her ear and penetrate herself with it, thus simulating, once again, a possible sexual assault. But through constant interpretative perseverance, Albertina gradually began to use the crayon as an aid to drawing, and she would produce pictures of increasing complexity and sophistication. I would then study the pictures with her and would offer comments on her use of colour and shape, carefully noting the tiny differences in form and style from week to week. Over the course of psychotherapy, Albertina must have created well over one thousand crayon drawings, which became, increasingly, her principal form of speech.

My deep interest in Albertina's drawings and my close observational attentivity proved very containing for this patient—so much so that whenever my watchfulness faltered, even if only for a second, Albertina became enraged. On one occasion, during the sixth year of psychotherapy, as Albertina sat calmly and quietly, drawing with crayons, I sneezed: the first time that I had done so in her presence. Although she had not spat for quite a number of sessions, she then stood up, coughed loudly, and produced an enormous globule of spittle and projected this onto the floor. She also began to slap herself repeatedly on both the face and the hand. I interpreted, "I think you felt very hurt and angry when you heard me sneeze a moment ago. I think you felt that I was not thinking about you or paying attention to you in that moment but, rather, that I had been concentrating on my own sneezing. I think you started to hit yourself, because you really wanted to hit me, and I think that you spat on the floor to show me your anger." After I commented in this way, Albertina sat down again and returned to her drawing, reassured that I knew, only too well, how very much she needed me to attend to her in the most reliable manner imaginable, rather like a parent in a state of primary maternal preoccupation (Winnicott, 1956a).

Over the course of time, I also obtained a great deal of data about Albertina's growing sense of containment from the way in which she used the toilet, located one flight down from my consulting room. At the end of each session, the remarkably composed and tolerant escort would help Albertina put on her coat and would walk with her to the bathroom prior to setting off on the long journey back to her residential facility. During the early months of psychotherapy, Albertina would flood the toilet, splashing water hither and yon, decorating the bathroom with pieces of toilet roll, and also with spittle. But as time passed and as Albertina became increasingly contained, she began to treat the toilet more respectfully and more ordinarily. Towards the end of treatment, Albertina had become something approximating an "ordinary patient" who destroyed neither the consulting room nor the bathroom.

I had established a clear boundary regarding confidentiality at the outset of psychotherapy with Albertina's family members, with the escort, and also with the staff team at her hostel. I underscored that I could not discuss the details of the treatment with them. But, in order to support the family and the staff, one of my disability psychotherapy colleagues from our mental handicap department did, in fact, make herself available to Albertina's staff members to offer support and to help them process their feelings of hatred towards this very challenging, very vexing woman. This proved an essential adjunct to the psychotherapy, and just as I began to acquire an increased capacity to understand Albertina, so, too, did her carers. To everyone's relief and delight, Albertina gradually became more and more calm in her residential facility; and as the years unfolded, she stopped hitting other residents with objects, and her compulsive spitting became much less ferocious.

After eight years of psychotherapy, Albertina and I ended our work together. Her family could no longer pay the increasingly large fees at the care facility where she lived; consequently, they decided to place Albertina in a cottage owned by a very gracious second cousin, who lived far away, in the north of England. After careful consideration, we decided during the month of September that we would stop our work the following Easter, some seven months hence. As the Christmas break loomed, Albertina spat three or four times, which she had not done for many, many months. I made a simple interpretation about her anger and her sadness regarding the approaching pause in our work and about the ultimate ending of our sessions the following April. At our final December meeting prior to the Christmas period, Albertina spat, but on this occasion she actually reached into the box of tissues—the very first time that she had ever done so—and, like a more "normal" patient, she evacuated her bodily fluids into the paper, rather than onto the floor.

Albertina and I worked together for another three months in the new calendar year. In our final session—a very moving one for both parties, I believe—Albertina drew a very special picture for me of two interlocking circles. I hypothesised that perhaps the circles represented both Albertina and Brett Kahr, and that by having drawn the circles in this way, she wanted me to know that she would remember this experience, and also me, and that she hoped, perhaps, that I would remember her. She became teary and I, too, felt my eyes start to moisten. At the end of the final session, I said that I had very much appreciated having had the privilege of working with her and that I would remember her. And in her broken speech, she smiled at me, and murmured, "Bye Bweh . . . bye Bweh . . . bye", and she waved at me as she and the escort trailed off down the corridor and then out of the building.

Concluding remarks

The child psychoanalyst Dr E. James Anthony noted the paucity of papers in the psychoanalytic literature about encopretic patients who cannot contain their bodily substances. As Anthony (1957, p. 157) lamented, "Clinicians on the whole, perhaps out of disgust, prefer neither to treat them nor to write about them." In fact, although many clinicians have written about the *retention* of bodily fluids and products (e.g., Freud, 1905; Abraham, 1919; Sterba, 1934; Rosenfeld, 1968), far fewer have examined their *expulsion*! Indeed, when, during my work with Albertina, I had the privilege of consulting the distinguished child psychotherapist Mrs Frances Tustin, renowned for her work with psychotic youngsters, she told me in no uncertain terms that she had, in fact, terminated her work with patients who spat in her face, as she simply could not bear the experience (telephone interview with Frances Tustin, 22 February 1994).

Both Professor Sigmund Freud and Dr Carl Gustav Jung had encountered a number of patients who evacuated bodily fluids; and one senses from their correspondence that they found these cases so distressing and enfeebling that they wrote to one another about these challenging individuals in a gesture of clinical solidarity. Freud (1907) described a male patient who would spit, which he regarded as a gesture symbolic of ejaculation; while Jung, in reply, provided brief accounts of a number of institutionalised patients who not only spat (Jung, 1907c) but also drank urine and ate faeces (Jung, 1907a), or who smeared themselves with excrement (Jung, 1907b). Nevertheless, in spite of these graphic descriptions, one has no sense that either Freud or Jung succeeded in working with these very challenging patients in a protracted psychoanalytic capacity.

Dr Karl Abraham (1917) did, however, examine the sadistic aspects of premature ejaculation, and Dr Bertram Lewin (1930) explored the psychodynamics of smearing, and a number of child mental health professionals have written about faecal soiling (e.g., Shane, 1967; Flynn, 1987; Forth, 1992), including Mr Paul Barrows (1996) who described encopresis as an attack on the parental couple and as an intrusion into their privacy. But on the whole most colleagues have not engaged sufficiently with the potential horror of patients who evacuate fluids, as most of us rely on our own capacity, and on the capacities of others, to maintain our secretions safely inside our bodies.

Drawing upon the sparse, but helpful, theoretical literature, and from my own clinical observations, I have come to conclude that Albertina spat for at least four particular reasons. First, having no capacity for more ordinary language, she did so as a means of communicating internal states of distress and disorientation. Second, she expectorated compulsively as a means of recreating possible sexual trauma, evidenced by her use of saliva as a lubricant that she inserted into her ears and, from time to time, into her vagina and anus as well. Third, Albertina used spittle, I suspect, as a primitive means of discharging sadistic libidinal strivings and as a vehicle for attacking hated persons in her memory (perhaps her mother and her father, and even the gardener). And fourth, Albertina spat as an expression of desperation, envy, and fury towards those who had failed to protect her. Fortunately, through ongoing, reliable, and consistent psychotherapy, I believe that I might have helped Albertina to achieve a reduction in a most unpleasant form of symptomatology, and that I assisted her to develop a calmer state of mind.

As any nursing mother or father of a newborn will appreciate, every human infant struggles to contain bodily fluids. Most reasonably healthy caregivers will experience toleration, even pleasure, when a baby dribbles or spits up milk. But through the course of development, most of us manage to confine our spitting and drooling to the morning and evening ritual of brushing our teeth or to the exchange of saliva during lovemaking. When we become ill, however, with a cold or catarrh or with influenza or other respiratory conditions, the containment of mucus, saliva, and other bodily fluids becomes more challenging. In the case of severely traumatised and regressed individuals such as Albertina, the normal human engagement with saliva can become extreme and perverse, with fluids used as a weapon against oneself and others, as a form of protection, and also as a means of communication.

One need not search very far in the historical literature to encounter horrific instances of spitting as expressions of profound violence. In 1938, David H. Buffum, the United States Consul in Leipzig, Germany—a witness to the horrific events of *Kristallnacht*, in which Jewish men and women suffered grotesquely at the hands of the Nazis—reported, "Having demolished dwellings and hurled most of the effects to the street, the insatiably sadistic perpetrators threw many of the trembling inmates into a small stream that flows through the Zoological Park, commanding horrified spectators to spit at them, defile them with mud and jeer at their plight" (quoted in Gilbert, 2006, p. 87). Several years later, in 1945, after the execution of the Fascist dictator Benito Mussolini, the inhabitants of Milan, Italy, spat upon the decaying cadaver of *Il Duce* (Farrell, 2003), prompting the British playwright Noël Coward (1945, p. 26) to quip, sardonically, "Mussolini shot dead and hung upside down in the street and spat at. The Italians are a lovable race."

In working with a compulsive spitter, one must navigate a great deal of hatred, desperation, and mess. Dr Wilfred Bion once told his students that, when treating an extremely ill and challenging patient, the clinician has two alternatives: either to abandon the analysis, or to write about it (Brendan MacCarthy, personal communication, 29 May 2002). I remain grateful to the many colleagues in the mental handicap team with whom I worked during the course of my treatment of Albertina, and to the supervisors and senior colleagues whom I consulted, who helped me greatly in my understanding of this challenging and, at times, quite nauseating case. Fortunately, fortified by these sources of support and by the pioneering efforts of leading disability psychotherapists and psychoanalysts such as Professor Nigel Beail, Dr Noelle Blackman, Dr Alan Corbett, Ms Tamsin Cottis, Mr Richard Curen, Dr Patricia Frankish, Professor the Baroness Sheila Hollins, Mr David O'Driscoll, Dr Valerie Sinason, the staff of Respond in London, and the founders of the Tavistock Clinic Mental Handicap Team, as well as colleagues at the Institute of Psychotherapy and Disability, contemporary mental health practitioners now have exemplars of inspiration and survival to whom we can turn for assistance in working with such complex and unusual individuals in distress.

Note

An earlier version of this chapter, entitled, "From the Treatment of a Compulsive Spitter: A Psychoanalytical Approach to Profound Disability", appeared in a special edition of essays on disability psychotherapy in the *British Journal of Psychotherapy* (Kahr, 2017a).

CHAPTER THREE

The intra-marital affair:
from erotic tumour to conjugal aneurysm

Als ob es vor seiner eigenen Ehe phantasiert wäre. (Freud, 1898a)
[It is as if he had constructed a fantasy before his own marriage.
(Freud, 1898b)]

Dr Sigmund Freud, Letter to Dr Wilhelm Fliess, 7 July 1898
[Freud, 1898a, p. 350; Freud, 1898b, p. 320]

Why do marriages explode?

I have always admired the loyalty of lifelong married couples. Let us consider, for example, the impressive marital history of one of the great forefathers of our profession.

On Saturday, 16 April 1938, Dr Edward John Mostyn Bowlby, a 31-year-old newly qualified English psychoanalyst, wed the beautiful Miss Ursula Longstaff, one of the seven daughters of a distinguished mountaineer. John Bowlby and his wife enjoyed a very happy marriage—one that lasted some 52 years, until Dr Bowlby's death on 2 September 1990. This solid, well–attached partnership has had a resounding impact across the generations; and it will come as no surprise that their son and daughter-in-law, Sir Richard Bowlby and Xenia, Lady Bowlby—themselves a loving and deeply attached married couple—have, either singly or jointly, served as generous supporters of various mental health organisations and charities over a lengthy period of time, including The Bowlby Centre in London, the Centre for Child Mental Health in London, as well as Attachment Parenting International and the Paracelsus Trust, among many others.

The long-term marital commitments so characteristic of the Bowlby family very much reflect, and have no doubt informed, the basic philosophical tenet of attachment theory—namely, that mental health and peace of mind stem in large measure from a profound immersion in ongoing, loyal, reliable, committed, intimate human relationships. And the Bowlbys, across at least two generations, if not more, have served as admirable, inspiring role models who know how to attach not only to each other but also to the professional organisations that they have supported, and continue to support, so generously and so lovingly.

Sadly, not all intimate partnerships can be as happy. Many spousal relationships terminate, as we know, in something akin to global warfare, in which, all too frequently, couples drop bombs upon one another.

With some 42% of marriages in Great Britain ending in divorce rather than death, we know only too well how greatly marital misery devastates our nation's psychological landscape, leaving unhappy, dysfunctional couples in a shattered state, more prone not only to mental illness but to physical illness as well. When marriages flounder or fail, partners suffer adverse psychological consequences, including, *inter alia*, an increased risk for depression, anxiety disorders, alcoholism, and suicidality, not to mention a raft of physical burdens, including a higher likelihood of developing cardiovascular disease, obesity, diabetes, dementia, and other potentially lethal medical conditions (Rankin-Esquer, Deeter, and Taylor, 2000; Meier, 2011; Kahr, 2012b).

In 2005, Professor Janice Kiecolt-Glaser, the distinguished psychoneuroimmunologist, published a landmark study with several colleagues on the adverse bodily consequences of poor marital relationships, discovering, *inter alia*, that physical wounds (e.g., cuts and so forth) endured by hostile couples will heal more slowly than those of couples who enjoy a more secure marriage. Indeed, hostile couples healed at only 60% of the rate of more harmonious couples and, similarly, produced more tumour necrosis factor alpha in the wake of an episode of marital conflict (Kiecolt-Glaser et al., 2005).

In a similar vein, more current research has continued to underscore the devastating physical impact of marital dysharmony; and colleagues at the University of Southern California and at the Davis School of Gerontology in the David Geffen School of Medicine, part of the University of California at Los Angeles, have reported that individuals in poor couple relationships, with insufficient spousal support, frequently suffer from higher levels of inflammation of biomarkers such as interleukin-6—a soluble protein that contributes to immune function and to the control of infection—as well as from higher levels of C-reactive protein—a blood protein that, when elevated, indicates the presence of often dangerous infections (Donoho, Crimmins, and Seeman, 2013). Thus, marital unhappiness can threaten our very physical wellbeing and even our mortality.

Furthermore, spousal dysfunction resonates across the generations; and the children of unhappy marriages suffer perhaps most of all. Dysharmonic couples will be more likely to produce children who become, like their parents, highly vulnerable and, consequently, more prone to psychological suffering, with a greater propensity for developing clinical depression, as well as a higher risk for educational failure, a greater tendency to physical illnesses, an increased likelihood of being hospitalised, and even an enhanced incidence of criminality in later life.

Above all, a miserable partnership causes deep pain and destroys the quality of life; for while nothing brings as much pleasure as marital joy, nothing causes as much suffering as marital injury. Indeed, many years ago, a patient, in the midst of a spousal crisis with her partner, wept, "Marriage is like open-heart surgery, but without the anaesthetic."

Even mental health professionals can experience marital woe. One of my psychological colleagues, who had recently celebrated his thirtieth wedding anniversary, quipped to me quite sardonically, "You get less for murder."

So, in view of the crippling emotional, physical, financial, and intergenerational costs of troubled marriages, what can we as mental health professionals do to treat those couples already mired in marital nightmares; and what, if anything, can we do to prevent future cases of dysfunction from developing? In order to approach such essential questions, we must first endeavour to understand more precisely what causes misery among intimate partners in the first place.

In 1914, not long after young John Bowlby's seventh birthday, the European continent erupted in the Great War, and Sir Anthony Bowlby, the distinguished physician (and father of the future psychoanalyst) helped to pioneer the field of modern military surgery. How the pre-adolescent John Bowlby would have understood the Great War, we do not know; but that intelligent, inquisitive surgeon's son might, even at the age of 7 years, have wondered whether one should blame the war on the Serbs for having assassinated the Erzherzog Franz Ferdinand and his wife, the Herzogin Sophie; or, whether one should attribute the responsibility to the perpetually belligerent Kaiser Wilhelm II. Older and more sophisticated people might have regarded this international conflagration as the inevitable outcome of the insidious arms race, or as the by-product of centuries of imperial oppression. Historians and political theorists alike have offered literally thousands of partial explanations of the causes of the First World War. And yet, alas, none seems completely satisfactory.

Just as scholars and commentators have suggested a welter of theories about the origins of the Great War, so psychologists and other mental health professionals have published a veritable litany of theories as to the origins of *marital* warfare. But what, precisely, causes spousal partnerships to explode like shells on the battlefields of France?

Throughout the centuries, pundits have proffered a multitude of explanations for the causes of infidelity: during the late fifteenth century, the now infamous German clerics Heinrich Kramer and Jakob Sprenger, authors of the influential tract *Malleus Malleficarum, Maleficas, & earum haereſim, vt phramea potentiſsima conterens* (known popularly, in English, as the *Hammer of the Witches*), first published in 1487, argued that spousal infidelity can be attributed entirely to the workings of the Devil (cf. Alexander and Selesnick, 1966). Fortunately, psychology has rather progressed since that time.

Basic textbooks of marital psychology generally attribute spousal difficulties to what we might think of as "external" forces that impact upon partners, such as a recent bereavement, unemployment, the birth of a baby, or the revelation of an extramarital affair. This seems a good place to start, for I have never encountered a couple whose relationship has become deliriously happy in the wake of the death of a family member or after a revelation of infidelity. But as psychotherapeutic workers, we have an obligation to dig deeper, and we have undertaken a training that permits us to do so. Thus, over many years, my colleagues and I have explored the more unconscious antecedents of these so-called "external" aetiological factors. Although losing one's job will increase one's likelihood of experiencing marital unhappiness, a psychotherapist must not only strive to discover the impact of job loss, but must also explore the unconscious ingredients—such as unconscious provocation or unconscious self-sabotage—that may have contributed to the individual being dismissed in the first place. Similarly, we know that an extramarital affair can devastate those who become embroiled in such a conflagration, but as psychotherapists, we work painstakingly to help couples to understand the little-known or even secret psychodynamics that might have contributed to the forensic enactment of extramaritality in the first place.

Let us now consider the origins of the extramarital affair, in particular, as a paradigm for understanding the deeper roots of marital woe. Nothing eviscerates the soul of a marriage more than the cruelty and hurt experienced in the wake of an extramarital affair. Sometimes one partner in a marriage will flirt with an attractive stranger at a party. An interaction of this nature might seem reasonably harmless, but even an eroticised glance, which some might regard as trivial, can, in my professional experience, ruin a marriage. Yet, as we know, various forms of infidelity contain far greater savagery, such as had occurred when one of my male patients took his wife's sister-in-law to a hotel room for sexual intercourse while his wife underwent chemotherapy on the oncology ward at a nearby hospital as part of her treatment for a fast-metastasising cancer.

Extramaritality has bedevilled us since ancient times, in spite of the Old Testament injunction against infidelity; but in the absence of more securely attached babies who will grow up with a supremely internalised sense of loyalty, those of us who work in the field of marital mental health will be unlikely to witness the eradication of infidelity in our professional lifetime. In a large-scale research project that I conducted between 2002 and 2007, based on a randomised survey of more than 19,000 British adults (Kahr, 2007a), I ascertained that some 55% of adult men and women admit consciously to at least one, and often more, acts of infidelity; 36% of British adults have engaged in kissing outside the bounds of their intimate, ongoing partner relationship; 18% have given or have received oral sex with someone other than a regular spouse; and 5% have practised anal sex, likewise outside marriage.

Additionally, as many as 24% of Britons have experienced vaginal sex with someone other than a permanent partner—in other words, extramaritally. In order to contextualise these percentages better, based on a population of around 45 million adults in Great Britain, the data suggest strongly that some 10.8 million people have engaged in vaginal sex with someone other than a regular partner.

The consequences of such extramaritality can be disastrous; and we know only too well, from research undertaken in the Department of Psychology at the Catholic University of America in Washington, DC, that those who do engage in extramarital sex will be more likely to experience diminished marital satisfaction and will, ultimately, be more predisposed to divorce (e.g., Glass and Wright, 1977). So both the scope and the consequences of extramaritality must be considered little short of enormous.

But there may be another type of affair far more sinister than the extramarital variety, namely, a fantasy affair of a sexual nature—often conscious, but generally fuelled by unconscious phantasy constellations. I have come to refer to this as the "intra-marital affair" (Kahr, 2007a, p. 32). Of course, virtually every human being experiences sexual fantasies in the privacy of the mind, and sometimes people will masturbate to the thought of a sexual encounter with a good-looking stranger or passer-by. Such sexual fantasies range in intensity and frequency, from fleeting glances and thoughts to daydreams, masturbatory fantasies, coital fantasies, and so on. Often, such ordinary, normative fantasies have few adverse consequences and might, in fact, provide great pleasure and release. But when fantasies become fixed, repetitive, suffused by sadism, and tinged with trauma and destruction and with the vestiges of fragmented, disorganised attachment patterns, then the intra-marital affair can, even more than the extramarital version, become toxic and result in extreme marital upheaval and distress.

Let us explore the concept of the "intra-marital affair" by reference to some clinical vignettes.

Clinical material

The case of Marissa: Cruising with Tom

"Marissa", one of the participants in the British Sexual Fantasy Research Project, whom I described in greater detail in my earlier writings on sexual fantasies (Kahr, 2007a, 2008), spoke to me most revealingly about her private sexual thoughts. A reasonably healthy young woman with no overtly gross signs of psychopathology, Marissa explained that she enjoys only one fantasy during masturbation, namely, having sexual intercourse with the Hollywood film star Tom Cruise. As one of the most successful and highly paid actors in the history of the cinema, beloved by countless millions of people around the world, it should not surprise us that the handsome and charming Tom Cruise should appear as the mainstay in the erotic fantasy life of a young woman.

In my interviews with voluntary research participants, I would always enquire more deeply, in an effort to understand the particular aetiological factors that might have contributed to such a fantasy. For instance, why should Marissa fantasise about Tom Cruise rather than about Brad Pitt or, indeed, Robert Redford? And why should she fantasise about a *film* star rather than a *pop* star, or a *sports* star, or, for that matter, the ordinary boy next door? As our conversation unfolded, Marissa provided more details of the fantasy. In conducting sexological research, one would be a very poor interviewer indeed if one allowed a research participant to declaim, simply, that she fantasises about Tom Cruise. This tells us very little. One must, of course, investigate how the fantasy unfolds, and one must discover what Mr Cruise does to her and, likewise, what she does to Mr Cruise.

Eventually, Marissa explained that, while masturbating, she imagines that she mounts Tom Cruise, allowing him to penetrate her. Once again, this seems perfectly reasonable, and one suspects that many other people will have fantasised about sexual intercourse with the Hollywood actor in this way.

Marissa admitted further that the intercourse occurs, *not* in a bedroom, but in Tom Cruise's red sports car, which he drives at lightning speed down a busy, traffic-filled motorway.

Of course, the seemingly ordinary masturbatory sexual fantasy of "sex with Tom Cruise" has now become much more complex and enigmatic. Why does the intercourse occur in a sports car whizzing on a highway? Surely that might be dangerous. And why does Marissa fantasise that Mr Cruise drives a *red* sports car, in particular?

Earlier in our conversation, in which Marissa and I had explored key moments in her childhood, I learned that, at the age of 11, Marissa's 18-year-old brother "Barney", a newly qualified driver, had died in a car crash, on a motorway, having collided head-on with a large articulated lorry. Suddenly, the contours of the fantasy became infinitely more interesting and potentially more explicable. As we discussed the fantasy, I wondered with Marissa whether she had managed to deal with this most searing trauma of her life—the unexpected and tragic death of her beloved teenage brother—by *eroticising* the trauma, in other words, by turning a deadly car journey into rather a pleasurable one. After all, Tom Cruise had set the film industry ablaze in 1986 with his portrayal of a dashing, action hero pilot, "Lieutenant Pete Mitchell", in the movie *Top Gun*, followed shortly thereafter by his role as racing driver "Cole Trickle" in the 1990 film *Days of Thunder*, in which he managed to survive even the most dangerous of escapades.

Extraordinarily, and also unwittingly, Marissa had managed to make her brother's traumatic death more bearable by bringing him back to life in her fantasies, symbolically disguised as the phallic and potent Tom Cruise, thus turning her actual memory of a deadly, bloody car collision into an extremely pleasant one, infused with the presence of a handsome film star, immune from mortality. In the course of our interview, I constructed a detailed family tree with Marissa, and I soon learned that her brother Barney was born in 1962. To my surprise, I later discovered that Tom Cruise had been born in that very same year; and this revelation thus underscored Cruise's status in Marissa's mind as a symbolic sibling. Thus, in choosing Mr Cruise as her fantasy object, Marissa had managed to replace her dead brother Barney with a fantasy action hero who drives cars and helicopters, and who never ages or dies, *and*, who happens to be exactly the same chronological vintage as her dead brother.

I also wondered whether Marissa's insistence upon Tom Cruise driving a *red* car might in some way represent her fear that Barney's smashed car would have become quite bloodied after he had collided with the articulated lorry, and that by choosing to place Mr Cruise in a *red* car, she found herself, quite unconsciously, turning a bloody red car of death into a red-hot passionate love-mobile of sex. Furthermore, by fantasising that Cruise would penetrate her vaginally, Marissa had thereby succeeded in having a brother-substitute always *inside* her, not only in the concrete anatomical–genital sense but also perhaps in the sense of Barney being *internalised*, and of being held in Marissa's mind and in her memory.

In attempting to psychoanalyse a sexual fantasy such as Marissa's, I have derived great inspiration from Freud's observation about the importance of discovering the meaning of each element in the narrative. In other words, it becomes imperative to understand why Marissa would fantasise about Tom Cruise in a red car on a motorway, as opposed to Johnny Depp on a yellow bicycle in the countryside. In considering dream analysis, Freud (1923b, p. 116) wrote that the study of the dream resembles "the solution of a jig-saw puzzle":[1]

A coloured picture, pasted upon a thin sheet of wood and fitting exactly into a wooden frame, is cut into a large number of pieces of the most irregular and crooked shapes. If one succeeds in arranging the confused heap of fragments, each of which bears upon it an unintelligible piece of drawing, so that the picture acquires a meaning, so that there is no gap anywhere in the design and so that the whole fits into the frame—if all these conditions are fulfilled, then one knows that one has solved the puzzle and that there is no alternative solution. [1923b, p. 116][2]

Young Marissa had no boyfriend; therefore, her sexual fantasy—her intra-marital affair—did not impact directly upon a spouse as such. But how, then, might an intra-marital affair operate in the context of a long-term spousal relationship? And what havoc might it wreak?

The case of Adolfine:
The impact of the Holocaust upon sexual fantasies

"Adolfine", an elderly Jewish woman, and her husband "Melchior", a Christian man, had not had any sexual contact in over thirty years. The couple had explored psychosexual therapy, as well as massage and other forms of physical stimulation; and they had even attended short-term counselling, airing their grievances about the disappointments in their professional lives as well as their hurt feelings from childhood; but none of these interventions had made any impact upon their inhibited sexual situation. In desperation, Adolfine and Melchior embarked upon psychoanalytic couple psychotherapy with me, knowing full well that their sexual anaesthesia could not be cured in a mere six sessions.

Over time, as our working alliance developed, Adolfine managed to reveal that, as the daughter of a Holocaust survivor, she often thought about Nazis. In fact, even though she had grown up in the safety of Great Britain, her mother had not had such a luxury, having survived several years in an Eastern European concentration camp. Adolfine then confessed that, every time she would masturbate, she imagined being raped by a Nazi guard. This sexual fantasy had informed her private masturbatory world since adolescence, and it brought her not only much erotic gratification but also great shame and confusion. Imaginary sex with Nazis became, in effect, her "intra-marital affair". And then, after her marriage to the Gentile Melchior, she experienced a tremendous conflict each time she and her husband made love, because she found the bedroom far too crowded, full of SS officers in her mind.

In my earlier writings on sexual fantasy (Kahr, 2007a, 2008), I posited that intra-marital affairs—these private, shameful sexual fantasy constellations—often develop directly from traumatic experiences or from the fantasmatic reverberations of traumatic events. Adolfine enjoyed a physically secure childhood. No one had ever raped her, and she had never met a Nazi; but her mother *had*; and as a means of processing the mother's trauma, Adolfine began to develop Nazi-related sexual fantasies as an attempt to master her mother's trauma by transforming the actual concentration camp experiences into something more pleasurable, leading to orgasm. When a trauma-fuelled sexual fantasy becomes deeply entrenched, it functions rather like a toxic mass in the mind. I have come to think of this type of intra-marital affair as an "erotic tumour". And this set of trauma-laden thoughts becomes the basis of the intra-marital affair, which, when imported into a spousal context, provides the necessary and often sufficient bedrock for marital dysfunction, resulting, in severe cases, in what I have come to call a "conjugal aneurysm".

Adolfine's intra-marital affair consisted of sex with Nazis, but it became dominated by guilt and shame and eventually transmogrified, more severely, into an erotic tumour. And when, on one occasion, Melchior, the husband, in an effort to reactivate his virtually non-existent sex life with Adolfine, suggested that they try a role-play involving a boss and a secretary, Adolfine became horrified and persecuted and told me that, for a brief moment, she fantasised about Melchior wearing an SS uniform; consequently, she forced him to sleep in the spare room in order to protect herself from his advances. This experience proved deeply traumatising for the couple and transformed Adolfine's private intra-marital affair into an erotic tumour, which, when provoked interpersonally, metastasised into a veritable conjugal aneurysm.

So, briefly stated, I wish to propose that, lurking beneath the behaviours of a dysfunctional marriage, marred by extramaritality or by sexual anaesthesia, one often discovers the presence of an intra-marital affair—an affair of the mind, frequently sexualised through repeated masturbation—which, when ossified, becomes transformed into an erotic tumour, linked to trauma, which, in turn, may result in a deeply painful marital explosion or conjugal aneurysm.

I appreciate that this appropriation of terms such as "tumours" and "aneurysms" from the fields of neuropathology, cardiology, and vascular medicine may seem quite unpalatable to certain ears, but over the years I have found myself deploying these concepts more and more in my work with traumatised couples, and I have found that such ideas give credence to spouses' experiences of attempting to survive something truly horrendous. As one of my couple patients confessed only recently, "A conjugal aneurysm is absolutely right. When I found out that he had been sleeping with prostitutes while I was pregnant with our child, I really thought that my entire head had exploded!"

Having now sketched a landscape that hints at the ways in which trauma impacts upon fantasy, which, in turn, shapes our intimate relationships with partners, let us now explore the concepts of the intra-marital affair, the erotic tumour, and the conjugal aneurysm in greater detail by reference to two particular accounts based on intensive, ongoing, open-ended psychoanalytic work, first with an individual and, next, with a couple.

The case of Zebulon:
The psychodynamics of the "sting"

Thirty-year-old "Zebulon", a tall Caucasian man, first entered psychotherapy some years ago for the treatment of a long-standing, crippling depression, which cast a "black pall" over his entire life. Zebulon told me that he could not derive pleasure from anything, even though he had perfect physical health and held a reasonably prestigious job in a lucrative industry. Zebulon found his position at work extremely boring, and he complained bitterly that it did not allow him to use any of his creativity. Convinced that he could be a brilliant painter, Zebulon had, in fact, never picked up a brush in his spare time; instead, he just simmered, and he lamented that he would die undiscovered as one of the great artists of modern times.

Zebulon refrained from speaking about either his sexual preferences or his sexual fantasies for a very long time. Although he and his girlfriend "Bernadette" had once enjoyed a very vigorous sex life, he no longer found her attractive, and he always avoided her advances in the bedroom, preferring to masturbate whenever he could create the privacy to do so. He experienced Bernadette not only as sexually

undesirable but also as increasingly boring, and he became very critical of the quality of her conversation at the dinner table, lamenting
that she failed to sparkle or to amuse their guests sufficiently.

As the psychotherapy unfolded, Zebulon made great strides in
working through his depression, and after two years his "black pall"
began to lift, particularly after we had begun to explore the nature
of his early attachment to his parents, whom he found unavailable
and inattentive, and who had sent him to an old-fashioned English
boarding school, where he experienced enormous loneliness and
isolation. Gradually, through the unfolding process of verbalisation
and engagement within the psychotherapeutic relationship, Zebulon
could envisage some glimmers of hope, and he could start to believe
that he might not, after all, die alone in his flat, as he feared, with no
one to discover his body for days.

In the middle of the third year of our work, Zebulon entered my
office in a state of sheer panic. He confessed to me that, while trawl-
ing on the internet, he had discovered a truly amazing website fea-
turing photographs of scantily clad women with very large breasts.
I did not quite know how to respond to such an announcement. In
part, I felt greatly concerned in case his pornographic activities might
represent an attack on his girlfriend Bernadette; but I also regarded
this revelation of libidinal arousal as a sign that Zebulon might be
coming back to life, and that his interest in sexuality might have
begun to reawaken.

After having told me that this particular website featured
extremely busty women. Zebulon then blanched and murmured,
somewhat sheepishly, "There's something I've left out. They're not
just women with huge breasts. There's something else." I braced
myself for a fantastical announcement. Zebulon then whispered,
"They're all *black*." I arched my eyebrows, as if to say, "And . . . is
there a difficulty with that?", whereupon Zebulon elaborated, "My
parents would be horrified. They are so racist."

Eventually, Zebulon confessed that he has always found "black"
women much more erotically arousing than "white" women, but
that having grown up in a Colonial family overseas, he found this
a very shameful and transgressive admission. During his very
early childhood—before his time in boarding school—his family
employed many black household staff, including one, in particular, who looked after Zebulon with enormous care and attention.
It seems that this African nanny had taught Zebulon about sexual
matters and had long conversations with him about how one makes

a baby. Unsurprisingly, these dark-skinned women became an over-arching presence in his erotic life. As he revealed more and more about his sexual fantasies, he told me that he always thought about African women while having intercourse with his Caucasian, English girlfriend. He claimed that if his parents knew about this, they would "have a heart attack", and this thought rather contributed to his general sense of excitement.

Over the years, I have worked with quite a number of Caucasian Englishmen who grew up in the last vestigial outposts of the British Empire, surrounded by African or Indian women; and in many cases these men, like Zebulon, had developed an erotic preference for dark-skinned women in favour of the light-skinned women who often reminded them of their neglectful mothers. For a Caucasian man to fantasise about African women seems, at one level, not at all problematic. But for Zebulon, the African women who fuelled his sexual fantasy life, both masturbatorily and coitally, became figures of taboo who not only stimulated pleasure, but, who also caused guilt at the same time, especially in view of the fact that his patrician and racist parents would be so disapproving.

But what does this have to do with erotic tumours? Surely, an intelligent, university-educated 30-year-old such as Zebulon should be able to find a way to enjoy his legal fantasies of black women without too much psychological suffering.

Eventually, Zebulon told me a great deal more about the fantasies. As so often happens in psychotherapeutic work, a patient will provide some preliminary information during one session and will then return at a later date and enrich the narrative, often filling in the more embarrassing details, which he or she had omitted the first time around. As our sessions unfolded, Zebulon told me that he not only fantasised about black women, but that he imagined treating them with *extreme violence*, knocking them about and penetrating them with an enormous fantasied penis, which would make them "scream with pain". Suddenly, the potentially politically correct fantasies of interracial sexual attraction with adult females acquired a more sinister, forensic quality. But now, at last, Zebulon had begun to speak of this hitherto secret part of his psychological life, and he provided me with a rich portrait of his intra-marital affair and of the erotic tumour that informed it, created in an early childhood context of broken attachment relationships with primary caregivers.

Some six months after first having discussed these fantasies with me, Zebulon made yet a further confession. Not only did he sneak away from his girlfriend at the end of every evening and masturbate to photographs of busty black women on his preferred website, but he also found yet another website, which allowed subscribers to chat to one another live, online, with a view to meeting up in person at a later point for furtive sexual encounters. In fact, he began to "hook up" with several black women in this way, and he experienced much disappointment when some of them did not want to have "rough sex".

Naturally, these admissions alarmed me greatly, and I found myself increasingly concerned over the safety of Zebulon's one-night stands, and of Zebulon himself; and I shared these concerns with him as we redoubled our psychoanalytic efforts to understand both his fantasies and his behaviours. Furthermore, I could now begin to appreciate that his depression—his presenting symptom—served as a very important defence against an underlying world of deep rage and violence.

One day, Zebulon arrived at my office looking unusually tearful. He told me that, over the weekend, he had a truly devastating experience. On the Saturday night he went online and began to "chat" to a beautiful black woman whose internet photograph he had not seen previously on the website's catalogue. He described her to me as "fresh meat"—in other words, as someone who had only just joined the website. In the course of their cyber-conversation, this woman asked Zebulon, "Do you like it rough?" He typed back, "Yes, I do . . . but how rough do *you* like it?" The mystery woman replied, "*Very* rough", whereupon Zebulon became instantly tumescent, and arranged to meet this exciting woman one hour hence at a Central London hotel. Zebulon sent the woman details of the location, checked into the rented room, and proceeded to wait for his "hook-up". At last, he heard a knock on the door, and with huge anticipation, he opened it. But to his utter horror, he found himself face to face, not with a beautiful black woman in search of "rough sex", but with his Caucasian girlfriend Bernadette!

Apparently, I seem not to have been the only person concerned about Zebulon's state of mind. Bernadette had also begun to suspect that something might be amiss, and she had very deftly hacked into Zebulon's home computer and had discovered his internet activities and his penchant for sadomasochistic sexual encounters with dark-skinned strangers. Zebulon told me that the sight of Bernadette standing in the doorway, having caught him red-handed, actually induced cardiac palpitations, and he thought that he might die from the shock and from the mortification. Bernadette had set up a so-called "sting" operation and had succeeded in entrapping Zebulon in the most compromising of situations. Needless to say, their relationship exploded, and in spite of my efforts to refer them to a colleague for marital psychotherapy, their long-standing partnership disintegrated, perhaps beyond repair. This type of marital tragedy—by no means unusual among contemporary patients in psychotherapy—typifies the ways in which erotic tumours and intra-marital affairs erupt as conjugal aneurysms.

Though shaken by his experience in the hotel room, Zebulon nevertheless tried to turn the experience to his advantage, and in session after session he told me that he felt relief that Bernadette had ended their relationship, because he had always wanted to do so anyway. He now realised that he absolutely *had* to start dating Afro–Caribbean women, and that he regretted having wasted all of his twenties with "white girls". He exclaimed that his psychotherapy had helped him to discover his true sexual self, and that he could now put his parents' anti-black prejudices to rest. I had other views, I must confess, and realised that we had not come to the end of our work by any means; instead, we had only just begun to shine the psychological MRI machine on his erotic tumour—a tumour that consisted of hugely aggressive components, and which, if left untreated, could metastasise and render Zebulon a full-fledged forensic patient.

Hereafter, Zebulon and I had quite a number of discussions in psychotherapy about the potential unconscious meanings of sadomasochistic sex. He sang its praises and accused me of being stuffy and conservative, in spite of having written a book about sex (Kahr, 2007a). In fact, he made frequent reference to people of "your age", imagining me to be a good decade older than my actual chronological age. In the transferential atmosphere of the consulting room, I had become the disapproving father who needed to be slain. Although I did not, initially, succeed in diminishing Zebulon's taste for "rough sex", his psychotherapy offered him, nonetheless, an opportunity to attack an oedipal rival and to neutralise some of his deep-seated aggression. My work with Zebulon continues uninterrupted, and I remain hopeful that, as psychotherapy progresses further, we might be able to modify the force of his erotic tumour, which, until now, has rendered him so very vulnerable to the destruction of his intimate relationships and which has replicated his primitive attachment patterns.

Not all cases of conjugal aneurysm can be traced to such colourful narratives or to such evident traumatic experiences. Indeed, not all of our patients will have experienced devastating sibling loss, as in the case of "Marissa", or the effects of being a second-generation Holocaust survivor such as "Adolfine", or of being brought up by a host of nannies and then sent to boarding school, such as "Zebulon". One does not need to experience horror in order to develop profound states of fantasy that can, nonetheless, shape one's own inner world and, consequently, one's marital situation as well.

We shall now consider a piece of work from a long-standing couple psychoanalysis in which the pronounced intra-marital affair of one of the partners exerted an immense influence on the couple's capacity to function.

The case of Jeremiah and Pandora:
A man, a wife, and a computer

One would be hard pressed to find two more sympathetic people than "Jeremiah", a 73-year-old man with an affectionate twinkle in his eyes, and "Pandora", his 72-year-old spouse, blessed with a beaming smile. In the seven years in which we have worked together in couple psychotherapy, neither has ever missed a single session, neither has ever come a moment late, and neither has ever delayed paying an invoice. In the midst of sessions, they have always listened to one another respectfully and have never interrupted one another; likewise, they have invariably attended to my observations with similar consideration. Throughout our time together, they have worked very hard. Indeed, Jeremiah and Pandora might well be described as perfect patients.

And yet, shortly before they had first contacted me nearly a decade ago, they had experienced a veritable conjugal aneurysm: Pandora had exploded at Jeremiah, insisting that she could no longer remain his wife, in spite of having managed more than forty years of marriage.

But why did Pandora explode? Had Jeremiah committed a marital crime?

I can assure you that Jeremiah had no lipstick stains on his collar, no credit card receipts for hotel rooms in his trouser pockets, and no penchant for pornography. He had never beaten his wife; he had never failed to come home for supper; and he had always earned a good wage, which he shared generously. Why, then, did Pandora erupt aneurytically?

Jeremiah had never cheated on his wife *extramaritally*, but it must be explained that he *did* have a *girlfriend*, and he kept her photograph on his bedside table, in full view of Pandora.

The frame, however, contained a picture *not* of a *woman* but, rather, of Jeremiah's Dell desktop computer! Literally, he had taken a photograph of his computer, and he kept it thus enshrined in the marital bedroom, in spite of the fact that this same Dell desktop computer resided only a few feet away, in Jeremiah's study, next-door to the bedroom, where he could see the actual computer at any time.

Photographing one's personal computer and placing it in a frame by one's pillow would hardly intrigue a divorce lawyer. Imagine an aggrieved spouse asking a litigator to sue her husband for all his worth because he kept a photo of his computer near to hand! But Jeremiah's seemingly innocent, perfectly legal, and undoubtedly non-forensic love affair with his Dell desktop personal computer had, nevertheless, more sinister ramifications, as fellow clinicians might well already suspect.

Though charming, cooperative, and honourable, Jeremiah also suffered from a form of psychological retreatedness that often bordered on clinical catatonia. Some might suspect Jeremiah of suffering from Asperger's syndrome because of his love of computers and other metallic objects; but if pressed to formulate his character in traditional psychoanalytic diagnostic terms, I would argue, rather, for a catatonoid state of withdrawal that contained elements of psychic retreat, dissociation, and frozen immobilisation. During the first years of treatment, Jeremiah would, in sessions, often fall asleep as Pandora screamed at him, or he would turn his body away from her and from me and appear to be completely immobile, or he would simply giggle anxiously whenever accused of being impossible.

Jeremiah held a high-level position of responsibility in a scientific research laboratory, which allowed him to interact predominantly with machinery and not very much with people, as Jeremiah could not easily bear human contact. Indeed, he found people messy and unpredictable, whereas computers, by contrast, would never disappoint him and could always be counted upon to be reliable and controllable. And Jeremiah certainly craved control. In fact, he wore the very same suit and the very same tie to every single session, never varying his costume at all. And I must confess that it would be impossible not to notice that Jeremiah craved consistency in clothing because his necktie stood out in a shocking manner. In particular, he always sported a wide 1970s-style tie, festooned with embroidered frogs sitting upon toadstools. It looked like something that a vaude-villian might wear in a pantomime, rather than a suitable piece of apparel for a distinguished man of science. When I queried Jeremiah's necktie—struck with disbelief that a person could don this piece of costume week after week after week—he merely chuckled and told me that he liked it very much.

Jeremiah's extraordinary desire to preserve sameness drove Pandora nearly insane, especially when his wish for constancy resulted in disorder in their home. To my shock and despair, I discovered quite late in our proceedings that the couple had only one toilet in their house, and that it had not worked properly for more than fifteen years. Apparently, in order to flush the toilet, one would have to remove the lid and fiddle with the inner workings, and then fill the tank with a pitcher of water. When, rather naively, I asked why this couple—who *do* have financial resources—had not called a plumber fifteen years previously, Pandora sighed with exasperation and burst into tears, lamenting that Jeremiah refused to allow a plumber into the house, as he kept promising that he, a scientist, would fix the toilet, but he could never muster the energy to do so, being always too tired at night and on the weekends.

Naturally, I engaged Pandora as to why *she* had not called a plumber of her own accord. With great passivity and with lack of insight, she explained that she did not want to upset Jeremiah, as he hated having visitors in the house. The breakdown of the toilet—the very object that disposes of toxic substances—served as a potent metaphor of the breakdown in both Jeremiah as a man, and also in the marriage. No detritus could be removed, and everything remained stagnant, from the unchanging necktie to the impaired toilet.

And yet, in spite of this portrait of a horrifically claustrophobic marital state, full of psychological effluvia, Jeremiah did come for psychotherapy, as did Pandora, and he did wear an outlandishly colourful tie with images of frogs and toadstools, painted in bright colours. Pandora always wore lovely yellows and reds and enjoyed a flourishing social life on her own. As a couple, they presented as vacillating between faecal deathliness and vibrant hopefulness. I often interpreted that they had come to see a plumber called Professor Kahr to help them unblock the mess in their minds so that they could then call the local plumber who might one day unblock their lavatory!

Although I cannot on this occasion provide a detailed case history or an account of the intricacies of our psychotherapeutic work, I can explore the way in which the couple's marital breakdown stemmed from an eroticisation of early trauma, which became encapsulated in the singular symptom of the framed photograph of the computer on Jeremiah's bedside table, which brought Jeremiah deep comfort and Pandora great despair.

One will not be surprised to hear that, although neither Jeremiah nor Pandora had suffered any gross physical abuse or sexual abuse as children, each had experienced monumental abandonment by parental figures. Pandora grew up overseas, tended to primarily by servants and other caretakers. On many occasions, when her parents left the house for shopping expeditions (and took the servants with them to carry the parcels), they would lock Pandora in a bare bedroom for upwards of twelve hours at a time, so that she could not harm herself in any way.

Jeremiah, likewise, had kindly parents who worked as medical missionaries overseas; but in their zest to help the children of Africa, they completely neglected their own son; he described to me long days spent exploring the veldt, with no human contact for hours and hours. Once, at the age of 8, Jeremiah flew from Africa back to England without his parents. He sat next to an adolescent girl, aged 16 years or thereabouts, whom he regarded as quite pretty. Although Jeremiah did not speak a word to this teenager and she did not address him, he fell madly in love with her nonetheless; and after disembarking from the plane, he decided that she would be his best friend for life, even though he had experienced no contact with her and did not even know her name. For the next ten years or so, this mystery woman from the airplane held a position of supreme importance in Jeremiah's lonely mind; and in an almost delusional way, he convinced himself that he had a friend at long last.

Eventually, disappointed by humans on multiple occasions, Jeremiah turned to science and to computers as sources of order, predictability, liveliness, and animation. Pandora, by contrast, did have human friends aplenty, as she had suffered fewer trenchant abandonment experiences than Jeremiah. But she endured enough compromised early attachments to find herself drawn to a man who understood this most besieged part of her own history, and so, the two married. Neither had ever had any previous partners. Indeed, these two exceptionally lonely people had found one another, had clung to one another, and had remained ferociously loyal to one another; and yet, they had little capacity to enliven one another; and so, after decades of unflushed toilets, Pandora exploded and threatened to leave.

I must also explain that although Jeremiah never cheated on Pandora in the conventional sense, he certainly did cheat through his idealisation of his computer and through the almost erotic, shrine-like placement of the Dell photograph in the couple's bedroom. In this respect, Jeremiah did, indeed, conduct an intra-marital affair with his desktop computer. But he also conducted another affair—not an extramarital one but, rather, another intra-marital affair with another woman. Jeremiah had a massive preoccupation with an old, minor film star from the 1940s called "Pandora". He loved this performer so much that he created an online fan club devoted exclusively to the ancient actress. He had never met the cinematic "Pandora" in person, but he had studied her films with the assiduity of an archivist, and he even spent several hours each day updating the star's website in obsessional detail. Pandora, Jeremiah's wife, became further enraged that she, a one-time amateur actress, had become merely the *second* Pandora in her husband's life!

I shall now attempt to summarise my formulation as to how Jeremiah and Pandora ended up in this extraordinary state.

Jeremiah had suffered from a primary trauma during early childhood: a profound breach of security of attachment by otherwise well-meaning and compassionate parents, who projected much of their own hatred into their son. In consequence, Jeremiah grew up with an introject that screamed: "I am abandoned." In order to manage this horrible internal experience, he developed what I would regard as a desperate and perverse means of triumphing over the trauma, and he did so through eroticisation and through taking pleasure in inflicting an unconscious form of abandonment on his wife. Thus, by ignoring his spouse, by turning his back on her in sessions, by falling asleep in mid-conversation, by worshipping his computer, and by prostrating himself as chief fan to another woman called Pandora, Jeremiah succeeded in transforming the grammar of his abandonment introject. No longer would he be governed by the internal thought, "I am abandoned." Instead, he reversed the narrative so that now he became suffused by the erotic tumour: "*I* am *not* abandoned. But I will take great pleasure in abandoning *you*." Thus, a broken attachment became a tumour of the mind, and one fuelled by unconscious pleasure.

The force of Jeremiah's erotic tumour penetrated every aspect of his personal life and, in particular, his marital life. Pandora, a fine woman in many respects, tolerated her husband's neglect unconsciously, having become quite accustomed to spending long days imprisoned alone in her childhood home. In many ways, she became the perfect partner for Jeremiah. And yet, although she endured her husband's intra-marital affair and, indeed, sought it out in the first place, she also hated him for his constant retreats to states of intra-maritality; and eventually, when the precise quality of Jeremiah's emotional abandonment of Pandora became too unbearable—more than their original unconscious marital contract had stipulated—she threatened him with excommunication. The marriage became aneurytic, and Pandora's devastating bouts of screaming only served to render Jeremiah more withdrawn, more catatonic, and more intra-maritally preoccupied. Sensibly, and in desperation, the couple sought help.

It pleases me to report that after five years of once-weekly couple psychoanalysis, Jeremiah finally purchased a new necktie—a sober one that would befit a professional office—and he gradually began to alternate this one with his more comical frog tie. After six years of psychotherapeutic endeavour, Jeremiah finally called the plumber, and the couple has, for the last year, come to enjoy a toilet that works spectacularly well. And after seven years of sessions, Jeremiah and Pandora now delight in a more fruitful marital interchange. They have resumed a regular sex life that each finds satisfying, and they have enrolled jointly in a series of adult education classes. Sometimes they even go hiking together in a nearby forest—something that they had never done previously.

I have offered this distillation of the case of Jeremiah and Pandora as an illustration not only of the power of couple psychoanalysis to effect both symptomatic and structural change in the mind of two lonely, abandoned, long-term partners but also of the complex vicissitudes of intra-marital preoccupations of the mind. One not need engage in physical, forensic enactments of infidelity (as in the case of Zebulon) but one can, nevertheless, "cheat" quite spectacularly merely through the use of one's mind and render one's partner a psychological cuckold in the process. Not every erotic tumour results in infidelity, and not every intra-marital affair results in an extramarital one. But in every case compromised attachments and early traumata attack the possibilities of spousal security in later life.

Ruining one's marriage in seven easy steps

For many years, the traditional psychiatric community neglected to provide formal consideration of marital eruptions as a form of psychopathology. In 2013, however, the *Diagnostic and Statistical*

Manual of Mental Disorders: Fifth Edition. DSM–5™ of the American Psychiatric Association (2013) finally included marital breakdown as part of the official nomenclature of psychological disease, albeit in a somewhat marginalised manner, tucked away in the general section "Other Conditions that May Be a Focus of Clinical Attention", under the sub-heading "Adult Maltreatment and Neglect Problems", which include: "Spouse or Partner Violence, Physical (confirmed or suspected)"; "Spouse or Partner Violence, Sexual (confirmed or suspected)"; "Spouse or Partner Neglect (confirmed or suspected)"; and "Spouse or Partner Abuse, Psychological (confirmed or suspected)".

Undoubtedly, physical violence and psychological violence do contribute to marital breakdown. But what causes the violence and abuse in the first place? It may be that something dangerous has become activated in the mind of the at-risk spouse long before one partner strikes another and long before one partner humiliates or insults another, just as smoking to excess and eating a profusion of fatty foods cause atherosclerosis long before a myocardial infarction attacks cardiological health.

Of course, such traumata as physical violence and psychological torture will contribute to marital breakdown, as will catastrophic life events such as bereavement, family illness, unemployment, and so forth. But as psychotherapists will know, these "external" events serve only to impact upon an already ravaged "internal" world. And the field of couple psychoanalysis has made important contributions to our understanding of the ways in which the external stressors—however ghastly—exacerbate an internal landscape already marred by disorganised attachment patterns (e.g., Clulow, 2001a, 2001b), by long-forgotten traumata including misattunement and neglect, and, perhaps most viciously of all, by the transmission of unconscious parental sadism (e.g., Kahr, 1993, 2007b, 2007c, 2012a).

John Bowlby often criticised his psychoanalytic colleagues for privileging "fantasy" over "real-life" events in the genesis of psychological distress and symptomatology. But though Bowlby offered a much-needed corrective to the fantasy-dominated psychoanalysis of the 1940s, we now appreciate that these two concepts need not be polarised in such a dualistic way. In fact, a sensitive and nuanced appreciation of the interplay between internal fantasies and external traumas can provide the clinician with a very broad canvas of ideas and hypotheses upon which to draw in the context of the psycho-therapeutic session.

Some years ago, I worked with a couple who told me that when they first met at a cocktail party, they fell not for one another's biceps or bosoms, nor for one another's sparkling eyes or witty banter; rather, "Arthur" experienced a strong attraction towards his future wife when he noticed that she had a plaster cast on her arm, which had resulted from a fight with a previous boyfriend, while "Anoushka" felt drawn towards her future husband when she spotted that he had recently broken his nose playing hockey. These virtually unconscious, fleeting moments of recognition form the very epicentre of a couple's fantasy world—a shared unconscious phantasy, one might suggest—in which each had recognised an injury and a woundedness that brought comfort, familiarity, and a sense of belonging.

Another couple, "Benedict" and "Benita", likewise became attracted to one another's injuries rather than to one another's beauty, brains, or brawn. This couple had first met when Benedict fell off the back of a bus and landed right next to Benita—his future wife—then a hapless passer-by who went to offer help. In a marital session years later, Benedict told me that he knew he would have to marry Benita because she nursed him on the street so lovingly, while Benita told me that she fell madly in love with Benedict when she saw blood gushing from his injured body as a result of the fall.

Marriage emerges *not* from conscious attractions but, rather, from deep unconscious processes that frequently remain a secret even to the couple themselves. These rich worlds of fantasy—these intra-marital affairs—often become sexualised; hence, it will not be surprising to learn that Benedict insisted that Benita dress up in a nurse's uniform as part of their foreplay. This constitutes an erotic tumour—a fantasy that becomes so pervasive that it dominates all interchanges between a couple, often in destructive ways. Although Benita enjoyed playing nurse, she soon grew weary of this because she wanted Benedict to care for *her*; and when he would not, a conjugal aneurysm ensued.

Having now introduced terms such as the intra-marital affair, the erotic tumour, and the conjugal aneurysm, let me briefly outline my understanding of what I have come to regard as the seven sub-phases that might contribute to the creation of spousal nightmares:

Step 1.   A caregiver impinges upon an infant either through abuse or abandonment, or through misattunement, or even through the transmission of death wishes, or some combination thereof.

Step 2.   These "impingements", as Donald Winnicott (1960a, p. 591) would have called them, result in traumatisation and in compromised attachment patterns that collectively deprive the growing infant of a secure base.

Step 3.   The trauma produces symptomatology: most usually depression and anxiety. But sometimes traumatic experiences will become eroticised, as an unconscious means of providing the person with pleasure rather than pain.

Step 4.   In certain cases, the eroticisation of trauma becomes fixed as an internal template or introject in the mind, which operates unconsciously. Such an eroticisation of trauma becomes an "erotic tumour".

Step 5.   Erotic tumours, reinforced by perennial masturbatory activities, result in potent "intra-marital affairs", in which an individual becomes pathologically preoccupied and unable to provide ongoing, intimate relatedness with a partner.

Step 6.   Those who become particularly prone to intra-marital affairs, based on erotic tumours, will often become unconsciously attracted to partners with similar preoccupations. Frequently, these preoccupations will counterbalance one another, and a marriage might well survive. But in cases in which the marital system becomes subject to external stressors, the intra-marital affair will *often erupt into an act of unbearable cruelty.*

Step 7.   When the couple in question has little recourse to verbalisation or other forms of psychological support, a conjugal aneurysm will often result.

This model has proven extremely helpful to me over the years in charting the development of a couple's marital breakdown and in identifying the complex interplay of both internal and external forces that compromise a couple's sense of marital security. I hope that, by delineating this often convoluted sequence, marital mental health professionals might become increasingly aware of the points of vulnerability that force people to progress from one step to the next; and I trust that such a delineation will be of some assistance to colleagues in becoming more adept at providing understanding and treatment before couples reach Step 7.

Over the last thirty-five years or more, I have worked with couples who have treated one another with the utmost cruelty. One spouse failed to reveal his HIV status to his fiancée prior to their marriage, and this duplicity ultimately erupted in a conjugal aneurysm. Another spouse, while on holiday, emptied her philandering diabetic husband's supply of insulin into the Indian Ocean, resulting not only in a conjugal aneurysm but also in endangering her partner's life. And still another spouse inflicted a punishment on his partner by telling her that her mother had died, which proved to be a bald-faced lie. But marital "crimes" need not be at all spectacular. The very first couple with whom I worked at the Tavistock Marital Studies Institute, many years ago, complained about butter—quite *literally*. "Carlos" expressed utter mortification that "Claudia" had purchased the wrong kind of butter and had served this inferior brand with toast at the breakfast table. Carlos felt so forgotten, so misunderstood, and so poisoned by his wife that he grabbed a nearby standing lamp and smashed her over the skull in retaliation.

Offering one's spouse the wrong type of butter does not automatically provoke a conjugal aneurysm. But nursing a long-standing passion for violence in the wake of early experiences of abandonment and intrusion contributes to the eroticisation of cruelty; and sometimes it requires merely a stick of the wrong kind of butter to spark a war, just as the assassination of the Austrian archduke became the trigger for more than 37 million deaths.

Although psychotherapists and psychoanalysts have become increasingly adept at communicating with patients about trauma, we still remain less than fully capable of helping our patients to speak about their most private free associations and, especially, about their masturbatory and coital fantasies. Indeed, while conducting my research on adult sexual fantasies, I ascertained that fewer than 10% of British psychotherapists had ever treated patients who had reported private sexual fantasies in full detail at any point. Although the climate has begun to change and although we have, more recently, started to acquire a better "sexual interviewing skin" (Kahr, 2009, p. 7), we, as practitioners, must still continue to develop greater comfort in discussing sexual matters if we wish to help our patients to speak with us about the ways in which they masturbate to images of Nazis, or to violent activities with busty black women, or even to motorway trips with Tom Cruise … a seemingly ordinary sexual fantasy, but one that could also serve as a desperate attempt to master the trauma of sibling death.

In the midst of writing this chapter, I happened to read a research study, published in the *European Heart Journal*, by a team of cardiologists from the Harvard School of Public Health at Harvard University in Cambridge, Massachusetts (Mostofsky, Penner, and Mittleman, 2014). These researchers confirmed that, in the two-hour period that follows an angry outburst, each of us will be nearly four times more likely to suffer a stroke and nearly five times more likely to experience a myocardial infarction. Our undigested, unprocessed, unneutralised affects, born in the strangulating bosom of broken affectional ties and affect-dysregulating misattunement experiences, can result not only in conjugal aneurysms that cause marital death but also in subcranial aneurysms that result in biological death. Woe betide the psychotherapist who focuses solely on externals at the expense of complex, convoluted, and often invisible unconscious fantasies. And woe betide the patients whose psychotherapists look outward only at the manifest, rather than inward, towards the hidden and the subterranean.

Back in the fourth and fifth centuries, St Alexius of Rome had, according to a medieval account, abandoned his bride on his wedding night in order to live in poverty and to devote himself to Jesus Christ (Lynch, 1992). St Alexius may, undoubtedly, have loved his saviour, but he may also have suffered from an early medieval attachment disorder. St Alexius's love for Jesus may have represented not only piety but also an eroticised intra-marital affair, which left Mrs St Alexius lonely and bereaved. External explanations provide some insight into marital discord, but only a lens that penetrates the surface can offer us a more comprehensive picture.

Having completed this work in 2018—during the centennial year of the end of the First World War—I might perhaps conclude these musings on marriage by remembering the words from the preamble to the Constitution of U.N.E.S.C.O. [United Nations Educational, Scientific and Cultural Organization], founded in 1945 in the aftermath of the Second World War, which states, with unusual psychological prescience, "since wars begin in the minds of men, it is in the minds of men that the defences of peace must be constructed" (U.N.E.S.C.O., 1945).

Notes

Small portions of the material from this chapter have appeared in a different form in *Sex and the Psyche* (Kahr, 2007a) and *Who's Been Sleeping in Your Head?: The Secret World of Sexual Fantasies* (Kahr, 2008).

1. The original German phrase reads: "der Lösung eines 'Puzzles'" (Freud, 1923a, p. 6).

2. The original German passage reads: "Dort ist eine farbige Zeichnung, die auf ein Holzbrettchen geklebt ist und genau in einen Holzrahmen paßt, in viele Stücke zerschnitten worden, die von den unregelmäßigsten krummen Linien begrenzt werden. Gelingt es, den unordentlichen Haufen von Holzplättchen, deren jedes ein unverständliches Stück Zeichnung trägt, so zu ordnen, daß die Zeichnung sinnvoll wird, daß nirgends eine Lücke zwischen den Fugen bleibt, und daß das Ganze den Rahmen ausfüllt, sind alle diese Bedingungen erfüllt, so weiß man, daß man die Lösung des Puzzle gefunden hat und daß es keine andere gibt" (Freud, 1923a, pp. 6–7).

CHAPTER FOUR

Sexual cruelty in the marital bed: unconscious sadism in non-forensic couples

Oh! how many Torments lie
in the ſmall Circle of a Wedding-Ring!

"Sir Solomon Sadlife", in Colley Cibber, *The Double Gallant: Or, The Sick Lady's Cure. A Comedy*, 1707, Act I, Scene ii

When wedding dresses catch on fire

Back in the late tenth century, more than a millennium ago, an aristocrat named Foulques Nerra—sometimes known as "Fulk the Black"—reigned over the *comté* of Anjou in the heart of France. Both a devout Christian who had founded numerous abbeys and monasteries, and also a patron of architecture who had built many castles, Foulques Nerra had, additionally, established a school for the education of the poor. But like many medieval potentates, Foulques dedicated himself not only to charitable works but also to violence: over many years, he distinguished himself in bloody combat, defeating the forces of Conan, the *duc* de Bretagne, in 992, in the Battle of Conquereuil, killing his enemy's son, Alain.

Foulques Nerra did not, however, confine his murderousness to the battlefield. It seems that he also practised early-medieval siege warfare at home. In the year 999, Foulques had discovered his coun-

74

tess, Élisabeth de Vendôme, *in flagrante* with a goatherd. Desperate for retribution, the nobleman had his wife bedecked in her wedding dress and then burned alive in the marketplace of Angers, the capital of Anjou (Guillot, 1972; Seward, 2014; cf. de Salies, 1874), in an act described by one medieval source as an *"horribili incendio combusta"* (quoted in Guillot, 1972, p. 25, fn. 129).

It seems uncertain that the fervent French Catholics of the tenth century regarded the vicious, unspeakable immolation of the approximately 20-year-old *comtesse* Élisabeth an act of domestic violence. Steeped in a climate of spousal abuse and frequent executions, these medieval Angevins might well have conceptualised the burning as justifiable punishment for the adulterous sin of the countess. But from our twenty-first-century perspective, it would be impossible to regard this act of brutality as anything other than the most vicious of marital attacks. By setting fire to his wife—a crime that would today land a man in Broadmoor Hospital for the criminally insane—and by having insisted that Élisabeth, little more than a late adolescent, should be burned in the very gown that she had worn on the day of their wedding, Foulques Nerra has become immortalised as one of the most gruesome perpetrators of marital sadism in history.

Although we cannot excuse the murderousness of Foulques for this uxoricide, let us not forget that the Angevin count had done so because of his *wife's* infidelity with a farmhand. This tale from medieval French history serves as a vicious reminder that in many, if not all, cases of marital explosion, each member of the couple might have contributed to the final outcome in some way.

One could, of course, cite numerous other instances of sexual cruelty between spouses throughout the centuries. In fact, one need not search very far for evidence (e.g., Bloch, 1991; Bourke, 2007; Butler, 2007; Goldberg, 2008).

Consider, for instance, one of the cruellest forms of sexual sadism in marriage—namely, rape. Indeed, for many centuries men could, and did, readily force themselves sexually upon their spouses, claiming that the mere act of marriage constituted a woman's consent to intercourse in the first place. The eminent American sociologist and traumatologist Professor David Finkelhor studied spousal rape in Boston, Massachusetts; in a landmark study, he and his colleague Dr Kersti Yllo discovered that rape occurred in around 3% of these marriages and, further, that one would be much more likely to be raped by a formally married spouse or by a cohabiting partner than by a stranger (Finkelhor and Yllo, 1985). Extrapolating this data to a British sample, one could estimate that, based on Finkelhor's and Yllo's findings, some 600,000 British women might well have suffered formal rape at the hands of their husbands, and countless others have had to endure unwanted sexual contact of various types. Fortunately, although many countries worldwide—including, of course, Great Britain—have, in recent years, declared spousal rape illegal, many others have not; and at the present time, no fewer than forty-eight countries or territories, including Afghanistan, Bahrain, Ethiopia, Haiti, Iran, Laos, Libya, Morocco, Saudi Arabia, Syria, Uganda, and Zambia, do not prosecute men for raping their wives or for committing other acts of sexual sadism upon their wedded partners.

Gross sexual violence occurs far too frequently within the context of long-term marital relationships, and always with disastrous consequences, including the infliction of physical and psychological damage. Fortunately, most married couples never engage in such clinically sadistic behaviours. Indeed, the vast majority of intimate partners treat one another's physical bodies with a reasonable degree of respect, and refrain from the use of sexual force.

But one need not be a violent, acting-out, forensic patient—a rapist or a torturer, for instance—to perpetrate deep cruelty upon one's spousal partner. Often, some of the "nicest" people—including those from privileged, well-bred, well-spoken, and well-educated families—treat their intimates with shocking viciousness, either physical or verbal, during sexual encounters. Many people, in fact, will reserve their most primitive and aggressive urges *specifically*, if not *exclusively*, for their long-term marital partners. And often, in consequence, the bedroom will become a boxing ring in which otherwise normal-neurotic couples might come to concretise some of their most sadistic tendencies.

Although I began my mental health career working in the forensic field with murderers, paedophiles, arsonists, rapists, and others who had committed acts of shocking abuse, I have accumulated far more experience in recent decades with ordinary, warm-hearted, honourable, philanthropic, civic-minded people who vote for the Labour Party, who read *The Guardian* newspaper, who make charitable contributions to worthwhile organisations, and who volunteer from time to time at the local soup kitchen *by day*, but who, nevertheless, will sometimes—indeed often—become deceptive, contemptuous, humiliating, and vengeful towards their spouses *by night*.

Those of us who work in the arena of marital mental health, as couple psychotherapists, couple psychoanalysts, or couple counsellors, have a unique opportunity to discover the hidden shadows of normal-neurotic marriages at very close range. Indeed, we now understand far more about violence in the ordinary couple than in the forensic couple (cf. Welldon, 2012; Motz, 2014), in large measure because most severe forensic patients live in prisons or hospitals, where mental health colleagues have little or no licence or opportunity to work with the spouses.

In view of the increased understanding of violence—especially sexual violence—in non-forensic couples (e.g., Weitzman, 2000), what, precisely, have we come to learn, in more recent years, about the origins of such cruelty, about its function, and also, about its treatment?

In the pages that follow, I will offer copious clinical vignettes in an effort to sketch a psychodiagnostic terrain of the different types of sexual hurt inflicted by otherwise ordinary, law-abiding citizens. I will then provide some thoughts about how the psychological clinician can better engage with these stories in work both with individuals and with couples. In all instances, I have, of course, altered the names and other obvious identifying biographical details of the individuals and couples concerned. Otherwise, I have refrained from any distortion of the data that I have heard over the years in my consulting room.

A typology of neurotic sexual cruelty

Violence towards one's spouse manifests itself in many forms and will often be underpinned by eroticism. Indeed, in the non-forensic population, spousal sexual sadism exists along a continuum ranging from seemingly minor acts of unkindness and insensitivity in the marital bedroom, characterised by only small amounts of "acting out", to those of a more severe nature, marked by a very considerable degree of acting out and consequent destruction. Let us now explore the panopticon of the different degrees and varieties of sexual sadism in the marital relationship, which might form the template of a typology of sexual cruelty.

Bodily evacuation as a form of sadism

Betty and Archibald

In the non-forensic sample of individuals and couples that one meets in an outpatient setting—often in an independent psychotherapy office—one becomes immediately aware of a vast range of acts of sexual unkindness. At one extreme, I recall the case of "Archibald", a hospital administrator, and "Betty", a nurse: a long-standing married couple with six children, who generally enjoyed one another's company and who had a capacity to make one another laugh. Archibald and Betty presented for couple psychotherapy one year after the death of Betty's mother, a bereavement that had plunged her into a moderate depression. Betty's mother had provided enormous support to the entire family, helping to look after the six children; consequently, her death left Betty deeply heartbroken. Yet in spite of Betty's melancholia, the couple still enjoyed a vigorous sex life.

One evening, Archibald returned home from the pub, where this hulking man with broad shoulders had consumed twelve pints of lager in swift succession. Archibald could generally guzzle as many as eight pints without experiencing any adverse effects, but after twelve of them he felt more than unusually woozy. As he explained, Betty's newfound depressed mood states had caused him distress and consequently he treated himself to four additional pints in order to fortify himself against the gloomy atmosphere at home. Later that evening, after the children had gone to sleep, Archibald and Betty went to bed, began to fondle one another, and soon proceeded to engage in coitus.

In the midst of penetration, Archibald began to wretch. Fortunately, he removed himself from inside his wife and staggered off the bed; he then vomited profusely on the floor, covering Betty's discarded clothes. Although such an encounter between a drunk husband and a depressed wife would be of little interest to a family lawyer—one certainly cannot sue successfully for divorce as the result of a single episode of vomiting—Archibald's behaviour caused Betty great disgust, and for several weeks thereafter she developed a phobic anxiety that her husband might actually vomit upon her. In view of Betty's depression, she had *already* begun to feel disgusted and dirty, and thus, when her husband discharged himself in this manner during sexual intercourse, Betty felt that the external world of *vomitus* both confirmed and exacerbated what she had already begun to experience in her internal world, soiled by her recent bereavement.

When Betty disclosed this information during a couple psychotherapy session, Archibald—usually quite compassionate—told Betty brusquely, "Oh, for fuck's sake, woman. Get over yourself. I had a few too many drinks. I didn't slap you." This reaction served only to inflame Betty's deep unhappiness in the face of such an unpleasant sexual encounter with her husband, and she then burst into tears. It took a great deal of time as well as much slow, painstaking psychotherapeutic work to help Archibald come to understand the way in which he had felt burdened and resentful about his wife's depression, which had made him, in consequence, feel impotent and useless. Gradually, Archibald began to appreciate that he had found a way of concretising his rage through the evacuation of vomit rather than through the expression of angry words, and that he would, in future, become more aware—more conscious—of his tendency to act out in such a manner.

Cressida and Dexter

Another normal-neurotic couple, "Cressida" and "Dexter", had recently celebrated their silver wedding anniversary. During their first consultation for couple psychotherapy, Dexter, a professional athlete, admitted that during recent months he and Cressida, an unemployed artist, had begun to fight "a bit", and that their general medical practitioner had recommended "talking therapy". Although Dexter explained that he had agreed to attend for sessions, he had his doubts about psychotherapy, as he believed that he and his wife had only "one little problem". In order to prove to me that he and Cressida had, essentially, a truly great marriage, Dexter then boasted that he and Cressida "make love" every single night and that, consequently, they enjoy a highly satisfying sex life. During Dexter's introductory speech, Cressida became increasingly ashen, and she began to fume. When Dexter paused, I turned in her direction, whereupon she exploded. "A great sex life?" she cried. "You think we have a great sex life?" Dexter then began to stumble over his words, uncertain of how to reply.

At this point, Cressida blew up. She explained to me that, in reality, they do not "make love", and have, in fact, *never* made love— quite the contrary. She then elaborated that every night Dexter will take her into the bedroom, undress himself fully, sit astride her naked torso, and then masturbate furiously and ejaculate onto her face. By this point, he will have exhausted himself so much that he will generally fall on the bed and succumb to deep sleep until the morning. After narrating her account of this nightly scenario, Cressida burst into tears.

Dexter, an often charming man who had many friends and who frequently donated large sums of money to those in need, had absolutely no capacity to express any comfort, tenderness, or regret to Cressida as she cried and screamed in the consulting room. Instead, he explained that he simply cannot stop himself ejaculating so quickly because he finds her so irresistibly beautiful, and that he could never imagine being with any other woman. Although Dexter may have intended this as a great compliment, Cressida became even more enraged at this point; she shouted, "Yes, but why do you have to do it on my face? You make me feel so cheap. It's disgusting. And you never bring *me* to orgasm. You're so selfish. So cruel!"

One need not be a mental health professional to wonder why Dexter restricted his sexual activities to climaxing upon his wife's face and why Cressida—ostensibly horrified by this—had endured such a nightly ritual over many long years. What, then, permitted such a complex marito-sexual dynamic to persevere? It might be tempting to describe the couple's nighttime ritual as a type of sadomasochism, characterised by Dexter's sadistic ejaculation upon his beautiful wife, and by Cressida's masochistic enjoyment for participating in this situation. But as I began to understand the unconscious life of the couple more fully, I came to realise that sadomasochism does quite not accurately describe the situation.

Dexter grew up in the East End of London, the seventh child of very impoverished parents who lived in a tiny two-bedroom flat on a council estate. Dexter described the estate as "disgusting" and "dirty" but boasted that his mother prided herself on cleanliness and that in spite of the family's impecuniousness and grubby surroundings she had managed to create a completely spotless home. The mother never allowed Dexter and his siblings to play outside, for fear that they might muddy their clothing. And in spite of having little money for the water bill, each child had to bathe every single day. Dexter's mother, clearly an obsessional woman, also refused, during rare family holidays at the seaside, to allow her children to walk barefoot on the beach, in case one of them might step on something "nasty". Chuckling affectionately, Dexter explained, "My mother was such a fierce lady that any germs would have been far too frightened to enter the front door."

Cressida had a rather more complicated childhood, characterised by a neglectful, alcoholic mother and a father who treated her with a certain amount of sexual lasciviousness. Although Cressida's father never laid a hand upon her, she recalled that he took an inordinate amount of interest in the size of her growing breasts and in the length of her skirts, making daily comments about her physicality, which she found intrusive and infuriating.

As our work progressed, the couple confessed to me that each night, prior to their sexual ritual, they would drink a bottle of very fine wine at dinner and would then retire to the sitting room and snort some cocaine. This revelation helped me to understand more fully the way in which such complex, nightly sexual choreography could be performed again and again.

Dexter and Cressida had never had children, and they claimed that they had never wished to have any. In view of the frequent facial ejaculations, I wondered whether the couple had *ever* engaged in traditional coitus, and I enquired about this. Dexter replied that he and Cressida had attempted "old-fashioned" intercourse a few times, but that neither of them had really enjoyed it very much, and that he had a much more powerful orgasm by masturbating himself.

As our psychotherapeutic work proceeded, and as our shared understanding grew, I became increasingly able to speak quite frankly with this couple. Cressida presented the marital dynamic as a veritable crime scene in which Dexter, the perpetrator, committed a foul act upon her body, and that she had no part whatsoever to play in this abusive situation. Dexter, by contrast, considered himself to be a truly worshipful lover and would defend himself by explaining that most of his male friends had mistresses, or visited prostitutes, or watched pornography, but that he never cheated on his wife and that he still found her so very exciting and attractive.

I offered a rather different conceptualisation, which I shared with the couple in slow, methodical stages.

I hypothesised that the nightly ritual of Dexter masturbating upon Cressida had begun not in the bedroom, but in the dining room, beforehand, when each kept filling the other's glass with more "fine wine"; then the situation became fuelled even further in the sitting room, while each of them inhaled cocaine. I compared this routine to that of an athlete warming up before a sporting event, or that of an actor vocalising prior to stepping out on stage. By underscoring this portion of the scenario, I began to explore with Dexter and Cressida whether, in fact, they might both be equally complicitous in the unfolding of the sexual tribulation that would follow. At first Cressida refused to consider that she had any active role in this episode, but eventually, as her defences began to loosen, both she and Dexter could begin to appreciate more fully the way in which they had conspired *jointly, as a couple,* to script such an evening routine.

Integrating our growing knowledge of the biographies of both Dexter and Cressida, we then began to consider the ways in which their highly institutionalised nightly sexual ritual might represent not a creative engagement of lovemaking but, rather, an instance of what Sigmund Freud (1914, p. 490) had first identified as a "Wiederholungszwang" ["repetition compulsion"] in which people restage early childhood experiences relentlessly, without any conscious awareness of doing so.

As our sessions progressed over a period of many months, the couple came to understand more fully that Dexter had suffered from a lifelong obsessional neurosis, which he had kept secret from Cressida and, often, from himself. It soon transpired that he had internalised so many of his mother's injunctions about germs and filth that he had developed the habit of washing his hands twenty or thirty times per day—always furtively so. Whenever he touched his genitals, he would skulk away to the bathroom afterwards, ostensibly in order to urinate but, in fact, to scrub his organ several times with carbolic soap. Essentially, he found sexual activity particularly dirty, both physically and mentally, and it proved both shaming and relieving for Dexter to verbalise this secret at long last to me and to his wife. Eventually, he plucked up the courage to inform us that he preferred to ejaculate on Cressida's face rather than to insert his penis inside her vagina, as he regarded the female genitalia as particularly unclean. Naturally, such a confession hurt Cressida deeply, and she began to cry, but gradually she came to realise that Dexter's revelation did not surprise her in the least. In many ways, she had already known this about her husband and had already sensed his disgust of bodies in general.

I interpreted that Dexter's struggle to penetrate his wife vaginally not only stemmed from his fear of maternal disapproval and from a fear of contamination but also served as an expression of his hateful feelings towards women more generally, starting with his mother, who had controlled his mind and body so relentlessly, and ending with his wife, onto whom he transferred these powerful affects. Drawing upon the originary observations of Dr Karl Abraham (1917), one of Freud's earliest disciples, I tried to help the couple to understand that the act of ejaculation upon the woman's body might well represent an expression of deep admiration and excitement, but it might also, at the same time, constitute a form of angry soiling.

Cressida, too, eventually came to acquire a more sophisticated knowledge of her own role in facilitating what seemed to be, on the surface, an exclusively sadistic sexual interaction, with Dexter as the ejaculating perpetrator and herself as the unwitting collaborator. In fact, by drinking wine and by inhaling cocaine each night—the necessary preparation for the sadomasochistic sexual ritual—Cressida had assisted Dexter in setting the stage for this particular form of erotic theatre, recreating her own role as the passive victim of her father's lecherous and humiliating attentions during her childhood. But this time Cressida allowed her husband to ejaculate upon her face, repeating something unpleasant but also, then, allowing herself to attack Dexter afterwards, constantly insulting him, complaining about him, and humiliating him—something that she had never done with her more terrifying father.

Thus, the case of Dexter and Cressida allows us to consider the possibility that the foundation of an uncomfortable sexual scenario, laced with hatred, stems from early antecedents and then becomes re-enacted inexorably, and without conscious understanding. In this instance, both members of the couple used the marital bed as a laboratory for discharging, evacuating, and projecting early discomfort and disgust into the other: Dexter did so through ejaculation, and Cressida did so by permitting Dexter to treat her as a dustbin, so that she could then avenge herself upon him with cruel verbal taunts.

Regrettably, I cannot elaborate in more detail on the development of insight in this couple over the course of time, but fortunately, towards the end of treatment some three years later, Cressida and Dexter had begun to cultivate a much more loving, much more tender, and much less sadistic style of lovemaking, as well as a much less alcohol-dependent, drug-fuelled style of interrelating more generally. Neither member of the couple found our psychotherapeutic work particularly easy or enjoyable; and often, each would take potshots at me for "subjecting" them to such an arduous process, which I interpreted as a further expression of their wish to evacuate wounded and hateful feelings into the nearest object to hand.

* * *

In the two aforementioned vignettes—those of Archibald and Betty, the couple who turned the bedroom into a *vomitorium*, and of Cressida and Dexter, the partners whose marital chamber became an *ejaculatorium*—each member of the couple participated in equal measure in the creation of the sadistic sexual scenario, using the marital bed as a means of evacuating unpleasant, primitive affects rooted in early experiences. Although Archibald vomited on Betty's clothing and Dexter released his semen on Cressida's face, neither couple, to their credit, "acted out" beyond the confines of the marital relationship. All the partners managed to preserve their most particularly noxious feelings exclusively for one another, and they did so at the same time, and in the same room. In spite of their difficulties in the bedroom, these couples remained very much faithful and intact.

I would like to propose that such instances of evacuation, confined primarily to the sexual sphere, offer the clinician and, indeed, the couple, a great sense of hope. Prognostically, such couples manage treatment reasonably well, if not very well indeed, and will usually remain committed to their marriage; in my experience, they rarely divorce or experience what I have come to refer to as a "conjugal aneurysm" (Kahr, 2014b).

But sexual sadism can become much more complex, and once the enactments of aggressivity begin to emerge outside the bedroom itself, couples will often experience infinitely more distress. Archibald and Betty, as well as Cressida and Dexter, remained deeply committed to one another. In more advanced cases of marital infidelity—either psychic or physical in nature, and often both—extramaritality becomes the hallmark of cruelty.

The intra-marital affair and the extramarital affair

Elfriede and Francis

A middle-aged woman, "Elfriede", entered individual psychoanalytic treatment in order to overcome a long-standing inhibition in her professional work. An artist of considerable accomplishment, Elfriede had begun to "freeze" while in her studio, and for several years she could produce no work at all. Elfriede, married to her childhood sweetheart, "Francis", an ophthalmologist, often smirked with a considerable amount of contempt and would joke that she had married the only blind eye-doctor in the United Kingdom, because Francis did not have a clue about his wife.

Indeed, Elfriede led a double life. She sat at her computer for hours, masturbating to internet pornography and enjoying cyber photographs of handsome men. She also frequented clubs and pubs, wearing tight skirts with no underwear beneath, in the hope that some man would notice her and whisk her away, *Madame Bovary*-style, from her bourgeois life as a doctor's wife. As Francis worked incredibly long hours, Elfriede felt extremely abandoned, in spite of the fact that she enjoyed the financial security afforded by her husband's profession.

Often gripped by strong denial, Elfriede spent a great deal of her session time boasting that Francis had not the slightest inkling about her computer activities or about her many visits to bars; and though she felt triumphant that she could "cheat" on her husband in this way, she also became extremely desolate that her "blind" ophthalmologist could not see the extent of her unhappiness. Interestingly, although Elfriede devoted much time to the internet and to her erotic forays into the West End of London, she never actually succeeded in sleeping with another man. Various gentlemen had bought her drinks and had made passes at her, but something always stopped her from taking them to bed. Technically, she remained faithful to Francis, but in her private mind she had committed a multitude of infidelities, exemplifying what I have already referred to as the "intra-marital affair" (Kahr, 2007a, p. 32), as opposed to the more familiar extra-marital variety.

The intra-marital affair—a liaison that unfolds predominantly in the mind—may not leave lipstick stains on the collar or hotel receipts in one's handbag or trouser pockets, but this type of internal enactment can cause great psychological devastation nonetheless. Intra-marital affairs—these extraordinarily private and deeply consuming sexual fantasy constellations—serve a multiplicity of functions. In my earlier study of the traumatic origins of the sexual fantasy, I identified as many as fifteen possible conscious and unconscious functions of the sexual fantasy or intra-marital affair, including, *inter alia*, that of an unconscious attack on both oneself and upon one's partner (Kahr, 2007a, 2008).

Although sexual fantasies may often provide much private fun and pleasure and can frequently, in the context of a healthy marriage, become an additional reservoir of sexual creativity, such intra-marital affairs serve, for the most part, as uncomfortable refuges that help to alienate one spouse from the other. In more extreme cases, especially in those individuals with a pronounced history of emotional and physical trauma, intra-marital affairs often become ossified as "erotic tumours" of the mind, which come to dominate all aspects of psychic functioning in much the way that a brain tumour will destroy aspects of healthy cognition. When these erotic tumours erupt, they will often result in what I have earlier identified as the "conjugal aneurysm" (Kahr, 2014b).

I cannot, on this occasion, provide a more detailed study of either the aetiology or treatment of Elfriede's intra-marital affair, but I can confirm that she did, indeed, suffer profoundly, and that her private sexual preoccupations, which she had never articulated to anyone prior to the start of her psychoanalytic sessions with me, prevented her from enjoying either her professional work as an artist or her marital relationship with a somewhat emotionally unsophisticated but otherwise loyal and decent husband. Elfriede's intra-marital affairs—an expression of sexual sadism towards Francis—bedevilled her mind, but fortunately an immersion in a lengthy period of intensive, multi-frequency psychoanalytic work helped to contain and to work through the force of her intra-marital preoccupations, and thus prevent them from becoming ossified as an erotic tumour or exploding as a conjugal aneurysm.

To her great credit, Elfriede had come to seek help before she could destroy her marriage in a volcanic eruption; and having undergone protracted psychoanalytic treatment, her spousal relationship remains intact and enriched to this day. But other individuals and couples who suffer from the psychopathologies of sexual fantasy will often arrive at our consulting rooms only *after* the conjugal aneurysm has exploded with devastating consequences.

Gwilym and Hester

"Gwilym", a successful barrister, devoted his life to public service and had, as a result of his hard labours, developed a fine reputation in his field of legal expertise. He often showered his wife, "Hester", with expensive pieces of jewellery, and he always made a point of protecting his family diary so that he would never do any paperwork at weekends; instead, he spent every Saturday morning playing football with his son, and every Saturday afternoon accompanying his daughter to ballet classes. He devoted Sunday mornings to cooking an enormous roast meal, which he and his wife and children enjoyed greatly; and later in the day, Gwilym would supervise the pleasant ritual of watching a family-friendly film with his loved ones. On paper, he had the perfect life.

But every night, after Hester had gone to bed, Gwilym would sneak downstairs into his study, lock the door, and masturbate to a particular genre of internet pornography. Although he identified himself as "one hundred per cent heterosexual", he had become quite obsessed with pre-operative transsexuals and would climax to visual images of men who still retained their penises but who also sported newly developed, hormonally induced breasts, bedecked in lacy lingerie. These internet sessions caused Gwilym a great deal of shame, but they also provided him with a degree of unrivalled sexual excitement that eclipsed any pleasure that he had experienced with his otherwise beautiful and loving wife Hester.

As one might imagine, those who perform sexual activities outside the bedroom will wish to conceal their infidelities—even those of a "virtual" cyber nature—but, at the same time, many will also harbour an unconscious wish to be discovered, in the secret hope that, if this should happen, a marital crisis may be provoked and then, ultimately, treated. And although thus far Gwilym had succeeded in not arousing suspicion, eventually Hester had become increasingly aware of her husband's late-night disappearances; on one fateful evening, when Gwilym had failed to lock the door to his study, she burst in on him unannounced and found him engaged in a live "cyber-chat" with a male-to-female preoperative transsexual.

At this moment, Hester's world collapsed entirely; she not only screamed at Gwilym for his tremendous duplicitousness and "perversion", but she also railed at herself for her naïveté, recognising that she could no longer respect or believe the very special, beloved man in whom she had placed every ounce of her trust. At Hester's insistence, she and Gwilym then arranged a consultation to see me for marital psychotherapy.

Gwilym had never actually met a transsexual man in person. In fact, he never exchanged bodily fluids with anyone other than his wife. But his copious cyber activities, indicative of a strong set of intra-marital affairs and erotic tumours, provoked a conjugal aneurysm of great proportions, which made Hester feel that she had lived a lie throughout her entire marriage. I must confess that, upon hearing of this aneurytic spousal relationship, I initially assumed—quite wrongly, I must confess—that such marital turmoil could never be survived, and that Hester and Gwilym had come to see me in order to find a more human way of divorcing.

But the couple loved each other greatly, and after five years of psychotherapy had managed to come to experience understanding and even forgiveness. Once again, I cannot discuss the complexities of the treatment itself in the context of such a brief communication, but I can report that through our work, Gwilym came to conceptualise his need for a fantasied sexual experience with a male–female person as the result of much early deprivation from both his mother and his father. And Hester not only developed a greater, more sensitive appreciation of Gwilym's complicated sexual mind but also came to realise the ways in which her own infantile rage, never before contained or treated, had helped to provoke Gwilym to seek a Hester-free refuge in his study late at night.

* * *

The cases both of Elfriede and Francis and of Gwilym and Hester typify the widespread nature of what we might come to consider as "disorders of sexual fantasy" in otherwise healthy, law-abiding, and compassionate individuals. Neither Elfriede nor Gwilym had ever perpetrated acts of discernible cruelty against their children, their friends, their colleagues, or other members of society. Instead, they reserved their private sadistic attacks for their spouses and, ultimately, in view of the consequences, for themselves.

Elfriede and Gwilym—the two fantasists under consideration—differ from Archibald, who vomited on his wife's clothing, and from Dexter, who ejaculated on his wife's face. While Elfriede and Gwilym "acted out" *beyond* the space of the marital bedroom *behind* their partners' backs, Archibald and Dexter did so in the *presence* of their wives. Of course, I do not wish to propose so crude a theory as to suggest that those who perpetrate sadistic acts in front of their partners may be less dangerous than those who do so more secretively. The very reality of marital rape would completely contradict such an assertion. But I do wish to suggest that when the sadistic enactment occurs in full view of the partner, then the cry for help becomes more apparent more quickly, and each member of the marital pair has a greater opportunity for awareness and for seeking psychological treatment.[1]

Sadistic enactments as a defence against death

Sexual insensitivity, sexual thoughtlessness, sexual narcissism, and sexual cruelty can cause a great deal of distress to partners. Thus far, we have examined what might transpire when partners treat one another's bodies or bodily spaces with unkindness, or when spouses "cheat" on each other in a fantasmatic way, often assisted by the internet. But what happens when infidelity moves beyond the realms of fantasy and into the arena of bodily enactments with another living person outside the marital home?

For the non-forensic couple—those who never commit arrestable crimes such as rape or murder or domestic violence—sadistic infidelity may well be the most serious expression of cruelty, and it presents far greater challenges both to the couple and to the clinician.

Isaac and Jessica

"Isaac" had just turned 40. A successful banker with lots of money to spare, this man travelled extensively on business and, during his frequent trips abroad, he spent many evenings alone in luxury hotels. Separated from his wife "Jessica" and from his four young children, Isaac often arranged for prostitutes to visit him in his hotel suite. Having paid these sex workers, he would engage in a variety of complex sexual activities with them.

Although Isaac explained that he found most of these prostitutes to be "disposable", one young woman—a 19-year-old escort called "Katerina"—had really captivated him, and he began to meet with her more frequently, often flying abroad just to see her. Before long, Isaac stopped paying Katerina for sex; he eventually established her as a second spouse and even purchased a beautiful apartment for her. In due course, Katerina became pregnant with twins. As a result, Isaac eventually found himself supporting two wives and six children, as well as both a British and a Continental household.

Isaac's concretely enacted infidelity can be traced to a multitude of sources. But above all, we must note that this series of visits to prostitutes and the creation of a second marriage to Katerina all occurred in the wake of his fortieth birthday. During the course of one-to-one psychotherapy with this man, it did not surprise me to learn that Isaac's father had also had a conjugal aneurysm at the age of 40. He had left Isaac's mother in a most traumatic way: he had simply disappeared, abandoning both wife and son forever; 10-year-old Isaac never saw his father again.

To Isaac's credit, perhaps, he did continue to maintain very regular contact—physical, emotional, as well as financial—with his wife Jessica and with his four British children. He never abandoned them in the completely callous way in which his own father had done. Although Isaac had repeated a parental, intergenerational trauma, he had, at least, minimised the extent of the abandonment. But even though he did not disappear from the lives of Jessica and his children in the way in which his father had disappeared, Isaac nonetheless committed an act of great infidelity—a form of sexual sadism— which cost him dearly. Not only did he find himself crippled by the cost of maintaining his two wives, six children, and two household establishments, he also found himself virtually bankrupt after Jessica discovered his "double life" and sued him for divorce, winning an impressive settlement that cost Isaac millions.

As a man who had only recently entered his fifth decade of life, Isaac began to fear death greatly. Indeed, in the wake of his divorce, he found it extremely difficult to differentiate between the emotional death that he experienced when Jessica took the children and his own sense of having an ageing body that would some day cease to function. In our psychological work together, we gradually came to appreciate the way in which Isaac's attraction to prostitutes, and, in particular, to the youthful Continental Katerina, served as a means of eroticisation as a defence against deadliness: a common form of "acting out" in the middle years of life in which one replaces death with sex in the hope that the birth of a new baby will minimise the pain and the work required from each of us at facing the severe limitation of time.

Throughout his psychotherapy, Isaac struggled to appreciate the full extent of the way his deep infidelity and his creation of a second family with Katerina had caused immense pain to his wife Jessica and to his four children. During many sessions, Isaac referred to Jessica as a "fucking bitch" for having hired such a "shark" of a lawyer who kept asking for more and more money in the divorce settlement. Isaac experienced great difficulty appreciating his deep, sadistic betrayal of Jessica. Fortunately, as psychotherapy progressed, Isaac became increasingly sensitive, and he came to realise that his enactments had caused immense pain and suffering.

Lester and Martina

I conclude this portion of the chapter with one further clinical vignette, which illustrates, most shockingly, the true depth and the profound viciousness of sexual sadism in spousal relationships. "Lester", a businessman, and "Martina", a schoolteacher, had wed during their early thirties and had remained in a very long marriage of more than twenty-five years; but throughout their time together, Lester had cheated on innumerable occasions. The couple arrived at my office in a dreadful state because, one year previously, Martina had received a diagnosis of lymphoma, and had subsequently undergone several rounds of debilitating chemotherapy and radiotherapy, which caused her to lose all her hair and resulted in great nausea and fatigue. Owing to the gravity of her cancer, Martina had hoped that Lester would cease his infidelities and become a good caretaker; and, indeed, he did promise that he would look after her throughout this dreadful medical ordeal.

Tragically, Lester perpetrated one of the greatest acts of marital sadism that I have encountered in over thirty-five years of clinical practice. It seems that after Lester had dropped Martina off at hospital for her chemotherapy sessions, he would then, quite frequently, check into a hotel room around the corner from the hospital and have sex with Martina's younger and healthier sister, whom he had always fancied. A skilled philanderer, Lester had managed to keep the details of these furtive encounters secret from Martina, but her baby sister "Norma", riddled with guilt, confessed what had happened in order to clear her troubled conscience. To her great credit, Martina refrained from killing herself in desperation and also from injuring her husband and her sister, which many other women might have done in such horrific circumstances.

I could expound at great length on the psychodynamic aspects of this case and upon the role of the childhood histories of both Lester and Martina, as well as of her sister Norma, in creating such an unholy triangle. But in this context I have chosen to undertake the more primary task of describing a typology of sadism; and no discussion of the topic would be complete without providing an indication of the magnitude of cruelty in otherwise normal-neurotic marriages between essentially law-abiding, decent citizens. I can report with a heavy heart that in the midst of our efforts to unravel and treat this exceptionally painful conjugal explosion, Martina succumbed to her lymphoma; she died at the age of 56 years.

* * *

The cases of the 40-year-old Isaac, volcanically immersed in a profound mid-life crisis that prompted him to find a second wife and to create a second family, and that of Lester, a long-term marital despoiler who slept with his wife's sister during chemotherapy sessions, underscore the painful association between sexual infidelity, marital sadism, and the struggle with death anxiety. In each instance, one member of the couple endeavoured in quite a primitive manner to defend against the inevitability of ageing and death by introducing eroticism into the mixture, in the vain hope that by suddenly becoming sexual, one could deny the reality of an ailing body.[2]

Torching the marital bedroom

In 2007, I published the results of a five-year study, the British Sexual Fantasy Research Project, which surveyed and analysed the sexual behaviours and, in particular, the erotic fantasies of a randomised sample of some 13,553 British adults (Kahr, 2007a), supplemented by comparable data on some 3,617 American adults published the following year (Kahr, 2008). This study of British sexuality revealed that as many as 36% of adults, aged eighteen or older, have kissed someone other than a regular spouse or partner outside the marital relationship; 25% have fondled someone other than a spouse or partner; 18% have engaged in extramarital oral sex; 24% have experimented with extramarital vaginal sex; and 5% have practised extramarital anal sex (Kahr, 2007a). In each of these instances, men in partnerships indulged themselves more frequently than women . . . but not much more. For instance, although 28% of partnered males boasted one or more experiences of extramarital vaginal sex, as many as 20% of partnered females did so as well. Translated from percentages into actual figures, this suggests, as I have already indicated, that nearly 11,000,000 British adults have experienced extramarital vaginal penetration.

When we examine sexual fantasies, as opposed to sexual behaviours, the incidence becomes infinitely greater: hardly a man or woman alive will not have climaxed to the thought of sexual congress with someone other than his or her long-term partner. This should not surprise us, as the indulgence in sexual fantasy has for many centuries helped to protect us from actual, forensic infidelities. If we take a pretty co-worker or a handsome stranger to bed *in our minds*, we might, perhaps, be less likely to do so in the "outside" world.

But when one explores the content of many of these sexual fantasies, one finds that the average Briton often achieves climax by masturbating about extramarital sex, with as many as 41% of British adults having admitted to the erotic fantasy of sexual relations with someone else's partner. Furthermore, as many as 29% of the adult British sample reported having fantasised about being dominant or aggressive during sexual activity, and 33% admitted to comparable fantasies about being submissive or passive during sexual activity, while as many as 13% have enjoyed the thought of spanking someone else, and 12% have indulged in fantasies of being spanked. As many as 23% of adults reported sexual pleasure at the thought of tying up another person, and 25% of adults admitted to sexual excitement at the prospect of being tied up (Kahr, 2007a). Clearly, the interrelationship between sexuality, aggression, and infidelity remains extremely intimate.

In the preceding pages I outlined a typology of sexual sadism in the non-forensic couple: those partners who constitute the vast majority of the world's population. None of the members of the couples described herein have ever set their spouses on fire, as Foulques Nerra, the medieval Angevin *comte*, had done back in the tenth century. Indeed, none of the couples in my clinical survey had ever, to the best of my knowledge, received even so much as a parking ticket from the local traffic warden. Most of the men and women with whom I have worked have led reasonably exemplary lives, have paid their taxes, and have helped old men and women cross the road. They have, indeed, proved to be model citizens—except, perhaps, in the bedroom.

And whether by vomiting on, or near, each other, by ejaculating on each other, by masturbating to internet pornography throughout the small hours, by keeping a second home, a second wife, a second child in another country, or by sleeping with the sibling of one's spouse while that spouse undergoes chemotherapy, all of the aforementioned couples had found a way of expressing sadism, thus soiling the potentialities of the marital bedroom. In most cases, one partner holds the distinction of being the overt instigator of the cruelty. For example, in the case of Gwilym, the man who spent hours engaged in internet cyber chats with pre-operative transsexuals, any court of law would describe him as the perpetrator, and his wife Hester as the innocent victim. After all, *she* had never masturbated with a stranger over the internet. Only Gwilym had done so. Of course, *in sensu stricto*, only Gwilym had committed an act of infidelity, but those of us who work from a couple psychoanalytic perspective have come to realise that even though one partner engages in the forensic enactment of infidelity, both partners in a marriage may well have contributed to the creation of the unconscious emotional climate in which such enactments become possible, even necessary, in order to maintain psychological equilibrium and to protect the couple from even worse marital violence. When, during couple psychotherapy, Hester screamed at Gwilym, she did so with such ferocity that I often wished that I had brought a pair of ear plugs to the consulting room. I realised, of course, that any wife who discovered her husband *in flagrante* might wish to raise her voice in such a pained and anguished way. But as I came to know this couple better, I learned from Gwilym that Hester had screamed at him night and day, long before he had ever had access to something called the internet. The screaming in the consulting room became so persistent and so penetrating that, on one occasion, a colleague who works in the adjoining consulting room in my office building complained to me afterwards about the noise level. This vignette helped me to realise that although one member of the couple often commits the "crime", *both* will have facilitated its ultimate emergence.

People often lambast Freud for having foregrounded the importance of both sexuality and aggression as the dominant features of the human unconscious mind. Whether Freud overestimated the role of such basic drives remains a matter for debate. But as a couple mental health worker, I would even be inclined to suggest that Freud might have *underestimated* the role of destructive sexuality and aggression in the intimate partner relationship, because as a couple psychoanalytic practitioner, I often see evidence of little else.

Oscar and Priscilla

In the clinical consulting room, we invariably encounter proof of the painfully close admixture of these two most powerful drives. "Oscar", an elderly man, had developed a severe bronchitis, and he languished for days in the marital bed. Once, he asked his wife "Priscilla" to bring him a cup of hot tea to ease his aching throat. Priscilla returned with the tea . . . four and a half hours later, claiming that she had forgotten all about her husband's request and had become engrossed in watching a film. Oscar, too weak to move, could not shout to her for assistance. Even such a seemingly simple example of sadism in the marital bedroom underscores how one need not dress like a dominatrix and whip one's spouse in order to make the spouse feel quite horribly beaten.

Quincy and Rose

In most instances, such enactments in the bedroom might be described as deeply unconscious, and the vast majority of my patients have absolutely no idea why they engage in sexual cruelty in the bedroom. "Quincy", a man with whom I had worked on a one-to-one basis in individual psychoanalysis, spent many months explaining how much closer he had grown to his wife "Rose", and how their sex life had improved greatly in recent months. Imagine my surprise when one day Quincy told me that he had recently embarked upon an extramarital affair with a woman called "Saskia". Curiously, each time Quincy took Saskia—the new girlfriend—to bed, he could not attain an erection; but when he had sex with Rose—the wife—he managed to become completely tumescent. This made no sense to Quincy, and he joked that he would be remembered as "the only man in history who could fuck his wife but not his mistress". Through sustained psychoanalytic work, Quincy and I came to realise that this episode of marital enactment—taking a mistress—had occurred in the wake of his ninth wedding anniversary to Rose; and that this might mirror quite precisely the fact that his father had begun to live with a mistress shortly after Quincy's ninth birthday. Quincy found the parallel extremely striking and soon came to realise that he had become engulfed in the unconscious re-enactment of an early child-hood trauma, without realising that he had done so. A few weeks later he broke off his affair with his mistress Saskia, and he resumed his very satisfying sexual relationship with his wife Rose!

Thérèse and Ugo

Marital unkindness appears in many guises, and on the surface numerous acts of thoughtlessness seem to be devoid of a sexual substratum. During my very first consultation with "Thérèse" and "Ugo", a Continental couple, I took a moment to clarify the correct spelling of their names and to write down their home address and telephone numbers. I turned to Thérèse and asked, "Would I be correct that you spell your name with two accents—an acute accent on the first "e", and a grave accent on the second "e"?" She confirmed this to be the case, whereupon Ugo exclaimed, "My God, I never knew that you had accents on your name." Thérèse became utterly heartbroken that her husband of five years did not seem to know something as fundamental as the spelling of her name. It then emerged that this couple, in spite of their rows, had sex constantly; and it soon became apparent that their sex life served primarily as an erotic defence against talking to one another. They managed physicality very well, but they could not relate in any other way, not least in terms of basic literacy, emotional or otherwise.

Vincent and Wendy

Sometimes unkindness between couples may not seem unkind at all. "Vincent", a young college student, got drunk at a party and took "Wendy", another inebriated student, to bed. In his psychotherapy session he boasted to me that as Wendy had had too much to drink, he thought it best not to penetrate her, in case she might regret this in the morning. Vincent thus presented himself as a true gentleman. But as he lay on the couch in my office, free-associating, he began to reminisce about a newspaper article that he had read some years ago concerning an American university student—a male—who had entered a sorority house and had shot all the women dead with a machine gun. Although Vincent had, indeed, behaved in a thoughtful manner by not forcing himself upon a drunken female, his free association revealed that he found himself struggling with sadistic desires nonetheless—unsurprisingly so, in view of their ubiquity in psychological life.

* * *

In many respects, we save our most unkind components for the person we claim to love above all others. We do so, in part, *because we can*. If we offend the hostess at a dinner party by insulting her food, we know that we will not be invited back again, and thus we cannot "use" that venue as a vehicle for the discharge of sadism. But if we critique our spouse's food, we know that such a verbal evacuation must be tolerated and *will* be tolerated; and therefore, we continue to perpetrate the same unconscious crime again and again.

Sometimes, in more cynical moments, having spent long days in the office working with rageful couples, I do wonder whether we marry our partners primarily as an expression of love or, instead, as an opportunity to discharge hatred. Such a dynamic epitomises the shrewd observation offered many years ago by Donald Winnicott (1970, p. 262), namely, that *"What is good is always being destroyed"*, and that we all have a very powerful need to use and abuse objects as a means of equilibrating our own faulty sense of self (cf. Winnicott, 1969).

In an ideal world, the marital bed should be a place where a couple can experience tenderness, eroticism, bodily safety, and psychological comfort. It could, and should, be a space in which partners can find a refuge from the anxieties of the world or even dream creatively about how they might change the world. It might be a venue in which spouses can read a book, watch a film, welcome young children on a Saturday morning, play with the cat and dog, and, of course, sleep in peace. But owing to the widespread nature of early trauma and the sadism that devolves therefrom, the bedroom often becomes a place of cruelty, which can manifest itself in both gross and subtle forms, even among those who have no criminal history in other areas of their lives.

As mental health professionals, we must continue to become bolder, more adept, and more diplomatic at working with couples to help them to unearth, and then to articulate, the many ways in which sadism can blight the landscape of an otherwise non-sadistic marital couple. As we know, one need not set one's spouse on fire in order to torch the bedroom. Fortunately, as we become better adept at the art of couple psychoanalysis and couple psychotherapy, we will, one hopes, ultimately prove to be more effective at helping to extinguish these deadly marital flames.

Notes

An abbreviated version of this chapter has appeared in a book on the psychodynamics of sadism edited by Dr Amita Sehgal (Kahr, 2018b).

1. The disorders of sexual fantasy, as I have indicated, often serve as the bedrock of infidelity, either in the form of an intra-marital affair or an extramarital affair. When I first presented this essay to a group of mental health colleagues, a member of the audience asked whether I regard all affairs as inherently pathological. This particular individual noted that many couples engage in "swinging" or in "open marriage" and so forth; other audience members observed that the partner of a very ill spouse might sometimes take a lover (e.g., as in the case of an elderly man whose wife suffers from Alzheimer's disease and who might have another partner for sexual relationships). One would need a further chapter in order to provide a clearer answer to this question, which concerns both clinicians and ethicists. On this occasion, I cannot offer a fully articulated position about the inherent pathology or non-pathology of the extramarital affair—or the intra-marital affair, for that matter; but I can report that in all the couples who have presented for psychotherapeutic treatment, each affair or each instance of infidelity caused great pain and suffering to all the people concerned.

2. In the context of such a relatively brief communication, I have elected to focus predominantly on three particular types of sexual cruelty, namely, the use of bodily evacuations, the intra-marital affair and the extramarital affair (or the disorders of sexual fantasy), and, finally, the use of cruelty as a defence against

death anxiety. But couples have an infinite capacity to express marital sadism in other ways. One could, of course, also examine other varieties of potential sexual cruelty, namely, the withholding of sex as a form of aggression (e.g., Friedman, 1962; Grier, 2001), as well as the practice of bondage and dominance (or "consensual kink") as potential forms of sexual cruelty (Ortmann and Sprott, 2013). These complex subjects deserve much further consideration.

CHAPTER FIVE

Committing crimes without breaking the law: unconscious sadism in the "non-forensic" patient

If you had been chained up all your life you'd be vicious too.

Professor Sigmund Freud, commenting upon an aggressive police dog;
quoted by Dr Ernst Simmel, *The Psychoanalytic Quarterly*, 1940
[quoted in Simmel, 1940, p. 174]

The sub-clinical forensic perpetrator

In 1969, Peter Sutcliffe, a 23-year-old sometime gravedigger from the market town of Bingley in the West Riding of Yorkshire, attacked a female prostitute, hitting her on the head with a stone wrapped in a sock. The victim did not press charges, and consequently Sutcliffe remained at liberty. In 1975, some six years later, Sutcliffe attacked another woman, assaulting her with a hammer and also slashing her stomach with a knife. Over the following five years, Sutcliffe perpetrated many more offences that became increasingly violent in nature and resulted in the murder of many innocent women, whom he bludgeoned with hammers and skewered with screwdrivers (Burn, 1984). Regrettably, this extremely dangerous man would not be apprehended until 1981, more than a decade after his first detected offence. Having served several years in Her Majesty's Prison Parkhurst on the Isle of Wight, the authorities eventually transferred him to the high-security Broadmoor Hospital in 1984 and then, in 2016, to Her Majesty's Prison Frankland in the village of Brasside, in County Durham.

When Peter Sutcliffe—reviled in the press as the "Yorkshire Ripper"—stood trial, the court psychiatrists debated the appropriate diagnosis of this multiple murderer. But although those who assessed Sutcliffe clinically may have struggled as to whether they should classify him as suffering from paranoid schizophrenia or from a personality disorder, everyone would have agreed that he merited the designation of "forensic patient": someone whose substantial psychological illness contributes to the enactment of violent crime consisting of the destruction of property or attacks either on the body of another person or persons, or, indeed, one's own body.

When forensic mental health professionals and members of the public alike encounter multiple murderers, career paedophiles, serial arsonists, and marital rapists, few of us would doubt that these offenders have crossed a very dangerous line. Consequently, forensic patients will require special treatment, which, quite frequently, consists of confinement in an institutional setting and, wherever possible, psychological care as well—perhaps even the opportunity to undertake dynamically orientated psychotherapy.

Thankfully, most people who attend for psychotherapy have never perpetrated acts of gross forensic criminality and do not suffer from an overtly diagnosable mental illness. Most psychotherapy patients conduct their lives with considerable honour and dignity, and most will "contain" their violent impulses with a reasonable degree of success. We might refer to such individuals as "non-forensic" patients.

Although these predominantly law-abiding patients never commit murder, arson, or rape and never attack the bodies of small children, many of our otherwise "normal" patients have, nevertheless, perpetrated acts of violence, even criminality, that have often remained undetected. From time to time, those of us who work as clinical psychotherapists may find ourselves in the truly uncomfortable and morally agonising position of being the only people privy to confessions of such acts of destruction.

Of course, every human being—whether a forensic psychiatric patient or an upstanding member of the community—has the capacity to harbour violent thoughts and fantasies. In my aforementioned study of sexual fantasies (Kahr, 2007a), fully 29% of Britons admitted that they have experienced sexual fantasies of "playing a dominant or aggressive role during sex" (Kahr, 2007a, p. 588), while 7% had fantasised about "using a whip or paddle or cane or slipper or strap" (Kahr, 2007a, p. 588) on someone. Likewise, 23% of British adults have engaged in coital or masturbatory fantasies about "tying someone up" (Kahr, 2007a, p. 588), and 4% have enjoyed "gagging someone else" (Kahr, 2007a, p. 589). Some 1% of the respondents in my study admitted to having fantasised about "sex with a child" (Kahr, 2007a, p. 589). While the figure of 1% may seem mercifully small, one must remember that 1% of the adult British population represents, nevertheless, nearly half a million individuals.

In 2008 I obtained comparable data about the pervasiveness of aggression and cruelty in the sexual fantasies of ordinary American men and women aged 18 and older (Kahr, 2008). Clearly, we readily encounter sadism in quite a widespread manner in the so-called normal population.

One might assume that my data, though carefully collected through the use of an anonymised and highly respected computer polling research network, might, in fact, have provided only a very conservative estimate of the true state of affairs. After all, many respondents may not have wished to confess their more violent fantasies to a team of investigators. But those who did admit to masturbating about forensic activities did so without restraint. One of the participants in my survey, a man called "Yannis", revealed that he fantasises about "Taking all my enemies, anyone who's ever been cruel to me, and fucking them until they bleed to death" (Kahr, 2007a, p. 336).

My own findings on the prevalence of violent sexual fantasies underscore the work published two years earlier by Professor David Buss (2005), an American psychologist, whose large-scale investigation had confirmed that as many as 91% of American men and 84% of American women have experienced vivid, detailed fantasies of committing murder.

Obviously, masturbating about murder or rape in no way guarantees that one will actually perpetrate murder or rape in the forensic sense. But where does one draw the line? And to what extent do violent fantasies place a person at risk for an ultimate forensic enactment at some point in the future?

Over the course of several decades, I have become increasingly aware that many patients undergoing psychotherapy have, often quite unconsciously, progressed beyond the realm of masturbatory or coital fantasy and have committed acts of violence or have even broken the law. None of these patients has ever, to the best of my knowledge, perpetrated such grotesque acts of murder as the Yorkshire

Ripper had done, and none has ever attracted the attention of the police or the courts or the forensic psychiatrists. But in certain cases ordinary, seemingly "normal" or "neurotic" men and women have engaged in violence that has, from time to time, even resulted in the death of another human being.

I have come to think of such individuals as "sub-clinical" forensic patients, whose sadism—often deeply unconscious—has remained undetected for long periods of time.

In the pages that follow, I explore the psychodynamics of the so-called "sub-clinical", non-forensic patient, concentrating on how and why such individuals function in this quasi-forensic fashion. I also consider what impact this unconscious "criminality" might have upon these patients, upon their intimates, and, also upon the independent psychotherapist, working in a private office, who has undertaken to provide treatment.

In my experience, few, if any, practitioners of psychotherapy would deny that a capacity for violence lies at the very core of the human mind. Each of us has the potentiality to fantasise about murder, but most of us develop the capacity to harness and encapsulate such fantasies and to neutralise their toxicity through an investment in loving attachments and in creative sublimations.

And yet, in spite of the fact that most of us find it very easy to refrain from setting buildings on fire or assaulting our colleagues with hammers and knives, every single one of us has, at one time or another, committed a crime.

I shall never forget that, some thirty years ago, during my very first seminar as a young student at the Portman Clinic, Dr Mervin Glasser, then Medical Director at this specialist institution for the treatment of forensic patients, pontificated to my cohort of trainees that one need not be a murderer or a paedophile in order to be a criminal. As Glasser warned us, anyone who had ever taken a paper clip from his or her clinic office and used it to attach any *personal* papers, as opposed to *clinic* papers, had, in point of fact, committed an act of theft. As Dr Glasser spoke, a shame-filled hush descended over all the students in this seminar on the psychology of violence, as each one of us recalled instances of having rung our spouses from the clinic telephone, having nicked a pencil from the storeroom cupboard, or worst of all, having used a stapler for private purposes. Technically, we had all engaged in enactments of thievery. But did such activities really qualify us as forensic patients? When I confessed to my own training analyst later that day that I had, over the years, purloined a paper clip here and there, he merely chuckled. After all, he had treated *real* murderers and rapists in his time, and he simply analysed my guilt as a vestige of early childhood fears of having murdered my siblings in my mind: a criminal from a sense of unconscious guilt (Freud, 1916).

But . . . sometimes acts of cruelty and violence among the non-forensic population can be much more extreme, and over the years I have encountered numerous instances of such "acting-out" among the seemingly normal ambulatory patients with whom I have had the privilege of working in a private practice setting in a comfortable part of London.

Clinical case material

Gretchen

A woman called "Gretchen" arrived at my consulting room for a session in a state of fury. Her mother-in-law, whom she hated, had become frail and incapacitated after having broken a hip. Gretchen's husband had hoped that he and his wife might be able to offer his mother a bedroom in their large house, but Gretchen told me that she had adamantly refused to do so, because the presence of a mother-in-law would unduly restrict her own social life. Gretchen admitted that, although her mother-in-law had never done anything untoward, my patient simply and honestly did not wish to extend herself in this way.

I reminded her that she and I had devoted many previous sessions of psychotherapy to an exploration of her fantasy of being an "unwanted" child, in view of the fact that she had arrived some ten years after all of her other siblings. Consequently, Gretchen had come to think of herself as a "mistake" and carried a great deal of rage in her heart at all times.

I wondered whether Gretchen's attack on her fragile mother-in-law might well constitute a displaced attack on *her* mother of infancy. Perhaps by denying shelter to her husband's mother, Gretchen had succeeded in gratifying an unconscious wish to attack her own mother.

The patient then spurted out, "Why should I give my mother-in-law a room? I had to sleep on the staircase as a child!"

I enquired further and soon discovered that, during Gretchen's very early childhood, her father had lost his job, and that, consequently, the family had had to move to a much smaller house, with fewer bedrooms. And for a period of time Gretchen did, indeed, have to sleep on a mattress placed, unceremoniously, in the stairwell. In view of this, how on earth could she have developed sufficient generosity of spirit to have created, decades later, a bedroom for her sick mother-in-law?

In spite of my valiant efforts to explore and to interpret the interconnection between Gretchen's early childhood experience and her adult state of mind, she refused to alter her position with regard to her mother-in-law and explained with steely resolution, "I simply refuse to look after that woman. It's not my responsibility." Gretchen spoke with such ferocity that I came to regard her decision not as a lifestyle choice or as the assertion of her autonomy but, rather, as an expression of historical cruelty.

But does the refusal to allow one's mother-in-law to sleep in the spare room constitute a forensic enactment? After all, Gretchen broke no laws. But might she have committed a crime? In many respects, I would argue that for Gretchen to have made such a verbal pronouncement, prohibiting her mother-in-law from occupying the spare bedroom, does indeed qualify as a type of forensic gesture.

It saddens me to report that Gretchen eventually sent her mother-in-law to a care home, attended by a nurse. Six months later, the aged woman fell in the bath, suffered a heart attack, and died instantly.

Leonard

Let us also consider the case of "Leonard", a generally calm, quiet, creative gentleman who works long hours in a respectable profession and who pays all of his bills on time, yet who harbours strong anti-Semitic sentiments. During the course of a lengthy analysis, Leonard wondered on many occasions whether I might be of Jewish origin. Although I never answered him directly, I always explored what possible meaning or meanings such a preoccupation could serve. Leonard, a Labour Party supporter who read left-wing newspapers, knew only too well that his hatred of Jews had no rational basis. He even had Jewish friends. And yet, secretly, while lying on the couch, he enjoyed indulging in fantasies of Jew-killing.

When, after several years of treatment, I resolved to raise my sessional fee by a relatively tiny amount, Leonard, a wealthy man, exploded. He simply could not believe that after four years of work I would dare to do something so seemingly cruel, and he then explained that my ostensible outrageousness provided him with proof-positive that I *must* be Jewish. He began to rant with a fury that I had never before encountered in clinical practice, and he delighted in telling me that if he had worked in Auschwitz during the Second World War, he would have escorted me and my entire family personally to the gas chambers and would have poured the Zyklon-B poisonous pellets into the pipes himself, rejoicing in our agonising deaths.

It pleases me to report that Leonard's abusiveness has not resulted in my demise. In this respect, he has not committed a forensic enactment as such. But the quality of cruelty that he displayed in the transference very much mirrored the sadism experienced by his wife, whom he had often insulted viciously and whom he had occasionally struck with his bare hands, causing tremendous marital distress, threats of divorce, and legal consultations. Does Leonard qualify, therefore, as a sub-clinical forensic patient? If we agree to expand our definition of what constitutes the forensic state of mind, then this gentleman might very well meet the criteria.

Naomi

A highly seductive and flirtatious person, "Naomi" had no difficulty enticing numerous men into her bed. Physically very beautiful and superficially very charismatic, she often identified herself with the siren "Lorelei" who lured unsuspecting sailors to their doom. For three years immediately *prior* to the commencement of her psychotherapy, Naomi had a passionate affair with "Patrizio", a man who had hoped to marry her; but Naomi grew tired of this gentleman, and she dumped him unceremoniously. Distraught, Patrizio retreated to a pub and drank himself senseless in order to relieve his unbearable anguish. In a state of great inebriation, Patrizio tripped and plunged down a flight of stairs, injuring his neck and becoming partially paralysed. In spite of numerous pleas from Patrizio for a visit, Naomi refused to oblige.

Should we consider Naomi to be a forensic patient? Once again, she broke no laws and perpetrated no crimes that would excite a lawyer or a police officer or a court. In fact, on the evening that Patrizio became crippled at a pub in Clapham in South London, she had remained at home with her three flatmates in Highgate in North London. From a legal perspective, she had a perfect alibi. Nevertheless, she had unleashed a terrific degree of sadism upon her lover and, one might argue, had stimulated his deep pain and his consequent act of alcoholic self-harm, which resulted in the tragic damage to his spinal cord.

* * *

Marital couples, in particular, have a huge capacity to become violent in a sub-clinical manner. Often each member of the couple will comport himself or herself in life with great compassion and great dignity, but when the two partners interact as a couple, the sadistic underbelly of each spouse becomes infinitely more visible.

Over the years of working in private practice, I have encountered the most enormous array of acts of cruelty—both conscious and unconscious—committed by otherwise law-abiding and reasonably mentally healthy men and women. Some of these sadistic activities could, one suspects, be subject to prosecution if a member of the law enforcement community should ever come to know about them.

Elisabetha

One of my patients, "Elisabetha", for instance, told me that her ex-husband, whom I never met and whom I certainly never treated, would, when angry, pour a tiny number of drops of acid into shampoo bottles in the bathrooms of his friends' homes whenever he attended a dinner party. After Elisabetha discovered her husband's "sub-clinical" treachery, she knew that she would have to divorce him, and eventually, she did so.

Bradley and Ignatia

Another patient, "Bradley", threw a kitchen knife and a fork at his wife, "Ignatia", during a horribly heated marital row. Fortunately, Bradley missed Ignatia, albeit by only a few inches. Nevertheless, one wonders what would have occurred if he had had better aim, and whether this action should be considered forensic in nature, and if so, to what extent.

Olympia

And "Olympia", yet another patient, told me that she had discovered that her 14-year-old son had obtained a forged identity card, which he used to purchase alcohol. When I expressed concern, Olympia told me that she proposed to do absolutely nothing about this, explaining that most of her son's friends snorted cocaine and other dangerous drugs; therefore, her son's drinking did not concern her in the least. In fact, she hoped that, by turning a blind eye, her son might not progress beyond bourbon and vodka.

* * *

These clinical vignettes—all taken from private psychotherapy practice—raise the most enormous number of deeply disturbing questions. For instance, what might be, or, indeed, *should* be, the responsibility of the mental health clinician when confronted with such data? Do we simply listen to these recitations of cruelty in a "neutral" manner? Do we interpret the unconscious sadism vigorously and risk, potentially, becoming policemen or policewomen in the transference? Do we turn a blind eye ourselves? Or do we step out of our roles as private practitioners and speak to social services or to law-enforcement agencies?

As a very young student at the Portman Clinic, one of my colleagues presented the case of a man who had perpetrated various sexual crimes against children. The trainee psychotherapist became understandably agitated, unsure what her professional obligation might be. The seminar leader—a deeply compassionate and highly experienced psychoanalyst—spoke with resolution. He explained: "You have one responsibility and one responsibility only. You must persevere with the psychoanalytic work, and you must do nothing else. If you telephone the authorities, you will cause the patient to flee from treatment, and if that should transpire, then you will never have a chance to work through the patient's paedophilic tendencies."

This remark made a great deal of sense to me and to my fellow students at the time and allowed us to experience some psychological relief, knowing that we would not have to "turn in" our patients to the police. But in the intervening decades British law has changed dramatically, and various professional bodies have now come to adopt newer rules and regulations about mandatory reporting. It will therefore come as no surprise that most mental health professionals struggle to know whether they can, could, should, or must report their patients for criminal activities, even though psychotherapy offers—at least in theory—the pledge of complete confidentiality (Bollas and Sundelson, 1995).

Such matters become infinitely more complex, particularly as many psychotherapists and counsellors might have completed a prior training in medicine, in social work, in education, or in psychology—disciplines that do require their members to report suspected cases of child abuse and other crimes.

The story of Kristopher

Sometimes the private practitioner will be confronted by a particularly complex and challenging case of sub-clinical forensic enactment.

Many years ago, a local general medical practitioner rang me and explained that she had given my telephone number to a prospective psychotherapy patient in great need of help. She told me his name— "Kristopher"—and she explained that in view of the urgency of the situation, this gentleman would ring for an appointment forthwith.

The patient did, indeed, telephone . . . *two years later*!

In spite of the very long delay between the referral and the first telephone contact, I had remembered Kristopher's name from my earlier conversation with his doctor, and I agreed to offer him an appointment for the following week.

I saw this man for a first consultation in the month of January, on a cold and blustery day. To my surprise, Kristopher arrived wearing only a T-shirt and jeans, revealing an overly developed muscular chest, which he displayed prominently. Within minutes, he told me that he has suffered from a deep depression for as long as he could remember. He also reported that he has lived with the HIV virus for more than ten years.

Having already undergone psychotherapy many years previously, Kristopher had no difficulty providing me with a full recitation of his early childhood, during the course of which he had endured many traumata.

Towards the end of our first consultation, I asked Kristopher whether he might find it useful to return for a second consultation. He told me that he had very much enjoyed our conversation and that he would, indeed, like to see me again, but that he had left his diary at home, and that, therefore, he would call me later in the day to discuss his availability.

Kristopher did, in fact, ring, as promised, but *not* that January afternoon. Instead, he next telephoned me the following October— some *nine months later*—and requested a second consultation.

Naturally, I devoted most of my interpretative efforts to an understanding of the meaning of Kristopher's reluctance to engage in human contact and to his profound fear of doing so, as evidenced by the fact that he took two years to call me for his first appointment, and then nine months for his second appointment. Privately, I thought to myself that if we continued at this rate, I might not be alive to see his treatment through to a successful conclusion: no doubt a pertinent countertransferential response, stimulated by the patient's own anxieties about living in the shadow of a potentially deadly illness.

Kristopher told me without hesitation that he had delayed nine months before ringing me back because he had experienced me as extremely frightening, and he thought that I looked like a monster. He explained that he had found my physical appearance—especially my eyes—very, very scary indeed; but he also knew that I had come highly recommended, and so, in desperation, he thought that he would attempt a second consultation. He then stood up from the chair and moved to the far side of the room, near the door, and told me that he would prefer to sit on the floor, some nine or ten feet away from me, as he felt very much safer there.

I risked a transference interpretation at this point, and I wondered whether he had *really* experienced me as frightening and scary and thus needed to protect himself from me, or, whether, perhaps, he actually wanted to protect *me* from *him*.

The patient had certainly not expected such a frank comment, and it had rather startled him. In fact, he did not know what to say: he simply sat on the floor, staring at me with discomfort—quite a change from his otherwise free and easy revelatory style.

As the second consultation neared its conclusion, I knew that we would have to address the possibility of a third consultation, and I experienced considerable trepidation, knowing that Kristopher would find this both desirable and dreadful at the same time. Once again, he promised that he would ring me, and I then asked him how many months he would take to do so. Kristopher laughed and promised to call me later that day.

He then telephoned for his third appointment in March of the following year, only five months after his second appointment. I took some small sense of satisfaction from the fact that the gap between our sessions had begun to narrow and that perhaps Kristopher could, bit by bit, tolerate an increasing amount of human contact.

Eventually, he and I began to develop a deeper rapport, and he confessed that he no longer thought that I resembled a monster but, rather, merely a greedy Hampstead psychotherapist who charges high fees.

Although I suspected that Kristopher would benefit from extensive multi-frequency psychoanalytic treatment, I thought it quite unlikely that he would ever consider such an arrangement; so, upon discussion, we agreed to embark on once-weekly psychotherapy. I felt quite prepared to fail utterly with Kristopher, knowing the extent of his psychopathology. I appreciated that this very frightened individual, a sexually compulsive man who had had thousands of one-night stands with strangers, might experience the enforced intimacy of psychotherapy as somewhat akin to a prison sentence. But, I also appreciated that, in spite of the extremely long gaps between our appointments thus far, Kristopher also wanted to reach out for help, and, to his credit, he had refused to kill me off entirely.

To my surprise and delight, Kristopher did engage with our weekly appointments, although he invariably arrived late. Unlike other patients who occasionally ring the doorbell two or three minutes tardy after having rushed through traffic, this man always pressed the buzzer at exactly twenty-five minutes: halfway through the session. I interpreted to him that he really wanted me to know that fifty percent of him wished to engage and that the other fifty percent continued to find both me, and this process, rather scary. Kristopher still sat on the floor, explaining that he regarded the patient's chair—some six feet away from mine—as far too intimate.

After a year of late arrivals, cancelled sessions, and "forgotten" appointments, Kristopher finally began to attend on time, and he did, eventually, return to the chair, which I came to regard as a great achievement. Moreover, he could now confess two hugely important experiences of biography.

In our very first meeting, Kristopher had revealed to me that during his eighth year his mother had suffered a cerebral aneurysm, which resulted in her immediate death. I knew that such a trauma had left Kristopher alone and isolated, cared for only by a very bereaved and often absent "macho" father, who hated his feminised son. After his mother's death, in a desperate attempt to bring her back to life, Kristopher used to dress up in his dead mother's clothes. He and I had, of course, talked about the impact of this early, horrific trauma in virtually every session. But on this occasion, he confessed some further, previously unknown information about his mother's death.

I knew already that his mother had died in the family home at 4.00 p.m., shortly after the 8-year-old Kristopher had returned from school. But I did not know what had happened in the few moments immediately *prior* to his mother's death.

Apparently, Kristopher had asked his mother if she could teach him how to bake a cake, but she refused, explaining that she felt unwell. Kristopher pleaded, but to no avail, and in a state of protest he stormed out of the kitchen and began to play in the room next door. Shortly afterwards, he heard an anguished gurgling sound coming from the kitchen. With no one else in the house, Kristopher knew that this strangulating noise must have come from his mother's mouth, but the young boy, feeling angry and stubborn, did not return to the kitchen to investigate. Approximately one hour later, he did seek out his mother's company, and when he walked into the kitchen, he found her collapsed on the floor. Unable to rouse her, he ran next door to the home of a neighbour, who called an ambulance; but, alas, the paramedics pronounced her dead.

Kristopher related this story with a look of horror upon his face and then confessed that, through his negligence, he had killed his mother and had sentenced himself to a life of misery with a father who hated him and whom he reviled in return.

Shortly after having told me this deeply painful and highly important story about his mother's death, he also revealed that he had yet another secret to tell me—namely, that he had a tattoo on his back. Before I could respond in any way, Kristopher ripped off his T-shirt, exposing a full-length tattoo of a very terrifying sea monster, with gnashing teeth, blood-red claws, and fuming with smoke, which extended from Kristopher's shoulder blades to the top of his buttocks. As Kristopher stood before me in a state of semi-nakedness, he smiled, as if taking pride in having shocked me—which he had indeed done—and then he quickly pulled his T-shirt back on over his head and torso.

I commented on the importance of his revelation about his mother's death, and, with sympathy in my voice, I expressed deep concern and sadness, aware that as an 8-year-old boy he had had an unbearable shock. I then paused and interpreted further that by having just whipped off his T-shirt so abruptly he might have hoped that he could shock me by revealing the monster that he had carried inside himself all this time.

Kristopher listened carefully to my words, but he did not reply in a direct way. Instead, he sat silently, pensively, almost dreamily, listening to my comments. The silence continued. I then made one more remark and reminded him of how monstrous he had found me when he had first stepped into my office more than a year earlier. I interpreted that by having carried the guilt of killing his mother—by not having rushed to her side immediately upon hearing her gurgle— he had suffered under the weight of being a murderous monster all of his life. And I underscored that finding his own scariness unbearable, he took secret comfort in locating this frightening feeling into other people.

Kristopher burst into tears, and then he told me that he had, in fact, killed not *one* person, but *two*.

Through his sobs, Kristopher explained that he held himself responsible not only for the death of his mother but also for the incipient death of a former male lover whom he had infected with HIV.

The patient reported to me that, ten years previously, not long after he had received his HIV diagnosis, his boyfriend at the time, for whom he cared deeply, pleaded with Kristopher to have unprotected anal intercourse. Kristopher refused to comply with this potentially dangerous request, but the boyfriend kept insisting again . . . and again . . . and again. Eventually, Kristopher succumbed and consented to his partner's pleas for unsafe sex. Some months later, the boyfriend, too, received a similar positive diagnosis and subsequently became very seriously ill on many occasions.

Although the boyfriend remains alive to this day, Kristopher carries a terrific sense of guilt that he has, in fact, killed this man by having sentenced him to a life afflicted by a serious disease—albeit one that can now be survived due to the great advances in modern pharmacology.

I shall refrain from commenting upon the ethics of the increasingly common practice of HIV-negative adults actively seeking to become infected by HIV-positive adults, a phenomenon known as "pozzing" or as "poz-chasing". Some people may well regard such an activity as perfectly justifiable, assuming that the "poz chaser" will have offered "informed consent". But others among us might well regard this behaviour as an unadulterated example of suicidality or as the enactment of unconscious traumatic experiences. Never having met Kristopher's boyfriend, I do not know the meaning of his wish to be infected, but I did come to learn more and more about the awful psychological burden borne by Kristopher for having agreed to the plan.

In subsequent psychotherapy sessions, we devoted considerable attention to the possible interconnections between the death of Kristopher's mother and the "pozzing" of his boyfriend. I came to hypothesise that by infecting his boyfriend in the 1990s, at a time when effective medications had become more widely available, Kristopher had succeeded in both killing off his boyfriend by infecting him with a life-threatening illness and also, at the same time, in bringing him back to life by paying for the boyfriend's private medical care—something that, alas, he could not have done for his dead mother.

Although we could devote infinitely more thought to the case of Kristopher, and although I could describe the subsequent unfolding of his psychotherapy in much greater detail, I have chosen to discuss him in this context primarily as an illustration of the fact that one can be a murderer without having committed any crimes and without in any way having broken the law. Indeed, by having participated in consensual, adult sex with his age-appropriate boyfriend he had broken no laws, in spite of having known that he had already received a diagnosis of HIV. And yet, in view of Kristopher's traumatic history and his fear that he had killed his own mother, he lived with the burden of having committed not one murder . . . but two.

The private forensic practitioner

Thus far, I have presented a series of vignettes that demonstrate, I trust, that the community-based independent psychotherapy practitioner will often encounter very seriously violent individuals who have a capacity for great cruelty. But I have not, as yet, offered any indication as to the specificities of providing treatment in such a context.

How, then, does one work with the sub-clinical forensic patient in psychotherapy?

In order to consider the practicalities of psychotherapy for such individuals, we would require a much more extended discussion; but, in the meanwhile, we can consider a small number of key observations and recommendations.

First and foremost, unlike our colleagues who work in secure or semi-secure forensic institutions, supported by large multi-disciplinary teams of psychiatrists, psychologists, psychiatric nurses, social workers, and creative arts therapists, the independent psychotherapist functions in virtually complete isolation and must, therefore, consider his or her physical safety.

Clinical case material

Verna

When "Verna", a staggeringly beautiful fashion model dressed in a mini-skirt with stiletto heels, arrived in my office and explained to me that her boyfriend suffers from pathological jealousy and has, on many occasions, threatened to kill any man with whom she spends any time, I listened to her cordially, engaged her in discussion, questioned her as to the authenticity of her boyfriend's threats, and then promptly referred her to a Consultant Forensic Psychiatrist who worked in a secure institution. The community-based forensic psychotherapist must always be courteous and professional, but he or she need not be unnecessarily heroic and certainly must not be masochistic.

* * *

The private practitioner should not only consider his or her safety, but must also maintain very rigorous clinical boundaries in an effort to provide structure and containment for potentially violent patients. For instance, if an ordinary, reliable neurotic patient with a good track record of attendance asked me in a thoughtful and appreciative manner to reschedule a particular session in order to attend her daughter's play at school, I would not hesitate to be helpful. But if a sub-clinical forensic patient did likewise, I would, in most instances, politely decline to do so and would adhere stringently to the original appointment time. As the psychoanalyst Dr Hanna Segal (1973) had observed, when working with patients who struggle with time-keeping—a metaphor for their state of disorientation—the clinician must become the reliable clock. In this way, the psychotherapy can begin to serve as something of a secure base (Bowlby, 1988). Whenever Kristopher, the patient who had infected his boyfriend with HIV, asked for changes of appointment time, I invariably declined and found that as a result his attendance record at sessions actually began to improve.

In addition to the insistence upon physical safety and the maintenance of regularity and reliability—essential characteristics of *all* psychotherapeutic work but of special importance for the forensic psychotherapist—one must also avail oneself, quite classically, of the rich opportunities for analysis of the transference.

Luigi

A homosexual man called "Luigi" worked in a perfectly respectable profession by day, but in order to make extra money, he established a pornographic video business by night, in which he convinced handsome heterosexual men to masturbate on camera and then posted these amateur films on-line. As Luigi described to me the ways in which he would entice these ostensibly consenting adult males to perform sexual acts for him, I became rather concerned as to whether the men in question really understood the ultimate fate of their sex videos, and whether Luigi had truly provided them with the opportunity to offer informed consent. Although Luigi had committed no obvious crime—as any consenting adult male may agree to be filmed—this patient certainly flirted with sexual exploitation. As the treatment unfolded, I endeavoured to maintain my analytically neutral position but also continued to express vigilance and concern about the patient's after-hours business venture.

During the course of a psychotherapy session in which Luigi spoke quite painfully about his extremely difficult relationship with his emotionally distant parents, he began to cry as he recalled certain childhood memories. He told me that although he appreciated having thrice-weekly psychotherapy with me, he found the "exposure" of his mind, while free-associating on the couch, very difficult indeed. I interpreted that perhaps he harboured a wish to sit in the analytic chair himself and to place me on the couch instead, so that he could locate the feeling of being exposed into me, just as he did each night when filming these exposed heterosexual men who volunteered to participate in his pornographic videos. My comment rather surprised Luigi, who began to cry even more. Some months later he had acquired a much better understanding of the potential violence of his film activities, and soon thereafter he shut down his production company.

Theodore

A successful businessman, "Theodore", also taught me a great deal about the value of interpreting any signs of "criminality" that might creep into the transference as a creative and effective means of examining the ways in which patients might project their forensic aspects onto or into the psychotherapist. Each month I would present

Theodore with a bill, and each month he would pay me with a wad of cash, sealed in an envelope. When I tried to analyse his motivations for settling his account in this fashion, wondering why a businessman of his stature would not pay by cheque, he sloughed me off each time, explaining that he had a bit of spare cash lying around at home and that he needed to use it.

Extraordinarily, Theodore would often overpay me by £50. Consequently, I would then have to return this excess to the patient at the beginning of the next session. This enactment between us occurred for many months, until I interpreted to Theodore that perhaps he wanted me to know something about his own anxieties surrounding his business dealings, and that he struggled, perhaps, from a fear of some kind of criminality that he tried to project into me, secretly hopeful that I might pocket the extra £50 in an unethical manner. This interpretation provoked much useful discussion about Theodore's fears of being robbed of money—a metaphor for his memories of being robbed of love by his mentally ill mother decades previously— and of his wish to entrap somebody else and to shame them, as he had felt shamed throughout his childhood.

* * *

The notion of the sub-clinical forensic psychotherapy patient can hardly be described as a novel idea. Since the very inception of psychoanalysis, practitioners have encountered men and women who have expressed deeply violent conflicts while reclining on the consulting-room couch. As early as 1907, Freud treated a gentleman called Ernst Lanzer—better known to us as "der Rattenmann" ["The Rat Man"]—described by a friend as "a man of irreproachable conduct"[1] (Freud, 1909b, p. 159), yet who considered himself to be a "criminal"[2] (Freud, 1909b, p. 159), tormented by "some criminal impulse"[3] (Freud, 1909b, p. 159), owing to his violent and obsessive murderous thoughts.

Dr Donald Winnicott also encountered sub-clinical forensic enactments in his private practice in Central London on a regular basis. For instance, Winnicott's patient, Dr Margaret Little, a qualified psychoanalyst but also a very troubled, tormented woman, committed an act of violence at the very outset of her treatment. As Little recalled,

> In one early session with D.W. I felt in utter despair of ever getting him to understand anything. I wandered round his room trying to find a way. I contemplated throwing myself out of the window, but

felt that he would stop me. Then I thought of throwing out all his books, but finally I attacked and smashed a large vase filled with white lilac, and trampled on it. In a flash he was gone from the room, but he came back just before the end of the hour. Finding me clearing up the mess he said, 'I might have expected you to do that [clear up? or smash?], but later.' Next day an exact replica had replaced the vase and the lilac, and a few days later he explained that I had destroyed something that he valued. [1985, p. 20]

Winnicott tolerated the destruction of objects in the consulting room with grace and equanimity. In fact, during the 1960s, his niece, Miss Celia Britton, and her boyfriend took tea and cucumber sandwiches with Winnicott at the end of a working day and, while there, in his home, the elderly psychoanalyst pointed to a potted plant with a missing leaf. He explained to his niece and to her partner, "that plant saved my life. My last patient this evening tore it apart rather than me" (quoted by Jeremy Holmes, personal communication, 26 September 2015).

Not only did Donald Winnicott and his fellow psychoanalysts engage with ordinary patients who commit vengeful acts, but even non-psychoanalytic psychologists have come to appreciate the widespread prevalence of so-called "ambulatory psychopathy" or "subcriminal psychopathy". Helpfully, the distinguished American psychopathologist Professor Cathy Spatz Widom (1977) had, as a young researcher, first examined the phenomenon of violence among the non-institutionalised population, inaugurating a programme of study into sub-clinical psychopathy.

Thus, mental health professionals have a long familiarity with the challenge of dealing with violent thoughts and enactments among ordinary psychotherapy patients undergoing treatment in warmly furnished consulting rooms situated in pleasant parts of town!

What, then, might we reasonably conclude from this brief examination of the sub-clinical forensic psychotherapy patient?

First of all, we may take great comfort in the knowledge that most human beings manage to contain their violent impulses quite substantially, and that most psychotherapy patients do not enact their destructive, murderous fantasies in a deadly manner. Happily, the vast majority of men and women undergoing psychotherapy would be refused a bed at Broadmoor Hospital or at any other forensic institution.

And yet many non-forensic patients, by virtue of being humans who have suffered from impingements, misattunements, and even traumata during infancy and early childhood, carry within their bosoms a smouldering rage, which often provokes aggressive fantasies and which, from time to time, erupts in sub-clinical forensic enactments. Every psychotherapist must therefore become increasingly vigilant about the possibility of meeting a sub-clinical forensic patient at one or more points during the course of one's career.

Sub-clinical forensic enactments vary in depth, scope, and intensity. While Donald Winnicott had no difficulty surviving the destruction of one of the leaves of the potted plant in his Belgravia consulting room, other practitioners—myself included—have struggled greatly with the complexity and with the ethicality of possessing knowledge about individuals who lace shampoo bottles with acid and who willingly infect their sexual partners with the human immunodeficiency virus. Consequently, ordinary psychotherapeutic practitioners working in the community must come to acquire a strong forensic spine and a sharply focused diagnostic radar. In view of the fact that one will, from time to time, encounter scantily clad women who claim to have Mafiosi boyfriends, or businessmen who try to entrap one in an act of dishonesty through overpayment in cash, the private psychotherapy practitioner must endeavour at all times to remain within the bounds of professionalism in a rigorous and thoughtful manner and must find a way to create a medium secure unit of sorts in Hampstead or Harley Street, or in Crouch End or Kensington, without the aid of locked wards, teams of doctors and nurses, psychotropic medications, or the protection provided by the Mental Health Act 2007.

The jobbing psychotherapist must seek appropriate clinical supervision from an experienced forensic practitioner when confronted with unexpectedly violent or potentially violent patients and must, if at all possible, avoid the sin of being too naïve. Even the most loyal, honourable, and decent of patients can surprise us with acts of criminality, either symbolic or real.

In summary, I wish to propose that we must begin to think about creative ways in which we might helpfully expand the definition of the forensic patient. Obviously, our community-based patients do not pose a threat to our society in the way that Peter Sutcliffe—the Yorkshire Ripper—had done. No one need fear walking the streets of Central London and being assaulted by an accountant leaving my consulting room. But by internalising a forensic lens, the independent practitioner of psychotherapy will have the opportunity to become more sensitive to, and increasingly savvy about, the possible range and meaning of various enactments within daily clinical practice, owing to the fact that our caseloads may contain many more sub-clinically forensic patients than we might, at first, have fully appreciated.

As an independent psychotherapist who, years previously, had worked in forensic settings, and who undertook training in forensic psychotherapy at the Portman Clinic, I confess that I have found such experiences invaluable for my work with more ordinary patients. My immersion in the forensic world, and my continued association with forensic colleagues, has allowed me to become, I trust, more observant and even more suspicious about the potential sadistic underbelly of human behaviour. Such contact with the forensic world has, I believe, helped me to develop a greater awareness of the disturbing fact that every forensic patient had begun life as a "sub-forensic" or, indeed, "pre-forensic", or, even, "non-forensic" patient, prior to committing acts of violence. The community-based, independent psychotherapy practitioner might, therefore, find himself or herself in a valuable position to help identify and treat those patients who have not *yet* exploded and who have not *yet* become full-fledged forensic individuals. The traditional, classical, independent mental health professional working in private practice might, therefore, perform an increasingly important role in terms of prevention.

With greater exposure to forensic psychotherapeutic thinking, every mental health practitioner, of whatever core professional background or theoretical orientation, will have the opportunity to become increasingly sensitised to the nature and scope of violence in its many shapes and forms. Additionally, psychotherapeutic practitioners will develop an improved understanding of the fact that most, if not all, of our forensic and sub-clinical forensic patients have experienced a welter of traumata during the earliest years of life, which will have contributed hugely to the development of violent fantasies and behaviours in years to come.

Psychotherapists must begin to discuss our more frightening cases more fully, more regularly, and more honestly, so that we may all help one another to navigate complex ethical problems and also to verbalise our own countertransferential hatred (Winnicott, 1949b; Kahr, 2011a, 2015a, 2020) towards these patients. By doing so, we will become more proficient at facilitating the psychotherapeutic process.

How many of us have ever wondered what might have happened if, during his years as a struggling artist in Vienna, the young, impecunious Adolf Hitler had stumbled into Sigmund Freud's consulting room for treatment? Many dramatists have, in fact, written plays about such an imaginary encounter; for example, the 2007 radio play

Dr Freud Will See You Now Mr Hitler, penned by Laurence Marks and Maurice Gran. Although one suspects that Freud might well have failed to treat Hitler successfully, we must remember that even the son of Alois Schicklgruber and Klara Pölzl Schicklgruber had begun life as a non-forensic baby who then became a sub-clinical forensic man, prior to his eruption as a full-fledged proto-forensic mass murderer. If we intervene early in our community-based settings, we might, perhaps, be able to contain even just a little bit of the violence that surrounds us all too chillingly.

Notes

An earlier version of this chapter appeared in a Festschrift dedicated to the work of my esteemed teacher and mentor, Dr Estela V. Welldon (Kahr, 2018a).

1. The original German phrase reads: "ein tadelloser Mensch" (Freud, 1909a, p. 360).

2. The original German word reads: "Verbrecher" (Freud, 1909a, p. 360).

3. The original German phrase reads: "ein verbrecherischer Impuls" (Freud, 1909a, p. 360).

PART **II**

INFLAMING AND DEFUSING BOMBS

In all my wanderings round this world of care,
In all my griefs—and GOD has given my ſhare—
I ſtill had hopes my lateſt hours to crown,
Amidſt theſe humble bowers to lay me down.

Dr Oliver Goldsmith, The Deserted Village, A Poem, 1770, lines 85–88

CHAPTER SIX

Donald Winnicott's struggle
with hate in the countertransference

I don't know what to do with the hate.

Dr Donald W. Winnicott, "Trips into Partisanship",
unpublished manuscript, 1967
[Winnicott, 1967, p. 3]

Winnicott's "irksome" patients

According to the London weather report, Wednesday, 5 February 1947, proved to be a bitterly cold and dull day, with virtually no sunlight. Indeed, the entire winter of 1947, marked by arctic blizzards, power cuts, and a fuel crisis, could only be described as grim (Payn and Morley, 1982). That evening, the 50-year-old English paediatrician, child psychiatrist, and psychoanalyst, Dr Donald Woods Winnicott, trudged through the darkened, snowy streets of Central London, towards 96, Gloucester Place, not far from Baker Street, to read a paper to his clinical colleagues at a fortnightly Scientific Meeting of the British Psycho-Analytical Society. As a physician at the Paddington Green Children's Hospital, West London, and as a psychoanalyst in private practice on Queen Anne Street, not far from Gloucester Place, Winnicott had already accumulated a wealth of medical and psychological experience, and he had no difficulties writing about his work in great depth. But on this occasion he presented an unusually short essay—a mere six pages in length in its printed version—entitled, quite unremarkably, "Some Observations on Hate".

Though ostensibly straightforward as a topic, Winnicott's contribution seems to have provoked many of his colleagues. The late Dr Colin James (1991), a young physician who subsequently trained as a psychoanalyst, recalled that when he had first encountered Winnicott's paper, he found it shocking *in extremis*.

Unlike Winnicott's other scientific and clinical essays, virtually all of them "instant" classics, his 1947 essay on hate, published subsequently in *The International Journal of Psycho-Analysis* under the more Gothic title "Hate in the Counter-Transference" (Winnicott, 1949b), did not become an immediate success. By contrast to Winnicott's (1953) contemporaneous article on "Transitional Objects and Transitional Phenomena: A Study of the First Not-Me Possession", the essay on "Hate in the Counter-Transference" enjoyed a somewhat frosty reception. Although Anna Freud offered official approval of the concept of transitional objects, referring to Winnicott's work in her papers on "The Concept of Developmental Lines" (Freud, 1963) and "About Losing and Being Lost" (Freud, 1967), she had little regard for Winnicott's work on hate.

Indeed, in the decades after publication, Donald Winnicott's text on "Hate in the Counter-Transference" received very few citations in the psychoanalytic literature. In 1958, Winnicott (1958a) published his *Collected Papers: Through Paediatrics to Psycho-Analysis*, and he included both the "hate" paper and the "transitional objects" paper, along with several other chapters. When Dr Isidor Bernstein (1959) reviewed the American edition of this volume for *The Psychoanalytic Quarterly*, he singled out Winnicott's (1958b) work on transitional objects, as well as his studies on such diverse subjects as infant observation (Winnicott, 1941), the antisocial tendency (Winnicott, 1956d), primary maternal preoccupation (Winnicott, 1956b), and many others besides; but, quite tellingly, Bernstein made absolutely no reference at all to the paper on "Hate in the Countertransference" (now published without a hyphen) (Winnicott, 1949c).

Even today, Winnicott's article on transitional objects has far eclipsed the essay on hate. A quick computerised literature search on Pep-Web, the Psychoanalytic Electronic Publishing service, accessed on 15 July 2018, reveals a whopping 2,382 "hits" for the concept "transitional object", but only 246 "hits" for "hate in the countertrans-ference" (and only 72 "hits" if one hyphenates the term "counter-transference").[1]

What exactly did Donald Winnicott write about in his short paper "Some Observations on Hate" (referred to hereafter by its published title "Hate in the Counter-Transference"), and why precisely did his otherwise enthusiastic and appreciative colleagues overlook this paper for many decades?

Essentially, "Hate in the Counter-Transference" contains a vast array of deeply unpalatable thoughts. As psychoanalytic clinicians will recall, Winnicott (1949b, p. 69) began his essay by acknowledg-ing that the treatment of psychotic patients can be "irksome" and represents a "heavy emotional burden on those who care for them" (Winnicott, 1949b, p. 69). Winnicott observed that many psychiatrists, especially those who have not had the benefit of psychoanalytic expe-rience or training, will employ "the too easy electric shocks and the too drastic leucotomies" (Winnicott, 1949b, p. 69), and that one can regard such somatic interventions only as "awful things" (Winnicott, 1949b, p. 69). In other words, Winnicott lambasted much of the treatment of psychologically ill men and women as cruel; and though he acknowl-edged the extreme challenge of treating psychotic patients, Winnicott admonished his colleagues nonetheless, quite sternly, for relying too readily on what he regarded as sadistic attacks on patients' bodies.

But Winnicott critiqued not only non-psychoanalytic psychiatrists; indeed, he then offered some arguably unfavourable observations about *psychoanalysts* as well, noting that they, too, struggle with their hateful feelings towards their analysands. By accusing his colleagues of hating their ill patients, Winnicott may have cut his comrades to the quick, questioning, and ultimately undermining, the millennia-long Hippocratic ideal that physicians exist primarily to care for their patients and to heal them, not to hate them.

And then, as if to add insult to injury, Winnicott observed that not only mental health professionals harbour hateful feelings towards their patients, but so, also, does every mother towards her baby. Win-nicott (1949b, p. 73) declared resolutely that, "The mother, however, hates her infant from the word go." He even provided a list of no fewer than *eighteen* reasons why the ordinary devoted mother must hate her baby, not least because the baby displays a certain ruthless-ness towards the mother, treating her "as scum, an unpaid servant, a slave" (Winnicott, 1949b, p. 73).

Winnicott hardly deserves credit for being the first psychological professional to admit to hateful affects towards difficult patients. Even the most cursory review of Freud's letters will reveal his often abominable attitudes to those with whom he worked. As Freud (1928b, p. 537) wrote to his Hungarian colleague, Dr István Hollós, exploring his hatred of psychotic men and women: "Finally I confessed to myself that I do not like these sick people, that I am angry at them to feel them so far from me and all that is human."[2] But whereas Freud had confined these blunt remarks to his most *private* correspondence, Winnicott, by contrast, wrote about the ubiquitousness of hateful feelings in a professional lecture for colleagues, subsequently enshrined *publicly* in the pages of an international periodical.

Certainly, Winnicott had hatred on his mind for quite some time. On 15 October 1946, only weeks before his paper of 5 February 1947 to the British Psycho-Analytical Society, Donald Winnicott wrote an unsolicited letter to the newly ennobled William, Lord Beveridge, the noted British economist, social reformer, and parliamentarian, about Beveridge's much-discussed proposals for the creation of a National Health Service for Great Britain. Resenting Beveridge's (1942) plan to hold physicians more fully accountable to government, Winnicott (1946, p. 8) fumed that "It was true ignorance that allowed you to make medical practice subservient to politics instead of to science, but ignorance cannot absolve you of my hatred." In the very next paragraph, Winnicott (p. 8) elaborated, "How can I reconcile my admiration of your new work on behalf of our democratic value, and my hatred of you because of your irresponsible suggestions in respect of doctors?" By contemporary standards, we might admire Winnicott's frank prose, as well as his capacity to express himself in words in such a forthright manner, not to mention his ability to be comfortable with his own aggression. But one wonders what Lord Beveridge had made of Winnicott's letter, in which some unknown doctor had written to him out of the blue, explaining in two separate paragraphs that he hated him?

As we know, Winnicott has made an immense contribution to the study of psychoanalysis and to the understanding and treatment of the more unbearable patient by speaking about the hatred that practitioners can experience countertransferentially. With extraordinary sagacity, Winnicott (1949b, p. 72) wrote: "The analyst must be prepared to bear strain without expecting the patient to know anything about what he is doing, perhaps over a long period of time." In this respect, Winnicott clearly recognised the enormous labours that we as psychoanalytic practitioners must endure, biting our lips as we attempt to deal with the often vitriolic verbal assaults of our more vulnerable and volcanic patients. But what allowed Winnicott to become so astute, so pioneering, and so capable of *digesting* experiences of hatred in such a direct, honest, and public manner, especially at a point when his forebears, including Freud himself, had, by contrast, *enacted* their "hate in the counter-transference" in a more subterranean fashion, in the form of gossip, rivalry, and treachery, both within the consulting room and within the psychoanalytic institution at large? What alerted Winnicott to the study of hatred, and what factor or factors facilitated his comprehension of this critical thematic? In order to understand how Winnicott became so deeply sensitised to the arena of hatred, let us examine his life situation—culturally, professionally, and personally—in the years prior to the publication of his landmark essay.

The assault on psychiatric sadism

In the mid–1940s, Donald Winnicott ought, perhaps, to have been a happy man. After all, at 2.41 a.m., on 7 May 1945, General Alfred Jodl, the *Oberkommando der Wehrmacht* [Chief-of-Staff of the German Armed Forces High Command], signed the "Act of Military Surrender", thus signifying the end of the Second World War. After more than five years of having lived in a state of undoubted psychophysiological hyperarousal, avoiding the bombs of the Blitzkrieg, and enduring the many wartime losses and deprivations, jubilant Britons undoubtedly breathed a long-awaited sigh of relief.

But though Winnicott may have joined the celebrations on the Mall in front of Buckingham Palace, he had suffered immensely during the Second World War. His second cousin, Robert Richard Winnicott, died in Dieppe, in France, on 19 August 1942, on military service. Back in England, German shrapnel fell on the grounds of his family home in Plymouth, Devon, where his aged father, Sir Frederick Winnicott, lived with his two spinster daughters. The Germans had destroyed much of Plymouth, one of the most heavily bombed of British cities, and many of the buildings of Donald Winnicott's childhood had evaporated in the nightly infernos unleashed by enemy aircraft. And in London, where Winnicott lived throughout the Second World War, he heard on quite a regular basis the sound of bombs dropping; indeed, in 1944, a bomb exploded very close to his wife, Mrs Alice

Buxton Taylor Winnicott—a very accomplished potter. She seems to have escaped death only narrowly, but she did sustain an injury near her eyes (Brennan, 1944).

In view of the devastation experienced by British children and adults during the war, both at home and abroad, one would have thought that the ceasefire of 1945 would have delighted Winnicott immeasurably. But although the cessation of the carnage brought an end to the misery of many, V-E Day [Victory in Europe Day] symbolised merely the beginning of a more private, more agonising war for Donald Winnicott—one that unleashed a period of immense upheaval in his personal life and nearly killed him, and one that propelled him, paradoxically, to articulate one of the most controversial and, ultimately, most profound theories in the field of psychoanalysis.

As Britons everywhere immersed themselves in their peacetime employment, Winnicott returned not to cheering throngs but, rather, to a landscape of devastation, as he resumed his public sector work as Physician to the Paddington Green Children's Hospital, in West London, where he assisted innumerable youngsters who had suffered from the effects of the psychologically crippling evacuations, and whose fathers—and sometimes mothers—had, in many instances, died violently and often abruptly, either in combat overseas or in the London bombings. Likewise, he resumed his private practice on Queen Anne Street, in Central London, where he must, no doubt, have treated cases of war neurosis, broken marriages, and every variety of post-traumatic anxiety disorders. As Winnicott dealt with many instances of severe psychiatric distress in his professional work, he became increasingly enraged at what he regarded as the brutal, almost Nazi-like abuse of patients in British mental hospitals. Although Winnicott did not himself work in a psychiatric hospital at this time, he treated, nonetheless, many patients who *had* undergone incarceration in such institutions, and he knew all about the horrendous "snake pit" conditions (Ward, 1946).

At this time, only ninety psychoanalysts practised in Great Britain, and most had few, if any, private patients: a small and essentially ineffective army to service a population of some fifty million people, many of whom suffered from psychological illness (cf. Stephen, 1940). In view of the regnant organicist-somaticist paradigm promoted by the Maudsley Hospital—the veritable "Oxbridge" of mid-twentieth-century British psychiatry—the British Psycho-Analytical Society represented only a tiny speck in the landscape of medical and mental health services.

In the late 1940s, pharmacological treatments prevailed, consisting mostly of hypnotics, such as the sedative paraldehyde, the most common treatment for mental illness at that time. Paraldehyde had a foul taste and would often have to be taken with peppermint tea, or with ginger, to soften its ugly impact. Physicians also administered chloral hydrate, as well as barbiturates such as seconal and veronal, not to mention a multitude of bromide sedatives, as well as anticonvulsants such as phenobarbitone. In more extreme cases, psychiatrists would recommend prolonged narcosis (administered through a rectal mixture of chloral hydrate, barbituric acid, and paraldehyde), or insulin coma treatments, which would force patients to sleep for an average of twenty hours a day out of twenty-four, for periods ranging from ten days to four weeks. Patients who did not respond to pharmacological interventions would be subjected to electroconvulsive shocks or forced to submit to psychosurgical procedures such as lobotomy, known in Great Britain as leucotomy (Dax, 1949). Psychiatrists would even employ more radical treatments, such as electro-narcosis or electro-pyrexia, which combined electrical and pharmacological methods, often inducing high fevers (Anonymous, 1949).

In an effort to combat what he regarded as the unsanctionable cruelty of British psychiatry, Donald Winnicott (1943a, 1943b, 1944a, 1945c, 1947a, 1947b, 1951a, 1951b, 1956e) wrote a series of brave and bold letters to the editor of the *British Medical Journal* and *The Lancet*, the two leading medical weeklies, criticising these ostensibly scientific procedures as retrogressive and as "a wonderful way of doing psychiatry without having to know anything about human nature" (Winnicott, 1943b, p. 829; cf. Winnicott, 1943c, 1944b, 1944c, 1951c). Winnicott (1949e, p. 35) regarded leucotomy, in particular, as "the worst possible trend in medical practice", adding that, "Those who practise leucotomy are frightening patients very much more than relieving the suffering" (Winnicott, 1949e, p. 38). Essentially, Winnicott regarded the use of extreme somatic treatments as a form of hate in the countertransference, and he mobilised his own hatred to speak out against what he regarded as an iatrogenically induced form of brain damage inflicted upon patients suffering from essentially psychological illnesses. Winnicott wrote with considered venom and with relatively uncensored fervour. He also criticised at least one pharmaceutical firm, Genatosan, in Loughborough, Leicestershire, lambasting them for their support of physical psychiatric treatments, exclaiming, "I feel it must do your firm harm" (Winnicott, 1949h).

One must recall that Winnicott penned these critical letters and memoranda long before the formal development of the so-called anti-psychiatry movement and the critical psychiatry movement of the 1960s (e.g., Double, 2006; Heaton, 2006). Winnicott's vituperative outpourings, based on clinical experience and personal conviction rather than on any systematic long-term follow-up investigations, which would be required by contemporary medical researchers, provide an indication of the strength of his own struggle with his hatred towards psychiatric colleagues: a disdain that mirrors, perhaps, the way in which he had used the term "hatred" in writing to Lord Beveridge at this time.

Thus, we can begin to understand the beginnings of a background to Winnicott's paper "Hate in the Counter-Transference", knowing that, recovering from the ravages of war, Winnicott found himself dealing with innumerable psychiatric casualties, many of whom had undergone the more extreme forms of medical intervention: shock therapy and psychosurgery. One doubts that Winnicott would have written his paper in the early weeks of 1947 without having already immersed himself in at least three years, between 1943 and 1946, of letter-writing and campaigning against these treatments.

But let us recall that, in Winnicott's paper on hatred, he attacked not only the non-psychoanalytic psychiatrists for treating psychotic patients cruelly, he also alerted his Freudian colleagues to the burdens and dangers of working with extremely ill men and women, warning them that they, too, could fall prey to hatred, even in the relative physical safety of the fifty-minute hour. What, then, prompted Winnicott to become so very aware of his hatred for his psychoanalytic colleagues and his psychoanalytic patients?

Winnicott overwhelmed

Donald Winnicott always worked with challenging cases. His very first child psychoanalysis patient—a delinquent—taxed the budding psychoanalyst considerably. As Winnicott reminisced decades later,

> This boy attended regularly for a year and the treatment stopped because of the disturbance that the boy caused in the clinic. I could say that the analysis was going well, and its cessation caused distress both to the boy and to myself in spite of the fact that on several occasions I got badly bitten on the buttocks. The boy got out on

the roof and also he spilt so much water that the basement became flooded. He broke into my locked car and drove it away in bottom gear on the self-starter. The clinic ordered termination of the treatment for the sake of the other patients. [1956c, p. 306]

But as the Second World War unfolded, Winnicott's caseload, already titanic in comparison to that of his colleagues, increased in drama and intensity. As Visiting Psychiatrist to the Government Evacuation Scheme, Winnicott had the responsibility of travelling frequently from London to various parts of the counties of Berkshire and, principally, Oxfordshire, where he would work in a variety of hostels that accommodated wartime child evacuees. Many of these youngsters had already suffered from psychological difficulties before the fighting had begun; and undoubtedly, the traumatisation of evacuation and the Blitzkrieg exacerbated their already fragile ego structures. In one of his reports on the residential management of "Difficult Children", co-authored by Miss Clare Britton, the psychiatric social worker with whom he worked in Oxfordshire, Winnicott enumerated the plethora of behavioural symptoms that these youngsters would display, including bed-wetting, faecal incontinence, stealing in gangs, burning hay-ricks, train-wrecking, truancy from school, truancy from billets, and consorting with soldiers. Additionally, these difficult children displayed anxiety, depression, mania, sulkiness, personality deterioration, and lack of attention to clothing or hygiene, as well as "odd and insane behaviour" (Winnicott and Britton, 1947, p. 89). All in all, Winnicott (1948) estimated that, during the Second World War, he had assumed clinical responsibility for no fewer than 285 of these psychiatrically and behaviourally challenging children.

But Winnicott worked not only with the evacuated "truanters" of Berkshire and Oxfordshire, he also continued to offer treatment services at Paddington Green Children's Hospital. At some time during this period, Winnicott began to care for a deeply ill anorexic girl who suffered so profoundly from an incapacity to ingest food that she became dangerously unwell and required full-time hospitalisation. According to Miss Lilian Brooks (1971), a nurse, and later matron, at Paddington Green Children's Hospital, Winnicott proved to be a "tower of strength" with this anorexic girl, displaying immense patience. In fact, according to Matron Brooks, he visited the youngster every single day. I know from my interview with Miss Irmi Elkan, a social worker who knew Winnicott during the Second World War and who later became a psychoanalyst, Winnicott would feed this anorexic girl with milk from an eye-dropper (interview with Irmi Elkan,

6 October 1994). Regrettably, in spite of Winnicott's vigilant care of this young anorexic girl, she died in hospital, presumably from gross malnutrition and organ failure.

Miss Laetitia Ingleby

In addition to the children of Berkshire and Oxfordshire and the tragic anorexic teenager, Winnicott also had his hands quite full with a long-standing female patient who suffered from an extreme psychiatric illness. In 1931, Ernest Jones referred a very troubled girl, then 12 years of age, to his young colleague, Donald Winnicott. She would remain in treatment with Winnicott for approximately twenty years. In his initial report, Winnicott described his first meeting with the girl, whom I shall call, pseudonymously, Miss "Laetitia Ingleby".[3] He wrote: "At that time she was a wild creature with hair streaming out behind her and she had been throwing chairs at her mother" (Winnicott, 1949i). In a subsequent publication, he described her, undoubtedly, as a case of schizophrenia (Winnicott, 1964a), and reported that he had devoted some 2,500 hours to her care; in other words, he expended fully three months of his life on Miss Ingleby, stretched out over many years. From the very outset of their work, Miss Ingleby explained that she wanted to die, and she hoped that Winnicott would permit her to commit suicide for the right reason, and not for the wrong reason (Winnicott, 1964a).

Laetitia Ingleby came from a deeply troubled family: her father suffered from a masked psychosis, and her mother, though free of obvious psychiatric illness, struggled with anxiety and marked neurosis (Winnicott, 1949i, 1964a). Miss Ingleby had virtually no contact with her sister; and her brother, the only member of the family to whom she felt close, had died in the early part of the Second World War.

Winnicott (1949i) confessed that

> In my attempt to give her psycho-analytic treatment I failed after about five or six interviews; in fact I made practically no contact with her. This was in part due to my lack of experience and skill, but also due to the fact that she had a severe mental illness and I have always thought of her as at the core psychotic. [Winnicott, 1949i]

In spite of his lack of success at the outset, Winnicott persevered with the treatment, and he continued to work with Laetitia Ingleby for decades.

Winnicott would sometimes discuss this case with his brother-in-law, Dr James Maberly Taylor, a fellow physician and psychoanalyst. Round about the time that Winnicott wrote his paper "Some Observations on Hate", Dr Taylor counselled Winnicott:

> You spoke yesterday of your feeling that 'Laetitia' might break off. If the external mother is felt to be as bad as the internal mother then feelings of immense potency leading to murder or suicide might take the place of impotence + despair. [Taylor, n.d.]

As a former analysand of Melanie Klein's, James Taylor knew that the aggressivity displayed by Miss Ingleby served as a defensive veneer for more explosive and sinister emotions.

In view of her illness, Miss Ingleby required frequent hospitalisations, and Winnicott thoughtfully arranged for her admission to Great Britain's only psychoanalytically orientated psychiatric inpatient institution, the Cassel Hospital for Functional Nervous Disorders, located in Ham Common, in Richmond, Surrey, where many psychoanalysts and psychoanalytic trainees worked. At that time, no other Medical Director of a psychiatric inpatient facility would have allowed a psychotic person to leave the hospital daily for psychoanalytic sessions at a private office several miles away, but Dr Thomas Main, a young psychoanalyst who had undertaken his didactic analysis with Michael Balint, and his supervision with Anna Freud and Melanie Klein (Johns, 2009), understood the importance of sustained, ongoing treatment, and he authorised Miss Ingleby to travel daily from Richmond to Central London for regular work with Donald Winnicott.

Some years ago, I managed to locate and, subsequently, to interview the specialist psychiatric nurse employed to escort Laetitia Ingleby from the Cassel Hospital into Central London for ongoing psychoanalytic appointments. The task of doing so proved such a burden for the nurse, herself a "psychiatric casualty", that, having deposited Miss Ingleby at Winnicott's private office on Queen Anne Street, she would go to see a psychoanalyst in a nearby office in Beaumont Street, in order to undertake her own much-needed analysis. The nurse (who insisted that she remain anonymous) told me that Miss Ingleby could be very demanding and exhausting, but, as one often discovers with such people, Miss Ingleby also had many positive qualities, which no doubt sustained Winnicott's commitment to the patient. These virtues proved, however, few and far between. In his 1949 summary report on the patient, Winnicott (1949i) noted only one asset himself: "She had one positive feature which was that she had been to all the films that could possibly be seen and knew a very great deal about them."

Laetitia Ingleby remained a long-term clinical commitment for Donald Winnicott. In later years, Winnicott (1957, p. 113) wrote to Dr Thomas Main about her once again, reflecting that patients such as Miss Ingleby "could wear down all the available nursing and actual psycho-analytic personnel", and, further, that "The psycho-analyst's life is likely to be threatened by one or two of these patients who always happen to be in his practice" (Winnicott, 1957, p. 113). Clearly, Winnicott recognised the exhaustion that he experienced from dealing with Laetitia Ingleby, and he permitted himself to verbalise his countertransferential hatred to colleagues. Tragically, no amount of hospitalisation, nursing, psychoanalytic care, or other forms of support alleviated Miss Ingleby's distress, and after several unsuccessful suicide attempts (Winnicott, 1964a), she eventually took her own life. As late as 1969, Winnicott wrote a highly confidential (and hence, unpublished) letter to a medical colleague, in which he confessed that Miss Ingleby died, "due to a failure in my own reliability".

Mrs Gladys Watson-Dixon

At some point during the latter part of the Second World War, perhaps in 1944, Winnicott began to treat a patient in his private consulting room on Queen Anne Street: a married lady with a child, whom I shall call, pseudonymously, "Mrs Gladys Watson-Dixon". According to a cache of unpublished notes from Mrs Watson-Dixon, many written in fading pencil and hitherto neglected by archivists and historians, this lady proved to be rather challenging. Although Winnicott never recorded a formal psychiatric diagnosis—at least none that survives in the available records—few mental health professionals would doubt that this patient displayed many of the classic symptoms of either a malignant hysteria or a borderline personality disorder, tinged with a highly eroticised transference. One need read only a small fraction of the surviving papers to realise the deep neediness and desperation of Mrs Watson-Dixon. For instance, on 13 September 1944, she wrote to Dr Winnicott: "I'm sorry I burst out like that in the middle of your work. Don't throw me over altogether. I do value the little bit of you that you are able to give me." Furthermore, she exclaimed, "I need a fairy godmother who can do things. Clean the house, feed me", thus providing us with some evidence of her yearning and perhaps of her regressive state of mind. On yet another occasion, Mrs Watson-Dixon wrote, "I'm very sorry I rang you up. I wish I had not done so. The only thing to do now is to decide not to ask your help at all ever again. This simplifies things a bit. It is easier to just feel awful and get no help than to feel awful, ask for help and then feel that one had no business to ask."

Winnicott saw Mrs Watson-Dixon several times a week, and, owing to her relatively straitened financial circumstances, he refrained from charging her an analytic fee. From time to time Winnicott did indeed treat patients for no fee, especially during the early years of his practice, in order to develop his breadth of clinical experience (Winnicott, 1978), and Mrs Watson-Dixon certainly seems to be one of these charity cases. Reading through the documentation, one soon discovers that Winnicott analysed Mrs Watson-Dixon at a whole range of times, thus suggesting that he would fit her in when he could, rather than fill up a regular, reliable treatment hour in his crowded timetable. This haphazard scheduling arrangement induced more wrath and pain from the patient, who complained, "Don't offer me times + things. I can't possibly know what I'm going to feel like on Thursday. In any case the whole thing is best left alone. I don't believe that you want to help me now at all. So I'm going to forget now that you ever have. You will help me best by ignoring the whole thing."

Within a short period of time, Winnicott's failure to provide a secure framework for Mrs Watson-Dixon's treatment sessions resulted in a torrent of rage. In an undated note, the patient complained, "You can't fool me. You never wanted me as a patient." She excoriated Dr Winnicott further, accusing him of exploiting his patients, and reprimanding him, "I think that you want to die famous." Mrs Watson-Dixon spewed forth all sorts of complaints, impugning Winnicott's motives towards his patients: "What you've learned from them you will put in [a] couple of books + everyone will say 'Isn[']t D^r W [a] marvellous, wonderful person', and you will be as pleased as punch. You get involved in too many people. This you do on purpose so that [you] can sort them out + use what you want out of them for later on."

In view of the fact that Winnicott found himself working with a patient who barged into his office in the middle of his sessions with other patients, only to criticise him bitingly, one wonders perhaps whether Winnicott had raised the idea of referral to a colleague, or even of termination of the treatment altogether. The patient responded to Winnicott's probable "hate in the counter-transference" with great hurt and great venom and then wrote an eight-sided handwritten letter to Winnicott, which she entitled "This is the Worm which is Eating Me". In pained, colourful language, Gladys Watson-Dixon emoted: "Now the time has come when you have finished with me. You don't tell me so in so many words because that would put [you] in a very poor light. You are too clever for that." Additionally, she attacked the psychoanalyst by stating, "My faith in you + all human nature is completely shattered."

After having examined the surviving materials about Gladys Watson-Dixon, one feels sympathy for Donald Winnicott, having had to endure the vitriol of a clearly distressed psychoanalytic patient, arguably in a state of heightened negative transference. But similarly, one also experiences concern for the patient, particularly when one discovers that Winnicott had treated her in a potentially uncontaining manner, violating the classical boundaries of traditional psychoanalytic practice. For instance, we know that he not only worked with her for no fee (a practice that might be considered highly seductive by an hysterical or borderline patient), but he also cancelled many of her appointments (thus stimulating rage and abandonment anxiety), and he saw her *at least* once on a Sunday (a clinical practice in which Winnicott engaged throughout much of his professional career).

Having investigated this case further, I have now established the true identity of "Mrs Gladys Watson-Dixon", and I have discovered that this woman occupied a rather unusual place among Winnicott's psychoanalytic patients during the 1940s. Not only did she attend Queen Anne Street for psychoanalytic treatment, but throughout this entire period of time she also worked both for Donald Winnicott, and for his wife's brother, the psychoanalyst Dr James Taylor, as their secretary. Taylor had observed Winnicott flirting with Mrs Watson-Dixon, and he wrote to admonish his brother-in-law: "Now for the pot calling the kettle black! Can't you stop (what I call) making love to 'G.'? It seems to me rather unmerciful. I mean the sort of thing you do when you address the letter to her in different shapes. However that's your affair + hers but not entirely because I do get mixed up in it."

Mrs Watson-Dixon's duties as receptionist and secretary included answering the telephone, opening the door to patients, and cleaning the consulting room. Additionally, Winnicott often called upon her to undertake various domestic tasks. From time to time, he asked her to look after his wife, Mrs Alice Winnicott, who suffered from emotional difficulties of her own. On at least one occasion, Winnicott despatched Gladys to Alice Winnicott's office, the Claverdon pottery at Upchurch, in Kent, quite a few miles outside London. The burdens of having to care in some capacity for the wife of her employer-cum-psychoanalyst proved too distressing, and after one of her visits to Mrs Winnicott, Gladys Watson-Dixon actually experienced an hallucination about her employer's spouse, which she reported thus to Dr Winnicott: "I had a vision of her dead in the road because she had had [an] accident because I hadn't gone to look after her." One need not be a clinician to spot Gladys's all-too-evident death wishes towards Winnicott's wife. On another occasion, Winnicott seems to have asked Mrs Watson-Dixon to wait at his private house in Hampstead, North London, to take delivery of a piano. Gladys did so, in spite of being ill, and then she lamented that she had got some "fluff" on her shirt, perhaps an indication of her feelings of fragility and contamination.

Eventually, the muddled boundaries between Gladys Watson-Dixon and Donald Winnicott became too complex, too entangled, and too murderous in tone; consequently, Winnicott raised the possibility that she might prefer to work with another psychoanalyst. In due time, both the secretarial and clinical relationship between Watson-Dixon and Winnicott came to an end. Eventually, though we do not know how this happened, Mrs Watson-Dixon became more equilibrated. Perhaps Winnicott did, indeed, refer her to a colleague for more traditional treatment. Perhaps she experienced relief at not having to perform menial chores for her psychoanalyst.

In the end, Gladys moved out of London with her husband and their child.

The inpatients at Pilgrim's Lane

During the mid–1940s to late–1940s, the case of "Gladys Watson-Dixon" proved by no means unique for Donald Winnicott. Throughout this time, he worked continuously with many regressed, fragmented, troubled and, even, violent adults and children. Circa 1947, Winnicott began the analysis of yet another very needy and tormented woman, who would remain in treatment with him for nineteen years, not terminating until 1966 (Winnicott, 1966). This type of long-term work—not uncommon for a psychoanalyst— took its toll.

We know from other clinical correspondence—now in restricted archives until the mid-twenty-first century—and from my interviews with patients, colleagues, and relatives, that Winnicott often used his wife Alice Winnicott as an honorary co-therapist. From time to time, Winnicott invited patients to his private home, Sydney House, on Pilgrim's Lane in Hampstead, North London, where he and Alice would spend time with them together. Winnicott could not protect Sydney House from the intrusions of psychiatric patients. Elisabeth Ede, the daughter of Winnicott's oldest friend Harold Stanley Ede (better known as "Jim" Ede), often spent long periods of time with Donald Winnicott and Alice Winnicott at Pilgrim's Lane, along with her sister Mary Ede, owing to the fact that their parents travelled extensively. Elisabeth Ede (later Dr Elisabeth Swan) recalled that Winnicott talked about his child psychiatric patients quite a lot, and that he spent much time with patients on the telephone, explaining that some of them might actually commit suicide if he did not speak to them (interview with Elisabeth Swan, 11 December 1994).

Some of the patients even moved in for a time. At least as early as the 1930s, a woman called Miss "Louisa Benedict" lived at Pilgrim's Lane, although we know nothing about this lady. Years later, in 1945, a gentleman, whom I shall call Mr "James Dawkins", wrote, thanking Winnicott for treating his daughter: "I know that the constructive, vital friendship which you and Mrs Winnicot [*sic*] gave to her at a time in her young life of very profound darkness was of incalculable worth and played, I am sure a very great part in leading her forward to the happiness and fullness of her present condition." Many, many other patients sent letters of thanks to Winnicott in which they conveyed their good wishes to Alice Winnicott for her friendliness and helpfulness.

Through my archival and interview researches, I have now identified *at least* six patients who lived at Sydney House during the 1940s: a young truanting boy; a young male student; a female student who had a breakdown during her work as a nurse; the daughter of a troublesome social friend; a more severely ill female psychiatric patient; and a vulnerable woman who cooked for the Winnicotts. As a long-standing childless man, Winnicott may have endeavoured to satisfy his urge for having children of his own by housing the challenging offspring of other people. As a clinical researcher, he justified this very rough-and-ready form of residential milieu therapy as a means of providing a home for those who had none.

Whether Winnicott's experiments in living represented a neurotic deviation from standard psychoanalytic technique or a compassionate form of helpfulness and a fulfilment of his deeply entrenched Wesleyan spirit of community service, one cannot know with complete certainty. After all, throughout the history of medicine, and the history of psychiatry in particular, one encounters many instances of physicians caring for patients in their own homes. In fact, in Gheel, in Belgium, the entire community had, over many centuries, devoted itself to the residential treatment of the emotionally unwell (Duval, 1867). But whatever Winnicott's motives—whether meritorious or masochistic—living with disturbed patients, especially when he had already found himself saddled with a troubled wife, produced burdensome consequences.

Famously, Winnicott wrote about one of these inpatients in his paper on "Hate in the Counter-Transference": the now widely known case of the 9-year-old boy who came to stay in his house on the aptly named Pilgrim's Lane. Winnicott (1949b) recorded that this London youngster, a chronic truanter, sought refuge in one of the psychiatric hostels providing shelter for child evacuees in Oxfordshire, where Winnicott worked during the Second World War. As Winnicott (1949b, p. 72) explained, "I hoped to give him some treatment during his stay in the hostel, but his symptom won and he ran away as he had always done from everywhere since the age of six when he first ran away from home." Ingeniously, the young boy escaped back to his native London, and in an effort to care for him, Winnicott explained that, "My wife very generously took him in and kept him for three months, three months of hell" (Winnicott, 1949b, p. 72). As he remembered, "He was the most lovable and most maddening of children, often stark staring mad." Living with the Winnicotts in Hampstead proved to be quite an experience, not only for the boy, but for Donald and Alice as well; before long, the youngster became assaultive in the house, and, as Winnicott (1949b, p. 72) confessed, "It was really a whole-time job for the two of us together, and when I was out the worst episodes took place."

Winnicott admitted that although tempted to hit the boy, he never did so, explaining that he had become, by this point, consciously aware of his own hate in the countertransference and therefore did not need to enact his hatred unconsciously, either through physical assault or punishment. He did, however, need to resort to other physical measures, explaining that,

> At crises I would take him by bodily strength, and without anger or blame, and put him outside the front door, whatever the weather or the time of day or night. There was a special bell he could ring, and he knew that if he rang it he would be readmitted and no word said about the past. He used this bell as soon as he had recovered from his maniacal attack. [1949b, p. 73]

In many respects, this young boy served as Winnicott's paradigm case for understanding and, consequently, managing his hatred in the countertransference. As Winnicott (1949b, p. 73) explained, "The important thing is that each time, just as I put him outside the door, I told him something; I said that what had happened had made me hate him. This was easy because it was so true." He then added, "I think these words were important from the point of view of his progress, but they were mainly important in enabling me to tolerate the situation without letting out, without losing my temper and every now and again murdering him."

On the basis of my investigation of Winnicott's unpublished clinical notebooks, which I have had the privilege of consulting, I can now reveal that this little boy, whom I shall call, pseudonymously, "Archie Leggatt", came to live at Pilgrim's Lane at least as early as 17 January 1942. Already well known to the London Probation Service for his delinquent activities, Archie found himself in the custody of the Tooting police station in South London. On 16 January 1942, Winnicott had collected young Archie from Tooting and returned him to his mother; but while Winnicott talked with the mother, Archie escaped. With extraordinary cunning, the boy found his way to North London, only a short distance from Winnicott's private home. Winnicott received notification from the Hampstead Police Station that Archie had come north, and on the following day Winnicott collected him from the station and took him back to live at Pilgrim's Lane. On 19 January 1942, Winnicott fetched Archie's clothes from his mother's home. By March 1942, the pressure had become too immense, and Archie went to a remand home. On 27 March 1942 he appeared in the Juvenile Court in Brixton, and by 16 April 1942 he would be transferred to St Joseph's School in Orpington, Kent, an "Approved School", at which point, his name disappears from the relevant clinical notebooks.

During this entire time, Winnicott found himself managing yet another complicated clinical situation as well. His wife Alice, in spite of being intermittently troubled by a whole host of psychological difficulties ranging from narcolepsy to auditory hallucinations, had obtained a post as a volunteer at Napsbury Hospital, a large psychiatric institution in Hertfordshire, where she used her considerable artistic talents to work as an untrained art therapist of sorts. While painting and drawing with patients, Mrs Winnicott made the acquaintance of a young person called "Susan" (a pseudonym) whom she befriended; and before long Susan, who had survived many courses of electroconvulsive shock, moved into Pilgrim's Lane, sleeping in the Winnicotts' guest bedroom. It soon became very clear that Susan might benefit from psychoanalytic treatment, and Winnicott entrusted this to his much-cherished colleague Mrs Marion Milner, who practised psychoanalysis from her private residence on Provost Road in Chalk Farm, not far from Winnicott's Hampstead home. Susan attended for daily sessions with Marion Milner at Provost Road, and Winnicott paid for the treatment. Additionally, he supervised the case, and he seems to have done so to good effect.

Susan suffered from extreme experiences of depersonalisation and from a fragile ego structure. I discussed the case with Marion Milner, whom I first interviewed in 1985 and with whom I spoke on many occasions thereafter, and she told me that she regarded Susan as schizophrenic, but that other colleagues had described her, subsequently, as borderline (interview with Marion Milner, 16 February 1985). Whatever the diagnosis, Susan certainly demanded much care and attention, and felt herself to be completely disconnected from the world. As Susan wrote to Marion Milner in 1959, after fifteen years of analysis: "I am in the world for the first time" (quoted in Milner, 1969, p. xix). Before having met Marion Milner, Susan exclaimed that, "I gave up my life."

Some years before her death, Marion Milner revealed that throughout the course of this analysis, Susan lived with Donald Winnicott and his wife Alice (interview with Marion Milner, 16 February 1985). Marion Milner subsequently confirmed this fact to the psychoanalytic historian Professor Judith Hughes (letter to Judith Hughes, 8 April 1986, cited in Hughes, 1989). Marion Milner did not, however, inform either Professor Hughes or me that, throughout much of this same time period, Milner herself underwent personal analysis with Winnicott, and that she did so *not* in Winnicott's office on Queen Anne Street, in Central London, but, rather, as I subsequently discovered, in Milner's private residence. We do not know precisely why Winnicott treated Marion Milner in her own home (Dragstedt, 1998; Pearl King, personal communication, 19 June 2002). Perhaps he indulged her, as she had a full caseload in her own right and might not have had the time to travel to Queen Anne Street. Milner (2012, p. 233) claimed that he did so, quite simply, "out of kindness".

Milner's correspondence with Winnicott, as well as other information gleaned from my private conversations with both Marion Milner and with "Susan" herself, indicate the complexity of Winnicott's clinical life away from Paddington Green Children's Hospital, away from the London Clinic of Psycho-Analysis (whose Child Department he directed), and away from his private office in Queen Anne Street. Eventually, Winnicott discontinued his somewhat unorthodox psychoanalytic treatment of Marion Milner and appeared in person at the painting school in Suffolk that Marion Milner attended in order to inform her of his decision (Margaret Walters, personal communication, 18 November 1998). Winnicott then sent her to Dr Clifford Scott, a close psychoanalytic colleague who had already treated Winnicott's wife Mrs Alice Buxton Taylor Winnicott, and who, in 1948, would ultimately begin to treat Miss Clare Britton, the woman who would become Winnicott's second wife (Kanter, 2004; cf. Pearl King, personal communication, 19 June 2002). Winnicott himself had at least one session of treatment with Scott as well (Mahony, 1997).

Winnicott's broken heart

Certainly, Winnicott's clinical work with troubled patients burdened him considerably. But, in addition, he had to endure the anticipated closure of his hospital at Paddington Green, the taunts of organically orientated paediatricians who ignored or ridiculed his psychological work, as well as his burgeoning battle with Kleinian colleagues amid the infamous Controversial Discussions within the British Psycho-Analytical Society. Winnicott may have had no safe haven at this time. But whatever *professional* workplace struggles Winnicott had to navigate as a paediatrician, child psychiatrist, and psychoanalyst, these pale in comparison to his infinitely more complicated and traumatic domestic life.

In 1923, the 27-year-old Donald Winnicott had married an older woman, Miss Alice Buxton Taylor, a talented painter and potter, whom he had met, in all likelihood, as a fellow student at the University of Cambridge. Early photographs reveal Alice Winnicott as not a very beautiful woman, but one possessed of a winning smile. Prior to her marriage, Miss Taylor had studied Natural Sciences and worked, subsequently, as a researcher in the field of optical glass, during which time she sustained a substantial blow to her cranium from a very large and heavy pendulum in a laboratory (Anthony Bradshaw, personal communication, 23 March 1996). Whether she suffered any permanent neurological damage remains questionable, but throughout most of her adult life she struggled with narcolepsy and would frequently fall asleep in dangerous locations—particularly behind the wheel of her automobile in mid-traffic (interviews with Joyce Coles, 18 December 1994, 5 March 1995).

Although Alice Winnicott worked creatively as a potter and even supervised a business that produced glazed earthenware, she became increasingly unstable in many respects as the 1930s and 1940s unfolded. For instance, in addition to her frequent narcoleptic episodes, she would often become very forgetful (interviews with Joyce Coles, 18 December 1994, 5 March 1995). On one occasion, while glazing some pottery in her kiln at Pilgrim's Lane, Alice neglected to watch over the burning, and in the process she caused a very dangerous explosion, thus unleashing a bomb in her own home. Furthermore, she developed a hugely erotomaniacal obsession with T. E. Lawrence [Thomas Edward Lawrence], better remembered as "Lawrence of Arabia", and she started to hallucinate that Lawrence would transmit special messages to her through the mouth of her pet parrot (interview with Anthony Bradshaw, 18 February 1995).

Alice Winnicott developed a strong interest in psychiatric matters through her husband's work and, perhaps, through her own struggles as well; and Donald Winnicott's extensive surviving correspondence reveals that Alice came to know many of her husband's patients and had endeared herself to them in the process. Eventually, she became a volunteer at a psychiatric hospital, where she met "Susan", the woman who would come to live at Pilgrim's Lane.

According to Winnicott's sometime analysand and disciple Masud Khan (1987, p. xvi), Alice Winnicott "went mad"; as a result, Winnicott had to nurse her, and "taking care of her took all of his youth" (Khan, 1987, p. xvi). Retrospectively, while one cannot readily determine the precise nature or extent of Alice Winnicott's difficulties, they undoubtedly caused great distress to Winnicott himself. Certainly, Alice had psychoanalysis from Winnicott's colleague, Dr Clifford Scott, at least as early as 1938 (cf. Winnicott, 1938, 1939).

Whatever Alice Winnicott's psychiatric status, she also suffered greatly from sexual anxiety. According to testimony from Alice's niece by marriage, Mrs Elizabeth "Betty" Bradshaw, Donald and Alice Winnicott maintained separate bedrooms at Sydney House on

Pilgrim's Lane, and Alice died a virgin, never having consummated her long marriage (interview with Elizabeth Bradshaw, 18 February 1995). Apparently, Winnicott discussed this situation with a number of intimates during his lifetime, and his lack of sexual satisfaction caused him much private grief, especially as it prevented him from becoming a father in his own right. One cannot, of course, attribute the lack of marital sexuality entirely to Alice Winnicott. Many colleagues have hinted that Winnicott himself suffered from impotence. Indeed, it may well be that Winnicott's own sexual inhibitions—if true—had prompted him to consult Ernest Jones in 1923, which he did at the time of his wedding. Jones then referred Winnicott to his younger colleague, James Strachey, freshly returned to England after having undertaken a didactic analysis with Sigmund Freud in Vienna. Winnicott remained in psychoanalytic treatment with Strachey for ten years; and during this time, he certainly spoke of his marital difficulties and of his sexual struggles. In an atrocious breach of confidence, James Strachey then blabbed about Winnicott's erectile difficulties to his own wife, the psychoanalyst Mrs Alix Strachey, and in a notorious letter to her husband, she wondered whether Donald Winnicott—her husband's analysand—would ever "f–ck his wife all of a sudden" (Strachey, 1924, p. 166).

In view of the complexity of his marriage to Alice Winnicott, triggered in part, perhaps, by an unconscious rescue phantasy to cure his depressed mother of childhood (Kahr, 1996a; Rudnytsky, 2011), Donald Winnicott began to seek solace outside his marriage. During the Second World War, while himself employed by the Government Evacuation Scheme, he met Miss Clare Britton, a young psychiatric social worker and Welfare Officer for the Oxfordshire County Council; and before long the two had become romantically involved.

The surviving correspondence between Donald Winnicott and Clare Britton provides clear evidence that their relationship had begun professionally and platonically. On 4 January 1943, Miss Britton (1943a) wrote to Dr Winnicott: "I hope that you + Mrs Winnicott had a good Christmas—or at any rate a good rest." This sort of letter seems to indicate an ordinary, friendly collegial relationship. But by the spring of 1943, the two had developed a greater intimacy, and it seems that Winnicott had asked Clare to purchase a necktie for him (Britton, 1943b). By July 1943, Miss Britton (1943c) encouraged Winnicott to see a production of William Congreve's late-seventeenth-century play *Love for Love*, which she described as *"really* bawdy + highly seasoned!"* And by October of 1943, Winnicott had met one of Clare's two brothers (Britton, 1943d). Eventually, the growing personal and professional intimacy became too powerful, and the couple embarked upon a sexual relationship. Winnicott must have found Clare Britton quite a relief, as she had no discernible psychiatric difficulties and must have proved a great source of comfort. Clare Britton also engaged with the specificities of Winnicott's professional work. She regarded him as a genius and became enamoured by all of his psychoanalytic theories, something that Alice, the potter, could never do.

Winnicott thus found himself tormented by conflict. Although he desperately yearned to marry Clare and rid himself of the burden of Alice, he could not do so for two pressing, conscious reasons. First of all, he felt immensely guilty and worried greatly as to how the vulnerable Alice would manage without him. And, second, he could not risk offending his nonagenarian father, Sir Frederick Winnicott, born in 1855, who, like many Britons at the time, regarded divorce in the family as a disgrace and a scandal. In Great Britain, throughout much of the twentieth century divorce constituted such a source of shame that even King Edward VIII succumbed to the pressure to renounce the throne in 1936, after he had chosen to marry a divorcée, the American socialite Mrs Wallis Warfield Simpson. And the stigma lingered. By 1951, only some 2.6% of the married population of England and Wales proceeded with divorce, as compared with approximately 12.8% in 1988, for example (Kiernan, 1991), and with infinitely higher rates today. Even as late as 1955, divorced people could not enter the Royal Enclosure at Ascot (cf. Mannin, 1971). Winnicott decided that he would have to wait until after his father had died. But Sir Frederick Winnicott had reached his nineties with much vigour, and he showed no signs of decease.

Winnicott became increasingly tormented by his internal and external life. Can it be any wonder that he wrote "Some Observations on Hate" in 1947?

By 1948, the situation had become even more acute. With a monstrous workload, a house full of psychiatric patients, a troubled wife, and a secret extramarital affair, Winnicott began to crumble. In November of 1948, Mrs Gladys Watson-Dixon, Winnicott's complicated, demanding former secretary-patient, miscarried her second child, and she pressed Winnicott to visit her at her home outside London. She sent a letter to Winnicott, describing her aborted pregnancy: "The whole thing fell out in the bedpan absolutely complete." Winnicott did visit Mrs Watson-Dixon. Alas, he could find no respite from psychiatric patients in any corner of his life, other than in his relationship with Clare Britton.

On 31 December 1948, Sir Frederick Winnicott died, at the age of 93 years, of a lobar pneumonia, compounded by senility. Also, during this time Donald Winnicott (1949b, p. 71) began to have psychotic-like dreams. In one of his dreams, he noted, "I had no right side of my body at all. This was not a castration dream. It was a sense of not having that part of the body." He also reported that he had begun to do "bad work" (Winnicott, 1949b, p. 71). Unsurprisingly, he started to feel physically ill. On 8 January 1949, just over one week after the death of Sir Frederick Winnicott, Donald Winnicott had a portable x-ray of his heart and lungs taken at the Paddington Green Children's Hospital. Dr George Simon (1949), an Assistant Radiologist at St Bartholomew's Hospital, interpreted the findings and detected no abnormality. But Winnicott's impulse to consult a physician proved prescient. He sensed that he might be on the verge of a significant illness.

Winnicott did not look after himself especially well at this time. In January of 1949 alone, he worked with some twenty-five different private patients, two of whom he saw five times weekly. He treated two other patients twice weekly. He also conducted regular clinics at the Paddington Green Children's Hospital on Tuesday mornings and on Friday lunchtimes.

On Friday, 28 January 1949, Winnicott psychoanalysed a female five-times-weekly patient at 9.45 a.m.—a hugely unwell person who often required a hot water bottle from Winnicott's secretary, Joyce Coles, after sessions (interviews with Joyce Coles, 18 December 1994, 5 March 1995). At 10.45 a.m., he provided a session to a training analysand. He then left Queen Anne Street and travelled to West London for his 12.30 p.m. clinic at the Paddington Green Children's Hospital, returning to his private consulting room in order to see a qualified psychoanalytic colleague, who had come at 3.00 p.m. for a re-analysis. At 4.00 p.m. he met with one more patient, finishing work at approximately 5.00 p.m., an unusually short day for Winnicott.

In all likelihood, sometime during the late afternoon of Friday, 28 January 1949, Winnicott developed a coronary thrombosis (Coles, 1971; cf. Winnicott, 1949f), which had begun when he exerted himself by turning the crank of his automobile (Ruth Brook Klauber, personal communication, 25 April 1996). He would not return to work until Monday, 9 May, 1949.

Winnicott took to his bed, but he kept a telephone by his side (Caine, 1949) and he continued working, ringing patients and colleagues, when he might have rested. Alice Winnicott proved the worst of nurses and, according to the testimony of Mrs Joyce Coles, she would often leave Winnicott alone, untended, in his bedroom, and would sometimes forget to bring him any meals (interview with Joyce Coles, 18 December 1994).

Winnicott's personal correspondence from this period indicates that he kept the full awfulness of his marital situation hidden from his oldest, closest friends (Bagenal, 1949a). Mrs Alison Bagenal (1949b), a much-loved friend whom he had met during his student days at the University of Cambridge during the Great War, wrote, "Donald, I wish we had been able to help more with Alice—I feel we let you down." Later, she expressed her regret, "Dear Donald I am afraid you must have suffered a great deal" (Bagenal, n.d.).

Upon recovering from his heart attack, Winnicott's thoughts turned almost immediately to his 1947 paper, "Some Observations on Hate", delivered over two years earlier. Winnicott promptly unearthed his typescript, and he began to make revisions. On 26 April 1949, he dictated a letter to Dr John Rickman, an Editor of *The International Journal of Psycho-Analysis*, and asked, "Do you remember my giving this lecture in 1947? I have considerably simplified the introduction." He asked Rickman, "Do you think it is getting any nearer towards something which the Journal would like to have?" (Winnicott, 1949g). Clearly, Winnicott seemed extremely keen to have the typescript published, and he had his secretary, Mrs Joyce Coles, send the letter out to Rickman before Winnicott had either read it or signed it.

Now convalesced and back at work, Winnicott began to sleep in his consulting room (interview with Joyce Coles, 18 December 1994). He no longer wanted to share a house with the spouse toward whom he felt, no doubt, increasingly resentful. Some time thereafter, Winnicott took his wife out for lunch and told her that he must leave her, and that he had found someone else with whom he wished to spend his life. Then, after making this announcement, Winnicott returned to his consulting room to continue his working day. According to Joyce Coles, Alice burst into his set of rooms on Queen Anne Street in a tormented state and attempted to barge into her husband's inner office in the midst of an analytic session. Mrs Coles had to bar the door bodily. Alice finally relented (interview with Joyce Coles, 18 December 1994).

Having made the decision to leave his wife and his "inpatient" clinic at Pilgrim's Lane, Winnicott experienced a new sense of freedom. On 18 May 1949, only days after he had resumed work with patients, Winnicott (1949d) returned to the British Psycho-Analytical Society and delivered the first half of his now-famous paper on "Birth Memories, Birth Trauma, and Anxiety". Having confronted death, he turned his attentions, quite understandably, to its obverse. His creativity began to surge even further, and by the autumn of 1949 his collection of radio broadcasts on *The Ordinary Devoted Mother and Her Baby: Nine Broadcast Talks. (Autumn 1949)* appeared in print (Winnicott, 1949a). In October and November of that same year, he delivered eight more talks for the British Broadcasting Corporation, securing his reputation as England's leading communicator on psychological ideas for the general public. Winnicott had returned to life. On 28 December 1951, he would marry Clare Britton, and he would remain very happily married to her for nearly twenty years. Not only did Winnicott enjoy a sexual relationship with his new wife, but Clare shared in all of her husband's professional triumphs, and she became a true, mature partner.

Winnicott had endured many bombs throughout the 1940s. But we must recognise that he had hurled many of these into his own consulting room, and into his marriage as well. Finally, from 1951 onwards, aided by a much more stable second wife and by the fruits of his lengthy experience of psychoanalysis between the 1920s and 1940s (Kahr, 1996a), he would, at last, begin to defuse his own bombs.

The legacy of a masterpiece

"Hate in the Counter-Transference" can be read in its own right as a sturdy clinical contribution that continues to provide ongoing inspiration to generations of psychoanalytic workers (e.g., Epstein, 1977; Frederickson, 1990; Gonçalves, 1996; Kahr, 2007b, 2012a). In fact, this classic essay need not be located in an historical framework in order to be understood and appreciated. But by contextualising Winnicott's work both biographically and historically, the paper becomes, I contend, much richer and, hopefully, much more engaging to a contemporary readership.

First and foremost, "Hate in the Counter-Transference" represents a vital attack on the brutality of twentieth-century organic psychiatry—a subject that psychoanalysts have often tackled, but none so bravely as Winnicott himself. Surgical and electrical treatments of mental states have a long, venerable, and deeply entrenched history—so much so that non-organicists would find it difficult to undermine their popularity. But Winnicott's salvo against what he regarded as the cruelty of these procedures remains a model of bravery not always apparent within the history of psychoanalysis; and his attack on psychosurgery, in particular, proved all too timely, for in 1949 Professor Antônio Caetano de Abreu Freire Egas Moniz received the Nobel Prize for Physiology or Medicine for his work on leucotomy as a treatment for psychosis. But though psychosurgery seemed poised to conquer psychiatry, it gradually became unmasked as a failure of extreme proportions. The virtual disappearance of psychosurgery, as well as the reduction in the use of electroconvulsive therapy for the schizophrenic psychoses, provides great support for Winnicott's foresight and prescience and owes something, perhaps, to Winnicott's clarion call (cf. Valenstein, 1986).

But, second, "Hate in the Counter-Transference" constitutes a most vital study of the hatred of the *non-psychiatric* psychoanalyst and psychotherapist and therefore foreshadows the subsequent study of abuses, both gross and subtle, perpetrated by psychoanalysts, whether sexual or seemingly less dramatic, yet nonetheless quite troubling, such as exploitation, or breaches of confidentiality (e.g., Walker and Young, 1986; Gabbard and Lester, 1995; Kahr, 1995c; Celenza and Gabbard, 2003). In spite of the fact that Winnicott himself became embroiled in the complicated case of Masud Khan—one of his own analysands who often practised abusively (Godley, 2001a, 2001b; Kahr, 2003; Hopkins, 2006)—Winnicott's paper helps us, nonetheless, to understand the potential for enacting one's hostility in an unconscious manner. Through his work in this area, we have come to understand that unless one has access to an analyst, a supervisor, or a collegial peer group that can provide support for the "irksome" and burdensome work that we undertake, often with extremely ill individuals, practitioners might find themselves at greater risk of conscious or unconscious perpetration of insensitivity or, even, cruelty.

Third, Winnicott has helped us to recognise something of the eighteen separate reasons why parents come to hate their children. Because infants often treat mothers, in particular, like "scum", even the most healthy of mothers will experience murderous impulses towards their offspring. Adult support for the mothers and fathers and other primary caregivers of babies will, therefore, be crucial. In this respect, Winnicott's 1949 paper prefigured the now widespread recognition that nursing mothers may be prone to puerperal illnesses and, hence, will require regular emotional sustenance from spouses, families, midwives, health visitors, and physicians alike.

Yet in addition to the "scientific" content of Winnicott's contribution, his essay on "Hate in the Counter-Transference" represents a poignant piece of writing suffused with autobiographical themes and confessions that serves as a potent reminder that even the best-educated, best-trained, and most experienced of our colleagues may struggle in the work, especially when engaged in pioneering activities at the forefront of practice. After all, Winnicott had received no formal training course in the psychoanalytic treatment of psychotic or borderline patients. Writing with great candour, he regarded himself as a "research analyst" (Winnicott, 1949b, p. 69) to these individuals, ever aware that, in order to reach these patients, one would have to undertake path-breaking, primary clinical research, to see what might be of help and what might be of harm (cf. Winnicott, 1962, 1963a).

Regrettably, Winnicott's research experiments with severely ill patients often got the better of him. Like Marie Curie handling radium for the first time (e.g., Giroud, 1981; Pflaum, 1989), Winnicott did not always appreciate the dangers inherent in his clinical endeavours, or the potential costs of working with so many ill patients simultaneously, or of inviting many of them into his home. Fortunately, later generations have managed to learn from Winnicott's experiences, and we now benefit from a more clearly articulated theory of psychoanalytic boundaries, which none of the early practitioners quite understood. It might well be the case that many of our contemporary psychoanalysts would have practised exactly as Winnicott did had we lived and worked in the 1940s or before (cf. Kahr, 1999c, 2006a). And yet, in spite of the costs that Winnicott bore from housing the inpatients of Pilgrim's Lane, one must also admire his unwavering commitment to helping the ill. As a Wesleyan Methodist, Winnicott adhered to a credo of performing unceasing charitable works, as the Christian leader John Wesley had done. Had Winnicott lived today, he would, in all likelihood, have offered food and shelter to the homeless mentally ill, overlooked by most people on the streets of many large cities.

To conclude, it would be only *too easy* to praise Winnicott for his insightful paper on "Hate in the Counter-Transference", or, to lambast him for being a "wild analyst" and also a masochist for having undertaken so much dangerous and debilitating clinical work. But to do so would only allow us the primitive comfort afforded by idealising our heroes and denigrating our enemies. Although Winnicott *did* engage in technical experiments with his borderline and psychotic patients, sometimes holding their hands, sometimes serving them soup, sometimes sitting with them on the floor while listening to the radio, he did this very sparingly indeed. In most instances, he practised a classical technique, which he referred to as *"standard analysis"* (Winnicott, 1962, p. 166). In 1956 Mrs Jane Shore Nicholas (formerly Mrs Jane Khan), underwent full analysis with Winnicott for four or five years, and she described him as "so reliable" (interview with Jane Shore Nicholas, 21 August 2009); she enjoyed a completely neutral, boundaried, and classical experience of treatment.

Having now interviewed dozens of Winnicott's former patients, including many of the notable patients contained within his writings, ranging from the "String" boy (Winnicott, 1960b) to "The Piggle" (Winnicott, 1977), I can confirm that for a great many people Winnicott proved to be a life-saver. Furthermore, a substantial number of patients consulted Winnicott only *after* they had dropped out of failed analyses with ostensibly boundaried, classical practitioners. Only with Winnicott did many of the more regressed patients experience safety and understanding of the most profound variety. Indeed, I can now report that even "Gladys Watson-Dixon", the woman with whom Winnicott had worked in a somewhat non-traditional manner, ultimately came to have a very good life, and remained in fond correspondence with Winnicott. Moreover, she even came to visit him towards the end of his life in order to discuss one of her children.

Winnicott-bashing has become increasingly popular since his death (e.g., Segal, 2006). But before we allow critical colleagues to consign Winnicott to the dust-heap of psychoanalytic history, let us remember the words of the patients themselves, whose plentiful testimonials serve as a potent reminder of the still-inspiring work of this towering figure in our field. After Winnicott's death in 1971, one of his patients described him as a "great healer". Another patient reminisced: "He helped me so that I could be prepared for life + death. I got so much from such a little contact with him." A mother of yet another patient wrote, "I cannot imagine how my husband and I and "Daisy" (to say nothing of the rest of the family) could have coped with her illness without the absolute sense of support that we all felt from Dr Winnicott. Now that I think about it it seems like a miracle that he was able to see "Daisy" three years ago when she was so ill and see her through. My husband and I felt that Dr Winnicott did for "Daisy" what no one else could have done for her. Liking her when she was rather unlikeable and letting her be—which seems to have helped her a lot."

In similar vein, Winnicott's former analysand, the psychotherapist Dr Harry Guntrip (1971), encapsulated the gratitude of patients quite perfectly in his letter of condolence to Clare Winnicott: "Your own personal loss is greatest, but I think more people will share this sense of loss, than would be true of any other analyst." And perhaps Dr Margaret Little (1971) epitomised the widely held posture of gratitude among his patients most compellingly in her condolences: "You know that but for his care + loving-kindness I would have been dead or in a chronic schizophrenia long ago."

On 24 November 1992, Her Majesty Queen Elizabeth II delivered a speech at the Guildhall in London, remarking memorably that, in the past year, she had experienced an *"annus horribilis"* (quoted in Hamilton, 1992, p. 1). The Queen did not exaggerate. In the preceding weeks and months, her daughter, Her Royal Highness The Princess Royal (better known as Princess Anne) divorced her husband, Captain Mark Phillips; her second son, His Royal Highness The Duke of York (better known as Prince Andrew), announced that he and his wife, Her Royal Highness Sarah, The Duchess of York, would be separating; and, most shocking of all, her eldest son and heir, His Royal Highness The Prince of Wales (known universally as Prince Charles), indicated publicly that he and Her Royal Highness The Princess of Wales (the much loved Princess Diana), would also separate. Then, the Queen's second home, Windsor Castle, caught fire, destroying much cherished property and, no doubt, many memories for the monarch as well. Fortunately, having already survived the Second World War and the bombing of Buckingham Palace, the Queen persevered in spite of this dreadful chapter.

In 1949, the year of his first coronary, Winnicott, too, had an *annus horribilis*, preceded by several *anni horribiles*. But like Queen Elizabeth, his nearby neighbour in London's Belgravia, he, too, survived. Commenting on the evolution of his technique, he observed, in 1962, "I am not like what I was twenty or thirty years ago" (Winnicott, 1962, p. 169). Perhaps Winnicott's many years of personal psychoanalysis, his healing second marriage to Clare Britton, and the enduring satisfaction of curing or soothing so many hundreds of patients, not to mention the long-term benefits of his relatively stable childhood and his lifelong commitment, as a Wesleyan Methodist, to public service allowed him to transmute his *anni horribiles* into a powerful clinical contribution, rendering subterranean hatred conscious and thus transforming hate into knowledge, and also hate into love.

Notes

1. In 2011, Pep-Web provided a ranking of the most popular articles on its database. "Transitional Objects and Transitional Phenomena: A Study of the First Not-Me Possession" earned pride of place, followed by "Hate in the Counter-Transference". In 2018, these two papers by Winnicott continued to occupy first and second place, respectively, among the "Most Popular Journal Articles". This information might well prove to be misleading. Certainly, *contemporary* researchers who use Pep-Web have come to relish Winnicott's "Hate in the Counter-Transference", but this represents a very recent scholarly situation. If one studies the citation of "Hate in the Counter-Transference" by psychoanalysts in the 1940s, 1950s, 1960s, and 1970s, one finds that the essay appears only very infrequently indeed in bibliographies (Kahr, 2020).

2. The original German sentence reads: "Ich gestand mir endlich, es komme daher, dass ich diese Kranken nicht liebe, dass ich mich über sie ärgere, sie so fern von mir und allem Menschlichen empfinde" (Freud, 1928a).

3. In preparing this chapter, I had the privilege of examining many of Donald Winnicott's unpublished case notes and much of his clinical correspondence, as well as many private archives belonging to some of Winnicott's former patients and colleagues. I also had the benefit of many extended interviews with the late Mrs Joyce Coles, who worked as Donald Winnicott's private secretary from 1948 to 1971, and who shared her extensive files of letters, notes, and other documentation with me, as well as her crystal-clear reminiscences. With the exception of the names of Dr Harry Guntrip (1975), Mr Masud Khan (1987), Dr Margaret Little (1985, 1990), and Mrs Marion Milner (2012), all of whom have written publicly about their analyses with Winnicott, I have in every other case employed pseudonyms to refer to the other patients mentioned herein. I have also referred to Winnicott's ex-analysand, Mrs Jane Shore Nicholas, the former wife of Masud Khan, by name. She had already granted permission for her story to be conveyed in Dr Linda Hopkins's (2006) superb biography of Masud Khan, and so her status as a sometime Winnicott analysand has already become more widely known and has entered the public record.

I have endeavoured to provide meticulous referencing for key pieces of information and for direct quotations contained herein; however, on a small number of occasions I have elected not to provide a detailed bibliographical reference to an unpublished item in an archival repository, as that would then provide an instant key to the identification of a particular patient. As both a mental health practitioner and an historian, I have a duty to protect the confidentiality of sensitive patient-related material, and I know that colleagues will appreciate such a responsibility, shared by us all. With reference to the letters of "Mrs Gladys Watson-Dixon" from which I have quoted, I have, on a small number of occasions, inserted bracketed words in order to provide greater continuity to some of her hastily written sentences.

CHAPTER SEVEN

"How to cure family disturbance": Enid Eichholz Balint and the creation of couple psychoanalysis

Bientôt nous plongerons dans les froides ténèbres.

[Soon we shall plunge into the cold darkness.]

Charles Baudelaire, "Chant d'Automne", Stanza 1, line 1,
in *Les Fleurs du mal: Poésies*, 1857

The prehistory
of couple psychoanalysis

In 2012, the distinguished actors Meryl Streep and Tommy Lee Jones starred in a Hollywood film entitled *Hope Springs*: a touching story about a long-standing couple whose marriage had become somewhat anaemic, and who, after several sessions with a therapist, portrayed in a sincere and tender manner by the comedian Steve Carrell, begin to enjoy a more lively intimacy once again. Clearly, couple therapy has become a fixture in popular culture; and in view of the increasingly frequent depictions of this modality in such popular television programmes as *The Sopranos*, *Desperate Housewives*, *House of Cards*, and *The Affair*, the image of the couple psychotherapist now threatens to eclipse that of the old-fashioned Viennese psychoanalyst, seated in a leather chair, while an individual patient free-associates on the couch.

Indeed, couple psychotherapy has become such an essential part of the contemporary mental health armamentarium that, in 2015, the Tavistock Centre for Couple Relationships,[1] the United Kingdom's leading supplier of both training in couple psychotherapy and in treatment, provided more than 17,000 sessions for approximately 3,500 couples (Tavistock Centre for Couple Relationships, 2015).

But from whence did couple psychotherapy originate? And how—especially in Great Britain, a country historically renowned for its reluctance to speak about intimate matters—did couple work become such an increasingly visible modality? *Who* invented British couple psychotherapy . . . and *how*?

For centuries, most troubled couples simply suffered in silence, or turned, perhaps, to prayer. Even seasoned psychiatric pioneers offered little comfort to spouses in distress.

In 1919, the famous ballet dancer Vaslav Nijinsky became psychotic, and his wife arranged a consultation at the Burghölzli asylum in Switzerland with one of Europe's premier psychiatrists, Professor Eugen Bleuler (1911), renowned for having invented the term "*Schizophrenie*" [schizophrenia]. Sadly, Bleuler provided little hope for the dancer's recovery or for the couple's happiness; and, damningly, he offered the following soul-destroying prescription to Nijinsky's wife: "Now, my dear, be very brave. You have to take your child away; you have to get a divorce. Unfortunately, I am helpless. Your husband is incurably insane" (quoted in Nijinsky, 1933, p. 410). In desperation, Madame Romola Nijinsky also consulted Professor Sigmund Freud, Dr Carl Gustav Jung, Dr Alfred Adler, and Dr Sándor Ferenczi, among many others (Nijinsky, 1933; Ansbacher, 1981; cf. Buckle, 1971). Yet none of these psychoanalysts provided any substantial support for either member of this troubled marital couple; consequently, Nijinsky spent much of the next thirty-one years in a catatonic stupor, while his wife embarked upon a series of lesbian affairs (Kahr, 1987; Nijinsky, 1991; cf. Ostwald, 1991).

Indeed, on the rare occasions when the early psychoanalysts *did* attempt to grapple with marital issues, they did so by treating the members of the couple *separately*, rather than *together*. In Vienna, Freud offered individual treatment to the American physician Dr Ruth Mack Brunswick, and also to her husband, the composer Mark Brunswick. But after lengthy analyses with Freud, conducted in parallel, the couple divorced (e.g., Roazen, 1975, 1995). To the best of our knowledge, this struggling marital pair never met with Freud for sessions at the same time. Freud treated many other couples in this fashion, with the husband attending at one hour and the wife at another; and those who participated in this arrangement often separated or ended up in sexless marriages.

This model of treating spouses individually remained the gold standard for much of the first half of the twentieth century. Psychoanalysts had simply not yet developed the clever idea of providing psychological therapy for both members of the couple *simultaneously*, in the same room at the same time.

Fortunately, throughout the middle years of the twentieth century, a seismic shift erupted in the clinical lens of psychotherapists and psychoanalysts alike, due, in large measure, to the devastations of global warfare.

In 1938, prior to the onset of the Second World War, some 385,000 British men served in the Army, the Royal Air Force, the Royal Navy, or the auxiliary services; but by the end of the war these numbers had increased more than tenfold, and by 1945, no fewer than 4,653,000 men had enlisted in the Armed Forces (Hancock, 1951). Sadly, many lost their lives in combat, as indeed did many civilians in bombings during the Blitz, leaving countless spouses abruptly widowed as well as untold numbers of children bereaved of one parent or orphaned of both.

When the war ended, the fighting forces returned home to mainland Great Britain, and one can only begin to imagine the complexities of integrating these veterans back into their families. Many would have suffered from post-traumatic illness or would have contracted sexually transmitted diseases from acts of infidelity with prostitutes or mistresses abroad. Many children failed to recognise their fathers, whom they had not seen for many years and, in some cases, had never met at all; and many other children became depressed from having had to endure evacuation to the countryside or even overseas (e.g., Bowlby, Miller, and Winnicott, 1939; Cosens, 1940; Anonymous, 1941; Bathurst et al., 1941; Winnicott, 1945b; Scott, 1948). Likewise, many wives may have taken lovers or may have harboured tremendous hatred towards their spouses for having left them to fend for themselves amidst the privations and dangers on the home front. Those marriages that had, in fact, survived the war did so under the greatest of strain.

Unsurprisingly, between 1939 and 1945 the number of petitions for the dissolution of marriage filed in England and Wales trebled, and continued to rise thereafter, on grounds of adultery, desertion, cruelty, lunacy, or the presumption of decease (Hancock, 1951). The landscape of British marriage in the immediate aftermath of the Second World War could best be described as catastrophic.

With an impoverished treasury, a blitzed landscape, and a malnourished population that had endured death, loss, abandonment, and traumatisation, marriages continued to crumble (cf. Haggett, 2012, 2015). British couples needed rescue, but to whom, if anyone, could they turn?

Enid Eichholz and the ravages of war

At some point during the 1940s, a woman called Mrs Enid Eichholz decided to do something proactive for troubled families and, in particular, for dysfunctional, traumatised marital couples.

Born in Hampstead, North London, on 12 December 1903, Enid Flora Albu attended school locally and then matriculated to Cheltenham Ladies' College and, ultimately, to the London School of Economics and Political Science in the University of London, where she obtained a BSc in Economics in 1925 (Hopkins, 2004). She married Robert Nathaniel Eichholz, a lawyer (Charles Rycroft, personal communication, 27 January 1996), and soon became a mother.

Round about 1934, one of her husband's German cousins came to visit and spoke of the horrors of Adolf Hitler's regime. Desperate to help, Mrs Eichholz established a school for German–Jewish refugee children. Through her work with these youngsters, she also began to provide assistance to adult refugees, some of whom came to live in her home (Rudnytsky, 2000).

Eventually, mid-war, Eichholz took up a posting at the Family Welfare Association, a charitable organisation that provided practical assistance for needy people in distress (e.g., Mowat, 1961; cf. Bosanquet, 1914; Hill, 1956; Darley, 1990; Lewis, 1991); and she inaugurated a series of citizens' advice bureaux in London. In this capacity, she visited the homes of the distressed, whom she described in later years as "people who had serious problems—relatives being killed, losing their limbs and their children" (quoted in Rudnytsky, 2000, p. 1). Mrs Eichholz had a mandate to advise these families about the benefits to which they would be entitled under the War Damages Act 1943. But family members surprised her by wanting to speak not about financial remuneration but, rather, about their private tragedies. Enid Eichholz approached her work at the Family Welfare Association with considerable trepidation, deeply conscious of "my lack of knowledge about human relations and how people wanted to talk" (quoted in Rudnytsky, 2000, p. 2). Nevertheless, in spite of her inexperience, she hoped that she might still be of use.

But how on earth did a lone woman, with only a bachelor's degree—and one in economics, no less—and with no clinical training of any kind, come to create a paradigm shift that would lay the groundwork for a new mental health profession—namely, couple psychotherapy?

Before examining in greater detail the ways in which the future Enid Balint began to create Great Britain's first marital psychotherapy institution, let us consider the broader socio-political climate, which would have encouraged the development of such a pioneering body of work. Eichholz's plan to provide some sort of intervention for troubled couples and families did not unfold in an historical vacuum. Her quest to offer support emerged amid the dissatisfactions with Great Britain's wartime administration.

Although Winston Churchill had served as an inspiring and ferocious prime minister throughout the Second World War, devoting his energies to the War Department and to the Defence Committee, after V-E Day Britons began to tire of his war-mongering and his passion for crushing foreign enemies and sought, instead, a far less bellicose leader (Harrington and Young, 1978). At this time the average housewife spent at least one hour each day queuing for inadequate food supplies; consequently, Britons craved a change of leadership, and, to the surprise of many, Clement Richard Attlee, Leader of the Labour Party since 1935 and subsequently Deputy Prime Minister with special responsibility for the Home Front, took control of the government with a majority of 146 seats (Beckett, 1997), thus ousting the incumbent bulldog Churchill. A former social worker in Stepney, in London's East End (Attlee, 1920), the new Prime Minister ushered in an overtly socialist government, which prioritised welfare over warfare and improvements at home over victories overseas (e.g., Attlee, 1954; Harris, 1982; Pearce, 1994, 1997).

Bespectacled and softly spoken, Clement Attlee wore his potency lightly. Many worried that he lacked the capacity to lead the country; indeed, the Conservative politician Duff Cooper (1945, pp. 356–357) described the new Prime Minister as "less impressive every time one sees him". Nevertheless, in spite of his bookish manner, Attlee devoted himself with tremendous zeal to the creation of a Post-War

Settlement, designed to improve the quality of daily life for Britons by counteracting the food shortages, high taxes, fuel shortages, and economic ruin, and by engineering the termination of American Lend-Lease aid. In point of fact, in an effort to improve both living and working conditions, Attlee's first Parliament passed no fewer than 347 Acts, thus masterminding the transition from a wartime to a peacetime economy through the introduction of a profound system of social welfare (e.g., Burridge, 1985; Pearce, 1994; Thomas-Symonds, 2010; Bew, 2016).

The National Health Service, inaugurated in 1948, became the flagship of Attlee's government, providing free health care for all (Hodgkinson, 1967; Webster, 1988). During its first year of operation alone, some 8,500,000 Britons received dental treatment and more than 5,250,000 people obtained spectacles. In total, physicians wrote some 187,000,000 prescriptions, often for long-standing health problems, previously neglected due to the prohibitive costs of private medicine (Pearce, 1994; Marr, 2007). Attlee's government guaranteed not only medical services but also, through the passage of the National Insurance Act 1946, government pensions, payment of funeral costs, fees to widows and to the handicapped, as well as increased unemployment benefits. Attlee's overt socialism allowed many to seek a range of assistance for domestic needs, thus foregrounding the family explicitly for the very first time (e.g., Marwick, 1982).

Yet in spite of Attlee's heroic efforts to create more jobs, provide free health care, build houses, train more teachers, offer pensions, care for widows, and such like, the government did not directly tackle the serious crisis within marriages during the post-war period.

Those who did require help generally turned to religion in the hope that God would deliver them from abusive husbands and unfaithful wives. Several enlightened clergymen did, however, collaborate with physicians steeped in psychological medicine in an effort to create a more enlightened form of intervention for troubled marital relationships. For instance, in 1938, the Reverend Herbert Gray, a Presbyterian minister, and Dr Edward Fyfe Griffith, a physician, founded the Marriage Guidance Council, an organisation that offered sexual and contraceptive advice to married couples (e.g., Griffith, 1981). And in 1946 a group of clerics established the Catholic Marriage Advisory Council, which provided support for couples through prayer (Harris, 2015). Without doubt, enlightened British reformers did not neglect the burdens of post-war marriage, though none had developed a consistent theory of marital dysfunction, nor a model of treatment that integrated the fruits of psychoanalysis—arguably the most profound body of knowledge about the role of early childhood experiences and unconscious processes in the formation of symptomatology.

Enid Eichholz recognised that a different space might be helpful: one that provided couples, quite simply, with permission to speak privately, in unrestricted fashion, much as Freud had done with adult patients more than half a century previously.

With the blessing of Benjamin Astbury, the General Secretary of the Family Welfare Association, Enid Eichholz organised a formal meeting on 22 January 1946, at 11.00 a.m., to mark the inauguration of the newly constituted Marriage Guidance Council and also to discuss the formation of a series of "Marriage Guidance Centres", in which those with troubled marriages could be offered interviews. The Marriage Guidance Council recognised that the valiant workers in its many citizens advice bureaux would not be sufficiently competent to undertake marital support; consequently, the organisation decided to engage qualified social workers, albeit few in number, in Great Britain after the war. Ordinarily, male professionals—physicians or clergymen—provided most of the psychological treatment at that time; indeed, at the Tavistock Clinic, female doctors could not work with male patients, only female ones (e.g., Rushforth, 1984). But Mrs Eichholz's new and enlightened Marriage Guidance Council conceded that male interviewers need not be required for sessions. Thus, Eichholz and her colleagues forged a path through which female workers could begin to engage with distressed marital couples. These female staff members—referred to as "secretaries" in spite of their social work qualifications—would hold meetings with family members and would thus be charged with the task of "diagnosing the trouble" (Marriage Guidance Centres Committee, 1946, p. 2).

Buoyed by the possibilities ahead of them, in February 1946 Mrs Eichholz and the members of the Marriage Guidance Council launched an ambitious scheme to open several marriage guidance centres in London, with units in some of the capital's most impoverished areas, namely, Bethnal Green, Shoreditch, North Islington, St Pancras, East Lewisham, Wandsworth, and also more centrally, in Westminster (Marriage Guidance Centres Committee, 1946). Soon thereafter, the Marriage Guidance Council changed its name to the Marriage Guidance Committee and, later in 1946, altered its name once more, to the Marriage Guidance Centres Committee (Marriage Guidance Centres Committee, 1946).

Most of the brief histories of couple psychotherapy in Great Britain claim that a woman called "Enid Balint" founded the first therapeutic organisation for troubled marriages—the Family Discussion Bureau—in 1948 (e.g., Gray, 1970; Clulow, 1990; Woodhouse, 1990); but the documentary evidence reveals quite compellingly that "Enid Eichholz" (not yet married to her second husband, Michael Balint) did so, and *not* in 1948 but, rather, in 1946. Thus, contemporary practitioners can now date our foundation two years earlier—more than seventy years ago—to a fledgling organisation known, not as the Family Discussion Bureau but, rather, as the Marriage Guidance Council, then subsequently as the Marriage Guidance Committee, and eventually as the Marriage Guidance Centres Committee.

Eichholz's newly launched centres certainly met a need within local communities. By December 1946, the unit in Lewisham had attracted some six new cases, that in Shoreditch three cases, and the one in Wandsworth four more (Marriage Guidance Centres Committee, 1946). Although this may seem rather a tiny number of families in distress, one must remember that during the late 1940s most Britons regarded the talking therapies with tremendous suspicion, referring colloquially to any psychiatrist as a "trick cyclist" (e.g., Muirhead, 1987, p. 124); therefore, those who did present for help—perhaps out of curiosity, perhaps out of desperation—should be remembered for their courage in having had the capacity to seek such as yet untried and untested professional assistance.

Alas, we know very little about the precise nature of the interviews undertaken by these "secretaries", nor the theoretical lens—if any—through which these women facilitated marital consultations in 1946. Furthermore, it remains very unclear to what extent Mrs Eichholz herself actually undertook the day-to-day clinical work; in fact, we have no surviving documentary evidence that she worked with couples or with families in a direct way at all at this time. But she certainly supported her "secretaries", and she maintained strong relationships with the hierarchy of the Family Welfare Association to ensure that her marriage centres would grow and prosper.

Enid Eichholz eventually came to recognise that in spite of her remarkable capacities as an administrator and, moreover, as the progenitor of original and path-breaking projects, she needed more help to provide a robust and systematic clinical foundation for the work undertaken by the secretaries. Having already admitted to her "lack of knowledge about human relations and how people wanted to talk" (quoted in Rudnytsky, 2000, p. 2), Eichholz knew that she would need to collaborate with some other person or persons who possessed a far greater understanding of the intimacies of family life.

The marriage of social welfare and psychoanalysis

At some point, probably during 1946 or 1947, Enid Eichholz had the opportunity to meet Dr Archibald Thomson Macbeth Wilson, known universally as "Tommy", one of the Tavistock Clinic's long-serving psychiatrists. The encounter between these two individuals sparked a remarkable revolution in the marital guidance movement.

Tommy Wilson had studied medicine at the University of Glasgow in Scotland, and then, after a period of teaching physiology in London, he became a Rockefeller Research Fellow at the Tavistock Clinic, ultimately joining its medical staff in 1939 (Dicks, 1970). During the Second World War, Colonel Wilson worked in both the Directorate of Army Psychiatry as a commanding psychiatrist (Ahrenfeldt, 1958; Dicks, 1970) and also on the staff of the Directorate of Biological Research. After the war, he began training at the Institute of Psycho-Analysis (Wilson, 1949).

A much-neglected figure in the history of psychoanalysis, Dr Wilson stood out from his colleagues as someone interested in working on the widest possible canvas. Unlike other practising Freudian analysts of the period who devoted themselves exclusively to five-times-weekly treatment of individual patients, Tommy Wilson had already pioneered the field of psychosomatic medicine in Great Britain, applying psychoanalytic ideas to the understanding of physical symptomatology and, in particular, to the dynamics of such conditions as peptic ulcer (e.g., Davies and Wilson, 1937) as well as haematemesis—namely, the vomiting of blood (e.g., Wilson, 1939). His study of peptic ulcers, in particular, undertaken in collaboration with Dr Daniel T. Davies, a physician at the Royal Free Hospital in London, proved quite landmark and earned pride of place as the lead article in the 11 December 1937 issue of *The Lancet*, one of the leading medical periodicals in Great Britain. Davies and Wilson examined some 205 cases of peptic ulcer and boldly concluded that fully 84% had developed after external stressors or traumata in the lives of the patients: a truly radical hypothesis in orthodox British medicine at that point in time.

Over the course of many years, Wilson worked closely in collaboration with eminent medical specialists in hospitals in an effort to forge a wider liaison among psychoanalysis, medical psychology, and general medicine. Wilson (1946) also studied the psychological consequences of servicemen returning home to Great Britain (cf. Ahrenfeldt, 1958), and he also maintained a strong interest in group psychotherapy (Wilson, 1947; Wilson, Doyle, and Kelnar, 1947).

Mrs Eichholz could not, perhaps, have attached herself to a more energetic or more organisationally creative physician, and she regarded her meeting with Tommy Wilson as rather "lucky" (quoted in Rudnytsky, 2000, p. 3). He introduced her more formally to the works of Sigmund Freud (Rudnytsky, 2000), and he invited her to meet with his clinical colleagues, offering her an *entrée* into the growing and thriving post-war community at the Tavistock Clinic. Before long, Mrs Eichholz became friendly with most, if not all, of the senior Tavistock psychiatric, psychological, and social work staff.

As a formal medical institution destined to join the incipient British National Health Service in 1948, the Tavistock Clinic could not receive donations of money from charitable organisations, nor could it, at that point, commission large-scale research projects. Thus, a group of forward-thinking mental health professionals and social scientists within the clinic community created the Tavistock Institute of Human Relations (TIHR) as a "twin" (Dicks, 1970, p. xiv) that could work alongside the Tavistock Clinic to promote psychodynamic thinking on a wider, non-clinical, applied scale (Dicks, 1970; Fraher, 2004). Tommy Wilson became the first Chairman of the Management Committee of the TIHR, and in this capacity he had the power to support projects such as Mrs Eichholz's Marriage Guidance Centres.

Eichholz soon began to attend seminars at the Tavistock Clinic, then located in its new post-war home at 2, Beaumont Street, in Central London, very close to Harley Street: the headquarters of the elite, private medical district. Founded in 1920 by the pioneering medical psychologist Dr Hugh Crichton Miller, the Tavistock Square Clinic for Functional Nervous Disorders championed the so-called "New Psychology" (Dicks, 1970, p. 1)—a non-sectarian catch-all name for the ideas of Freud, Jung, Adler, and others (e.g., Crichton Miller, 1921, 1922; cf. Culpin, 1924, 1927). Unlike the British Psycho-Analytical Society, which promulgated only Freudian theories, the Tavistock Clinic enjoyed a more eclectic and open-spirited approach to the treatment of the neuroses and actively sought to provide psychotherapy for those who could not afford private fees (Dicks, 1970), describing itself as a veritable "Harley Street for the anxious poor"

(Anonymous, 1934, quoted in Kahr, 2000, p. 399). Although Ernest Jones sternly forbade any members of the British Psycho-Analytical Society to teach at the Tavistock Clinic (interview with John Bowlby, 20 February 1984), the "Tavi", as it came to be known, encouraged the widest possible collaboration and facilitated its staff to develop outward-looking links.

Hugh Crichton Miller's successor, Dr John Rawlings Rees, fostered an even greater spirit of open-mindedness. Remembered as a "genial" and "rotund" (Dicks, 1970, p. 58) pipe-smoker with an "American personality" (Dicks, 1970, p. 59), J. R. Rees enjoyed bringing newcomers into the larger Tavistock Clinic family. Indeed, in 1933 he wrote that, "We give the warmest welcome to every sound new venture in this field of psychiatry" (quoted in Dicks, 1970, p. 60).

During the Second World War, Brigadier Rees became the chief psychiatrist for the British army, and he co-opted many of his clinical staff members and appointed them to key posts (Ahrenfeldt, 1958; Dicks, 1970; cf. Rees, 1945). By 1945, many of the Tavi psychiatrists had returned to civilian life and to their staff consultancies on Beaumont Street full of rich experience, as many had already experimented with group psychotherapy and therapeutic communities (Bion, 1948a, 1948b, 1949a, 1949b, 1950a, 1950b, 1951, 1961; Dicks, 1970; Gray, 1970; Bridger, 1985; de Maré, 1985; Sutherland, 1985; Trist, 1985; Harrison, 2000)—new discoveries that developed out of the sheer wartime necessity of processing large numbers of traumatised soldier-patients—and consequently the Tavi staff greeted Mrs Eichholz's efforts to work with marital couples and with families in a highly appreciative manner. Indeed, the post-war Tavistock Clinic, headed initially by Dr Wilfred Bion as Chair of the Interim Medical Committee, had already planned, quite explicitly, to grapple with "problems of engagement and marriage" (Dicks, 1970, p. 143), as well as with the "anxieties of the newly married in relation to home-making" (p. 143).

In 1948, Mrs Eichholz applied, successfully, to train as a psychoanalyst in her own right at the Institute of Psycho-Analysis, and she received a place in the new intake of candidates. She chose as her training analyst the venerable Quaker physician Dr John Rickman, a pioneer of psychoanalysis and medical psychology and sometime analysand of Sigmund Freud. Renowned for his openness and for his creative range of interests (e.g., Rickman, 1926a, 1926b, 1927a, 1927b, 1928, 1932, 1939, 1940a, 1940b, 1940c, 1947, 1948; Gorer and

Rickman, 1949; King, 2003a), not least for his work at the War Office Selection Board (Rickman, 1943; cf. King, 2003b), applying psychological thinking to the screening of military personnel, Rickman had a great capacity to encourage his students in the most generous of ways.

Miss Pearl King (personal communication, 4 November 2001), one of Rickman's analysands during the late 1940s and thus one of Enid Eichholz's analytic "siblings", told me that Rickman used to encourage his patients to speak in the fullest voice possible, not only figuratively but also literally. When, for instance, Pearl King had to deliver a paper, Rickman instructed her to visualise a physical barricade across the lecture room and insisted that she must work to project her voice *over* that barricade so that people at the back could hear her! Thus did he, one imagines, help his patients to become maximally vocal and impactful in their efforts and that Mrs Eichholz would have benefited hugely from having such a man as her training analyst.

Forging "marital" links:
Enid Eichholz as collaborator

Thus far, the Family Welfare Association's citizens advice bureaux had become transformed, first, into the Marriage Guidance Council, then the Marriage Guidance Committee, and ultimately, the Marriage Guidance Centres Committee. Circa 1948, Enid Eichholz's organisation changed its name yet again, adopting the title of Marriage Welfare Committee. Eichholz herself served as the Secretary, and she co-opted Dr Tommy Wilson to serve alongside her, as well as a young Scottish woman, Miss Isabel Menzies, a social scientist who also worked at TIHR (Lyth, Scott, and Young, 1988). Brilliantly, Eichholz had surrounded herself with a formidable group of outward-looking and forward-thinking men and women who had devoted themselves to bringing health—in all its manifestations—out of the clinic and into the community.

By 26 February 1948, the Family Welfare Association agreed that all new family welfare centres would hereafter be known as "Marriage Welfare Centres" (Marriage Welfare Centres Committee, 1948). Only later that year did Eichholz begin to refer to her new experiment by yet another new name—its sixth designation (!)—namely, the Family Discussion Bureaux (with "Bureaux" spelled in the plural rather than in the singular). Eichholz aimed high in terms of recruiting patrons to join the board, enlisting not only Tavistock Clinic and TIHR personnel but also physicians such as Dr Innes Pearse and Dr George Scott Williamson of the pioneering Peckham Health Centre (General Secretary, 1948; cf. Barlow, 1985).

Eichholz also co-opted the 40-year-old Mrs Lily Pincus, a Jewish refugee, to serve as her day-to-day right-hand woman, administering to the minutiae of Eichholz's growing series of projects (Marriage Welfare Centres Committee, 1948). Born in 1898 in the Austro-Hungarian city of Karlsbad as Lily Lazarus, she then distinguished herself as an administrative secretary in Potsdam, in Germany; in 1939 she fled to London with her husband, Fritz Pincus. Mrs Pincus would ultimately prove to be Mrs Eichholz's greatest institutional partner (cf. Cohen, 2013).

In mid-1948, Enid Eichholz (1948c) assumed the title of "Chairman" of the "Marriage Welfare Committee" (Eichholz, 1948c) and began describing herself and her female colleagues not as secretaries but, instead, as social workers. Even though not all of the clinicians had graduated from a recognised social work training, the adoption of such a title proved to be rather common at that time, in view of the dearth of recognised social work practitioners. By the summer of 1948, the "Marriage Welfare Committee" became rebranded as the "Marriage Welfare Sub-Committee"; and on the morning of 14 June 1948 Enid Eichholz, aided by Dr Tommy Wilson, convened a group of esteemed colleagues for yet another landmark meeting with the express purpose of discussing "the specialist services which can be arranged in connection with Marriage Welfare work to be undertaken by the Association" (General Secretary, 1948).

The invitees included Dr Tommy Wilson and Miss Isabel Menzies, both from the Tavistock Institute of Human Relations; Dr Thomas Forrest Main, the Medical Director of the Cassel Hospital for Functional Nervous Disorders; and also Dr John Bowlby (General Secretary, 1948).

One of Great Britain's most influential child psychiatrists and a passionate enthusiast for healing troubled families (e.g., Bowlby, 1949a), Dr John Bowlby had, of late, become a keen supporter of Enid Eichholz's efforts to work with turbulent marriages. As Director of the Children's Department of the Tavistock Clinic since 1946, he had already begun to offer consultations to parents in the hope of ameliorating the psychopathology of their children; consequently, he warmly supported the plan, which he described as one of "considerable importance" (Marriage Welfare Committee, 1948). In fact, Bowlby became so smitten by the project that he lobbied strongly for the establishment of a marriage welfare centre in Hendon, North London, where he consulted on two afternoons per week.

Extraordinarily, within the space of only two years Enid Eichholz had cultivated important links with some of the nation's leading mental health professionals and with at least three seminal psychological institutions: the Tavistock Clinic, the TIHR, and also the Cassel Hospital for Functional Nervous Disorders (Memorandum on Visit to the Cassel Hospital on Monday, 28th June 1948, by Mr. Astbury, Miss Menzies and Mrs Eichholz, 1948). With such support behind her, the Family Welfare Association agreed to fund the establishment of a number of better developed marital centres to replace the more makeshift ones first established back in 1946 in Bethnal Green, St Pancras, Wandsworth, and other communities. And on 20 September 1948, a certain Mrs Reynolds—whose forename eludes us—commenced her employment at the first properly funded and reasonably staffed marriage welfare centre at 21, Kempson Road, in Walham Green, in Fulham, London SW6, which opened to the public in early October 1948 (Eichholz, 1948d).

With the launch of the marriage welfare centre at Kempson Road, Great Britain now boasted a formal institution—albeit a small one—that could provide fledgling psychological treatment for couples in distress. Although the Catholic Marriage Advisory Council and the Marriage Guidance Council offered spiritual advice, medical information, and lessons in contraception, Enid Eichholz had created a space in which couples could talk about their private emotional life for the very first time and could begin to have an experience of being listened to by specialist social workers or caseworkers. And by late 1948 the Family Welfare Association had established marriage welfare centres in North Islington, South Islington, Kensington, Paddington, and St Pancras (Eichholz, 1948e).

By 1949, these individual centres had become known as family discussion bureaux (FDB), and Eichholz (1949a) gradually began to describe her centres as the "F.D.B. of the FWA"[2]—the Family Discussion Bureau of the Family Welfare Association. This pilot experiment proved highly successful, and Eichholz discovered that the application of a psychoanalytic approach to the study of marital distress resulted in the betterment of the couple relationship as well as in an improvement in the health of the children of couples who presented for treatment (Anonymous, n.d.).

Although the surviving archival materials from the years 1946 to 1949 offer a great deal of pertinent information about the development of the Family Discussion Bureau as an institution, they fail to provide much insight into the precise nature of clinical practice at this time. We do know, however, that Eichholz and her team worked with some very challenging marital couples. For instance, when Eichholz took some of the FDB cases to Dr Millicent Dewar's firm at the Cassel Hospital for Functional Nervous Disorders for discussion and consultation, Eichholz reported that Dr Dewar's team made very clear, if not dismissive, pronouncements. For instance, in reference to the case of a certain married woman, Eichholz (1950a) wrote, "they thought that she had too slight a therapeutic drive and did not like this case"; and with reference to a certain male patient, Eichholz (1950a) recorded, "they did not like this, thought the case was too bad from my report of it and would not consider for triage".

Nevertheless, cheered, no doubt, by the establishment of the various branches of the Family Discussion Bureau and by her increasing sophistication in psychoanalysis, Eichholz called upon many of the senior staff at the Tavistock Clinic for further assistance. In 1948, she drafted a letter to the Medical Officer of Health of Middlesex County Council (Eichholz, 1948a), asking for support of her "piece of experimental social work" and of her plan to provide "intensive case work on a small number of cases" (Eichholz, 1948a), offered by "highly trained social workers" (Eichholz, 1948a). She explained that she and the staff at her pilot centres endeavoured to research "some of the reasons leading to marriage break-down, and following from that they will hope to develop more effective methods of prevention and treatment" (Eichholz, 1948a). In true pioneer fashion, Mrs Eichholz (1948a) explained to the Medical Officer of Health that she wished to engage in "preventive work", in the hope of treating cases "at an early stage before break-down occurs" (Eichholz, 1948a). In this respect, Eichholz positioned herself, perhaps unwittingly, as a true pioneer of preventative mental health services—a concept that would not become more standard until approximately half-a-century later (e.g., Wurtele, Kvaternick, and Franklin, 1992; Willis, 1993; Barron and Topping, 2011; Harder, 2014)!

Such a forward-thinking approach to mental health work appealed greatly to Dr John Bowlby, who had already begun to devote himself wholeheartedly to the documentation of the adverse effects of early deprivations and separations and to the strengthening of family ties (e.g., Bowlby, 1939, 1940a, 1940b, 1944a, 1944b, 1946; cf. Kahr, 2015b). In an effort to be of assistance, Bowlby kindly offered to comment upon Mrs Eichholz's (1948b) draft document to the Medical Officer of Health. The following year, in 1949, Eichholz (1949i) expressed a strong desire to work with Bowlby directly at the Tavistock Clinic, but unfortunately due to staff shortages in his department, Bowlby (1949c), to his regret, could do no more than support her "important work" when he could. But, happily, he did arrange, most helpfully, for Eichholz to undertake supervision with Miss Noël Hunnybun, one of his cherished social workers. Bowlby (1949b) suggested that Eichholz might pay the "Tavi" two guineas per weekly supervision session, but Eichholz (1949j), in deep appreciation, offered to contribute more, exclaiming, "Please let me know if you feel that two guineas a week is enough as I feel I will be getting a great deal of help from other members of your staff as well as from her."

Eichholz soon found herself in supervision with a woman of exceptional skill and experience in mental health matters. Some fourteen years older than Enid Eichholz, the warm-hearted Noël Hunnybun—a pioneer of psychiatric social work—provided a great deal of nurture. On 11 August 1949, Hunnybun (1949) wrote to her new supervisee: "I shall look forward to our work together and hope that you will find it helpful. I must admit to some qualms at the prospect of supervising so experienced a worker as yourself, but anyway it will be fun I think, and very interesting, and I expect to learn from the experience." Thus the supervision began; and Hunnybun eventually charged Eichholz only one guinea per session, in contrast to the two guineas previously agreed by Bowlby (Hunnybun, 1950a). After having worked with Hunnybun for some time, Eichholz (1950c) wrote, "I feel that the charges you make shew in no way the amount of work I get from contact with you and supervision of my cases."

The partnership between Eichholz and Hunnybun proved of great importance; and Hunnybun provided not only clinical supervision but also career advice and even financial tips, explaining that Eichholz could claim her psychoanalytic training costs against income tax (Park, 1950)—by no means a common practice at that time. With tender, maternal affection, Miss Hunnybun wrote to congratulate Mrs Eichholz for having organised a conference about the work of the Family Discussion Bureau. Hunnybun (1950b) enthused, "I hope the Conference will be very successful and will help people to gain some understanding of the real meaning of training for work with human beings. It seems as if we have got to go a long way before people engaged in social work really understand the need for a careful training based on psychology."

After a year of formal supervision, the two women stopped referring to one another as "Miss Hunnybun" and "Mrs Eichholz" and began to speak more informally as Nöel and Enid. One senses that Hunnybun's benign supervision of Eichholz proved most deeply important at a time when Eichholz, as "mother" to the social workers and caseworkers at the burgeoning marriage welfare centres, had to give so much.

Sensibly, Eichholz not only sought further training and supervision for herself, but she also arranged additional training for her Family Discussion Bureaux staff. As a fledgling trainee psychoanalyst, she had become a student once again, and consequently she encouraged her new staff members to do likewise. In 1951, Noël Hunnybun organised a course—very possibly the first full-time, year-long psychoanalytic postgraduate training for psychiatric social workers and caseworkers—based in the Child Guidance Department of the Tavistock Clinic. With lectures by Dr John Bowlby on "Child Development and Personality Growth" and by Dr Elliott Jaques on the "Dynamics of Social Structure and the Processes of Social Change" (Syllabus for the Advanced Course for Post Graduate Case Workers, 1951), this training proved irresistible; and Mrs Eichholz sent two of her relatively new staffers, Mrs Judith Stephens and Mrs Antonia Shooter, to participate in this landmark course.

Miss Hunnybun (1951) honoured Mrs Eichholz and the staff at the Family Discussion Bureau by suggesting that not only might FDB students train at the Tavi, but perhaps Tavi students might also begin to participate in FDB seminars as well—no doubt a profound validation of the work that Enid Eichholz had begun to undertake. As Hunnybun (1951) wrote, "May I say how pleased we are to extend this invitation to your students and some time I should like to discuss with you the suggested reciprocation, whereby our case work students in the Advanced Course might be able to join in a discussion on advanced case work with your group."

With a number of active branches of the Family Discussion Bureaux (still spelled, at this time, in the plural), and with a small but sturdy staff team in place, as well as supervision from Noël Hunnybun, and support from such figures as Tommy Wilson and John Bowlby, and also fortified by her own training at the Institute of Psycho-Analysis and by her training analysis with John Rickman, Enid Eichholz had, by late 1949, truly created something from nothing.

A home in Chandos Street: towards solid foundations

Enid Eichholz's developmental work and her forging of rich professional alliances continued in an unrelenting fashion throughout 1949 and 1950. But she also began to undertake research and to apply for external funding. On 14 March 1949, she sketched out her intentions to commission a "Research Project into the Social Structure and Social Needs of Communities" (Eichholz, 1949a), in which she explained,

> The help needed by individuals in families from social workers is very undefined. That there are needs for help in family + community living there seems little doubt. What the needs are, and how, and by whom they can be met can only be discovered by research.

Consequently, she proposed the inauguration of an "intensive study" (Eichholz, 1949a) into the landscape of individual and family needs, to be undertaken by psychologists, social caseworkers, and "socioanthropologists" (Eichholz, 1949a); together, such a team could investigate healthy families and unhealthy families, in an effort to discover their "storm centres" (Eichholz, 1949a). Ideally, this research project would come to discover "how to prevent + how to cure family disturbance, and how to plan communities which are helpful to individual + family growth + maturation" (Eichholz, 1949a).

By 1950, Enid Eichholz no longer positioned herself as the untrained female social worker with a degree in economics who needed to align herself with potent male physicians for guidance and support. Colleagues came to recognise her as an independent expert in her own right and respected her hugely for what she had begun to achieve. For instance, in 1950, Tommy Wilson asked her to provide assistance to the distinguished psychiatrist Dr Alfred Torrie, who hoped to establish a group for expectant mothers. Eichholz (1950b) could state quite proudly that she and her team had *already* created such a group for postnatal mothers at the Fulham Maternity Hospital, where "we hear quite a lot about their feelings before the birth of the baby and during their time in hospital".

At one point in the late 1940s, while attending seminars at the Tavistock Clinic, Enid Eichholz met a most unusual man from Hungary. Dr Michael Balint, a physician and psychoanalyst, worked in the Adult Department at Beaumont Street. Analysed not by one, but by two, of Freud's closest disciples—namely Dr Sándor Ferenczi in Budapest, and Dr Hanns Sachs in Berlin—Michael Balint developed a reputation as a man of deep intelligence and charisma; and Enid wasted no time in recruiting him to offer seminars for her staff team. On 25 March 1949, she expressed her gratitude to the brilliant Dr Balint, noting, "I am sure you know without my telling you how helpful we are finding the seminars and how much we appreciate your being able to spare us so much of your time and interest" (Eichholz, 1949f). Before long, Enid had begun to consult with Balint about the growth of the organisation and about how to handle her staff members (Eichholz, 1949b, 1949g); by the summer of that year, she confessed, "I felt encouraged by our talk and look forward to finding out what we can do between us" (Eichholz, 1949h).

Michael Balint maintained a particular interest in the vicissitudes of adult sexuality as opposed to infantile sexuality, and he had recently published a seminal paper in *The International Journal of Psycho-Analysis*, "On Genital Love" (Balint, 1948), in which he wrote about the importance of treating one's lover with tenderness and respect and without any greediness, denigration, or humiliation. In March 1952, Enid arranged for Balint to deliver a seminar on adult sexuality—although, as she lamented to Nöel Hunnybun, "I am not sure whether he will be free to do this" (Eichholz, 1952b).

In spite of having separated from her husband Robert Eichholz, Enid and her estranged spouse had not yet divorced. Although still technically a married woman, Enid began to experience a frisson towards Dr Balint, and he seems to have shared these sentiments. Interestingly, when Enid struggled to find the monies to pay for Michael Balint's seminars, he graciously told her that she must not worry about such matters (Eichholz, 1949c). The affection between Mrs Eichholz and Dr Balint blossomed, and gradually the two began to enjoy an extramarital affair. Her growing relationship with Dr Balint, both professionally and personally, would open up enormous collaborative vistas for Mrs Eichholz in the decades to come.

By 1951, Enid Eichholz had, in only five years, assembled an impressive staff team of social workers and caseworkers and had recruited senior psychiatrists, social workers, and psychoanalysts to offer supervision and training; moreover, she had enlisted the services of researchers in anthropology and social psychology. She had forged collaborative links with the Tavistock Clinic, the Tavistock

Institute of Human Relations, the Cassel Hospital for Functional Nervous Diseases (e.g., Eichholz, 1949d, 1949e; Weddell, 1949), the Peckham Health Centre, and other organisations. She had elicited funding from the Home Office and from the Nuffield Foundation (Eichholz, 1950d). And she had helped to inaugurate a stream of publications (e.g., Menzies, 1949; Wilson, 1949; Wilson, Menzies, and Eichholz, 1949). Above all, she had incorporated psychoanalytic ideas into traditional social welfare casework for troubled marriages, families, and even children, and, had begun to transform the so-called "marriage guidance" profession, which, previously, had emphasised sex education and contraceptive advice, into a new profession of marital psychoanalysis.

By late 1951, Eichholz and her staff team, which now consisted of Mrs Lily Pincus, Mrs Kathleen Bannister, Mrs Joan Maizels, Mr Douglas Woodhouse, and others, could no longer squeeze into the offices of the Family Welfare Association on Vauxhall Bridge Road, near London's Victoria Station; and so Eichholz arranged to lease premises in the heart of Central London, at 4, Chandos Street, quite close to Harley Street. In doing so, she endeavoured to position the work as a clinical discipline, on a par with psychiatry and medicine more generally.

Spread over the second and third floors of Chandos Street and consisting of six large rooms, with specially dedicated lavatories for both male and female members of staff, the new offices boasted an inventory of ten Parker Knoll chairs, thirteen Pel chairs, and three wooden chairs, as well as three metal filing cabinets, three typewriters, five waste paper baskets, some woollen rugs and square matting for the floors, three coffee pots, two aluminium sauce pans, and, perhaps, most crucial of all, twelve sherry glasses (Inventory of Furniture at 4 Chandos Street, Cavendish Square, W.1.: 2nd & 3rd Floors. November 16th 1951, 1951). Ever conscious of the privacy required for such delicate clinical work, the Family Discussion Bureau would have to pay £7/10s for sound-proofing the door that separated the two interview rooms on the third floor (Bolland, 1952)—a sum that required special approval from the Finance Committee of the Family Welfare Association (Savage, 1952).

In October 1951, the new organisation opened its doors and began conducting some one hundred clinical interviews per month. Indeed, between 1 April 1951 and 1 March 1952, the Family Discussion Bureaux staff had facilitated as many as 1,175 interviews, with each case receiving on average five consultations (Eichholz, 1952a).

The clientele consisted predominantly of married couples, but the FDB also treated premarital couples, adolescents, as well as parents concerned about their children. Additionally, the staff held group sessions for school-leavers in Fulham, as part of a prevention pro-gramme (Eichholz, 1952a). During the academic year of 1952–53, the FDB had to manage a significant budget, paying some £2,025 in caseworker salaries, some £799 for clerical salaries, and £168 to Michael Balint for conducting clinical seminars (Family Discussion Bureau, n.d.).

By late 1952, Enid had become so very deeply ensconced in her psychoanalytic training, and also in her extramarital relationship, that she decided to resign as head of FDB: she surrendered her post to her stalwart deputy, Lily Pincus. When, on 2 January 1953, Enid and Michael married (Hopkins, 2004), the staff of FDB sent them a bowl (Balint and Balint, 1953).

From 1953 onwards, Lily Pincus undertook yeoman work to develop the sturdy and impressive foundations established by her predecessor. Dr John Sutherland (1955), the Tavi's new Medical Direc-tor, praised the Family Discussion Bureau for treating clients like people: "I certainly have a strong impression that for the FDB all of their clients are very much people + not bits of psychopathology." Indeed, he lamented that,

> I personally have a strong feeling that what has gone out of psycho-analysis is 'love'. We really produce high-powered interpreting machines whereas the FDB group have retained enough of their direct spontaneous feelings with the clients despite the attempt to understand the dynamics [Sutherland, 1955]

Enid Eichholz Balint could not have asked for greater recognition.

Although no longer the reigning leader of the Family Discussion Bureau, Mrs Balint remained a vibrant presence in the British mental health community. She not only collaborated extensively with her new husband on the application of psychodynamic ideas in the field of general medical practice, she also became a much coveted Training Analyst at the Institute of Psycho-Analysis (e.g., Rudnytsky, 2000), as well as a teacher, lecturer, and administrator. She came to be so much in demand that, even in her seventies, she worked between sixty and seventy hours per week (Balint, 1974) and could be reached by telephone only between 7.00 a.m. and 8.00 a.m. (Woodhouse, 1975).

No doubt Enid Balint enjoyed watching the constant growth of the organisation, which included the launch of a book-length publication, in 1955, on the psychodynamic approach to marital treatment (Bannister et al., 1955), and then, in 1956, the transfer of the FDB to the Tavistock Institute of Human Relations, and a change of name—yet again—to the Institute of Marital Studies. In 1959, the organisation relocated from Chandos Street to the Tavistock Clinic headquarters on Beaumont Street, and then, ultimately, in 1967, to the Tavi's new home in Belsize Park, becoming very much a central core of British psychoanalytic and psychotherapeutic life. After *five* further name changes from the Institute of Marital Studies, to the Tavistock Institute of Marital Studies, to the Tavistock Marital Studies Institute, to the Tavistock Centre for Couple Relationships, to Tavistock Relationships, the organisation and the profession it represents has developed from strength to strength, providing relief for untold thousands of couples and families for nearly three-quarters of a century.

A tale of two rooftops

Those of us who have followed in the footsteps of Enid Eichholz Balint have a great deal to learn from this bold and visionary woman. Even though she lacked clinical qualifications, she could, nevertheless, from the mid–1940s until the early 1950s, through sheer force, passion, and perseverance, make an outstanding contribution to the betterment of private life in Great Britain. And she created couple therapy through her brilliance at forging couple alliances with carefully selected colleagues, whether Wilson or Bowlby or Hunnybun or Balint or Sutherland or Pincus. Each of these professional "marriages" contributed hugely to the foundations of couple psychoanalytic work today.

Over the last thirty-five years, I have conducted numerous interviews with senior mental health professionals on several continents, collecting reminiscences about our forebears in the psychotherapeutic field. In the course of these interviews, I have heard many deeply unflattering, indeed ugly, stories about these great pioneers. But it may be significant that of the many people who graciously shared with me their memories of Enid Balint, not one single person had anything nasty to say about her whatsoever. In fact, her former patients and colleagues always described her as warm, as maternal, as generous, and as gracious. Indeed, one of my interviewees even characterised her to me, in no uncertain terms, as "the only compassionate person" in the entire Institute of Psycho-Analysis (Estela

Welldon, personal communication, 15 May 2015)! No doubt her basic mental health allowed her to form partnerships easily and pleasurably. A mad woman could not, it seems to me, have founded the field of marital mental health.

But to idealise Enid Eichholz Balint as kind and sweet would be rather too simplistic. She could, by her own admission, be nasty and aggressive (Rudnytsky, 2000), and she possessed cunning, wiliness, and even sexual charm. Indeed, Dr Estela Welldon, a noted psychiatrist, explained to me that men found Mrs Balint really quite "beautiful" and that virtually every man who met her soon became rather "smitten" (Estela Welldon, personal communication, 15 May 2015). Undoubtedly this sexual allure may have facilitated the development of her professional partnerships with some of the Tavistock Clinic's most sturdy men and even women.

While leading psychiatrists and psychoanalysts such as Dr Wilfred Bion, Dr Siegmund Foulkes, and Dr John Rickman treated British soldiers—all male—during the Second World War, Enid decided that she would look after the wives, whose emotional needs had remained neglected. When the men returned home, she defied all gender restrictions and cared not only for the wives *and* the husbands but also for the families. From the ravages of the Second World War, Enid—a true daughter of the Clement Attlee regime—created something moving and touching amid such unparalleled destruction.

It would be tempting to regard couple psychoanalysis as a mere extension of individual psychoanalysis, but this would be inaccurate. Freud, though savvy about the cruel psychodynamics of intimate relationships and about the infantile origins of sexual conflicts, did not distinguish himself as a clinical practitioner of couple relationships (e.g., Freud, 1905, 1909a, 1910, 1912, 1918, 1919). Indeed, in 1891, Frau Pauline Theiler Silberstein, the 19-year-old spouse of Freud's long-standing friend Eduard Silberstein, came to Vienna for a consultation with Freud (1928c); but sadly, either before or after having spoken with the future creator of psychoanalysis, she threw herself from one of the upper storeys of his home at 8 Maria-Theresienstrasse, and plunged to her death (Vieyra, 1989; Borch-Jacobsen, 2011).

Enid Eichholz Balint did rather better at rooftop consultations. As a schoolgirl at the Cheltenham Ladies' College in Gloucestershire, the young Enid Flora Albu had developed a reputation for being sensitive and sensible. When, on a cold night, one of Enid's fellow schoolmates sought refuge on the roof of one of the buildings, and none of the teachers could persuade this depressed and possibly suicidal girl to come back indoors, they sent Enid out to sit with her. Apparently, Enid perched herself neither too close to the girl nor too far away, and waited patiently until, in due course, the troubled student decided to return inside, much to everyone's relief (Balint, n.d.).

Perhaps, irrespective of one's training and influence, one also needs a very particular internal core and a zest for healing. Certainly Enid Flora Albu Eichholz Balint Edmonds[3] possessed just such capacities.

Enid Balint created partnerships. She nurtured partnerships. And she healed partnerships. Above all, she helped her colleagues to master the art of defusing marital bombs. Her collaborative model of creativity and of leadership remains an inspiration to us all.

Notes

A considerably shortened version of this essay has appeared in the journal *Couple and Family Psychoanalysis* (Kahr, 2017b).

1. In 2016, the Tavistock Centre for Couple Relationships became Tavistock Relationships, part of the Tavistock Institute of Medical Psychology.

2. In the interest of historical accuracy, I have maintained the unusual or idiosyncratic punctuation found in the original source materials.

3. Towards the end of her life, Enid Balint married Robert Humphrey Gordon Edmonds, a diplomat; she then became known, at times, as Enid Balint-Edmonds.

CHAPTER EIGHT

The ten best interpretations
in the history of psychoanalysis

> The LORD said, "If as one people speaking the same language they have begun to do this, then nothing they plan to do will be impossible for them."
>
> *Genesis*, Book 11, line 6 [New International Version]

Clinical case study

The case of Montgomery

Shortly before his sixteenth birthday, "Montgomery", a teenager from one of the most impoverished areas of South London, assaulted several little children for whom he babysat. Horrifically, he tied them up and molested each one of them in turn.

One does not become a vicious juvenile sexual offender overnight, and it will come as no surprise that Montgomery had suffered greatly during his own childhood. Shortly after his birth, his alcoholic father abandoned him permanently. And then, only a few months later, as Montgomery's mother pushed her newborn son in a pram, a drunk driver swerved onto the pavement and knocked her over, killing her instantly. Baby Montgomery sustained a head injury. Orphaned completely as an infant, Montgomery grew up, thereafter, in a series of foster homes.

At Montgomery's court hearing, the judge considered him to be at high risk for becoming a serial paedophile and sentenced him to several years in a remand home. Moreover, the judge also insisted that Montgomery should be mandated to attend psychotherapy. At this time, I worked in the forensic mental health field as a psychotherapist in a pioneering project that provided psychodynamically informed treatment for young sex offenders, in the hope that, by intervening early, we might prevent these individuals from perpetrating further offences upon their eventual release from custody.

Montgomery arrived at my consulting room, escorted by not one, but two, probation officers, who sat in the waiting area. I greeted Montgomery at the door, and I introduced myself: "Hello, my name is Brett Kahr. Please do have a seat." Montgomery looked at me with tremendous suspicion as he perched himself on a chair in my office. He then bowed his head and tucked his chin into his sternum, making no eye contact with me whatsoever.

It seemed disingenuous to ask Montgomery why he had come. He knew *precisely* why he had come and so, too, did I, having received copies of his court reports, probation reports, and psychiatric assessments beforehand. Instead, I paused and remained silent for a few seconds to see whether Montgomery wished to begin the conversation; but he remained sullen and downcast, and he said absolutely nothing. Hence, I felt pressurised to begin speaking. Although I cannot recall my precise words, as this meeting took place nearly thirty years ago, I believe that I had uttered something reasonably anodyne. I might have asked him to tell me about himself, or how he felt about coming to see me. My ordinary attempt at establishing some sort of verbal contact failed miserably, and Montgomery still made no effort to look at me or to respond in words.

My level of anxiety began to rise a little bit. I had, of course, worked with many forensic patients, and also with many adolescent patients; and I knew only too well that they often require a little bit of gentle coaxing to begin a session, unlike our educated, neurotic patients who cannot wait to narrate every detail of their complex life histories. After a further interval, I made another comment: "I would imagine that it must be very odd for you to come to see a psychotherapist." I also asked him how he felt about having to arrive at the clinic with two probation officers in tow. Once again, my curiosity failed to elicit any evident response.

Over the course of the next twenty minutes, I tried every trick in the book. I remained silent. I asked questions. I attempted to articulate something about how he might be feeling. I commented upon his silence. I scrutinised my countertransference responses for clues as to what I might say or do next. I even contemplated talking to him in teen language: "Yo, dude, what's the deal?"

I knew only too well that forensic patients who "act out" by committing crimes often have very poor verbal capacities and thus cannot easily transform their sadistic fantasies and feelings into words. While most normal or neurotic people have the ability to articulate their hateful desires, the forensic patient cannot do so and, hence, turns to enactment. In many ways, Montgomery's silence did not surprise me. This adolescent boy spoke not with his mouth but, rather, with his genitals.

Suddenly, while stewing in an increasingly uncomfortable silence, I realised that although Montgomery would tell me nothing about himself, I had already read an enormous dossier of reports about this teenage rapist; consequently, I knew a great deal about him in spite of his silence. It had finally dawned on me that he would have had to have recited his life history to a fleet of police officers, social workers, probation officers, and lawyers, on many previous occasions. Why on earth should he do so once again with me? Perhaps he assumed that he had no need to speak, knowing that, in all likelihood, I would already have studied his biography beforehand in intricate detail.

And then, at long last, it dawned on me, and a hypothesis began to form in my mind.

I remembered only too clearly that Montgomery's father had abandoned him after his birth and that, only a few months later, his mother died in a dreadful hit-and-run incident.

Bracing myself, I made an "interpretation". I explained, "You know, it does not surprise me that, in spite of my many attempts to speak with you and to learn something about you, I see that you have remained completely silent. I know that during your very early childhood, something really awful happened. Your mother died quite abruptly, and you suffered an injury to your head. And all because of some terrible drunk man who killed your mother with his car. And now, your probation officers have brought you here today to see a man called Brett *Kahr*. And how painfully ironic it must be that out of all the surnames in the world, you happen to be sitting with a person called Kahr, spelled 'K-a-h-r'. It sounds exactly the same as the car that hurt you and killed your mother.

You must be terrified that I might be an evil, drunken car that will run you over and kill you."

I took a large but silent breath, expecting that these words, too, would fall upon deaf ears. But to my great relief, Montgomery raised his head, stared at me with a look of anguish, and within seconds began to sob in an almost uncontrollable fashion. He cried for at least five minutes.

This comment—this "interpretation" of what I imagined to be a deep-seated, arguably unconscious terror—seemed to have made a huge difference. At last, Montgomery could begin to speak, and he then did so in a virtually uninterrupted fashion. He remained in psychotherapy with me thereafter—under escort—during which time he expressed extreme guilt for having sexually assaulted those small children.

Silence had not worked. Chit-chat and ordinary conversation seemed to have made no difference. Rogerian-style reflection about Montgomery's feeling states proved completely ineffective. But a good, old-fashioned Freudian transference interpretation, in which I, as the clinician, offered a tentative hypothesis about a deep unconscious anxiety that early traumata could be repeated in the here-and-now, succeeded in opening up a world of possibilities.

Interpretation and its suspicions

This clinical vignette about my first twenty minutes of contact with Montgomery—though touching, I believe—will hardly strike a die-hard psychoanalytic mental health professional as unusual or, indeed, original. Psychoanalytic practitioners have utilised the transference interpretation and, indeed, other types of interpretation for more than a century, and we continue to rely upon the interpretation as one of the most mutative ingredients in the psychological treatment process.

But not all mental health clinicians have become enamoured by interpretation, and some actively revile this form of intervention. Many humanistic, integrative, existentialist, and other non-psychoanalytic psychotherapists and counsellors disparage the interpretation as an old-fashioned, elitist, even snooty form of interaction in which the psychotherapist presumes to know more about the patient's internal world than the patient does. Over the years I have encountered many colleagues who work from systemic or cognitive-behavioural perspectives and who regard the Freudian-style interpretation as quite bizarre.

Certainly, patients who have undergone psychoanalysis have, at times, complained about having received stern interpretations, which their psychoanalysts have rendered coarsely or arrogantly, with a "sense of superiority" (Menaker, 1989, p. 191). Indeed, William Menaker, a young American who underwent psychoanalysis with Dr Helene Deutsch in Vienna during the early 1930s, recalled that, on one occasion, Deutsch had rendered an interpretation, upon which he reflected carefully. Having considered the interpretation, the patient responded to his analyst: "Maybe." Helene Deutsch replied in what the patient experienced as a most opinionated and cocksure manner, pronouncing, "Not maybe but yes" (quoted in Menaker, 1989, p. 148). This response thus created a climate of distrust towards Dr Deutsch.

More worryingly, Professor Eli Zaretsky, a tremendous psycho-analytic sympathist and author of a substantial history of psycho-analysis (Zaretsky, 2004), reminisced, nevertheless, about his own disappointing experience as an analysand. Zaretsky (2016, p. 458) recalled that,

> my doctor would offer an "interpretation" that would undo what I had said, or tried to say, an interpretation that would convey to me that I was lying to myself, that I did not know what I was feeling or what I believed. Understandably, this angered me so that my free associations started to be interrupted by Tourette-like intrusive thoughts such as "bullshit" or "asshole" or "this is complete crap". He underscored that, "my analyst made me feel ashamed, as did the continuous undermining of my perceptions achieved through each day's cutting interpretation. [Zaretsky, 2016, p. 459]

Many psychoanalysts have also struggled with interpretation and, especially, its misuse. As we indicated in the previous chapter, the distinguished psychoanalyst Dr John Sutherland (1955), then Medical Director of the Tavistock Clinic in London, wrote to his colleague, the pioneering marital psychotherapist Mrs Lily Pincus, about the ways in which many of his colleagues within the British Psycho-Analytical Society had become little more than "high-powered inter-preting machines". He claimed that as a result of this over-emphasis on interpretation, the profession had suffered greatly, prompting him to confess, "I personally have a strong feeling that what has gone out of psycho-analysis is 'love'" (Sutherland, 1955). Indeed, the tendency among British psychoanalysts to offer habitual interpretations, even at the very beginning of the session, produced "amazement" (Fenichel, 1942, p. 232) in some of the more measured practitioners from other countries.

During the 1950s, many of John Sutherland's colleagues shared his sense of disgruntlement at the ways in which certain psychoanalysts—especially those who had trained with Melanie Klein—had begun to fetishise the clinical interpretation, thus abusing the patient in the process. Dr Donald Winnicott, in particular, spoke out vociferously—indeed unreservedly—about how certain fellow psychoanalysts disgraced the profession through their valorisation of the interpretation. For instance, on 21 May 1959, Winnicott wrote an uncompromising letter to Dr Donald Meltzer, one of Melanie Klein's last analysands, excoriating him for having delivered a paper to the British Psycho-Analytical Society in which he provided ample evidence of making very long interpretations. Winnicott chastised Meltzer, noting that,

> it is only possible to make long interpretations like the ones that you reported under special circumstances and when the patient has a high IQ. It is unfortunate that the sort of presentation which you gave last night makes people feel that the followers of Mrs Klein talk more than their patients do. [1959, pp. 124–125]

He underscored that, "if the analyst makes too long an interpretation, the listener gets the impression that the analyst is talking to himself rather than to the patient" (1959, p. 125).

Winnicott knew, of course, about these lengthy, intellectualised interpretations, not only from Meltzer's paper, but also from his own multi-decade association with Melanie Klein herself, and, further, from what he learned from his wife, Mrs Clare Winnicott, then undergoing a training analysis with Mrs Klein. Apparently on one occasion Mrs Winnicott presented a dream to Mrs Klein, who then offered her patient an interpretation of its secret meaning fully twenty-five minutes in length. Outraged, Clare Winnicott fumed, "How dare you take my dream and serve it up to me?" (quoted in Grosskurth, 1981, p. 452); she then boycotted her analytic sessions for some time.

Apparently, Melanie Klein's interpretation to Clare Winnicott seems quite short by comparison to the one that she produced for Dr Clifford Scott, her very first training analysand at the Institute of Psycho-Analysis, back in the early 1930s. In 1982, Scott told the British psychoanalyst Mr Patrick Casement (personal communication, 19 March 2016) that on one occasion Melanie Klein had rendered such a very long interpretation—which she had, in fact, written down—that it took her two sessions to read it out to him!

With intimate knowledge of the brutality of long interpretations, one should hardly be surprised that in 1960, in his paper on "The Theory of the Parent–Infant Relationship", Winnicott proclaimed that the psychoanalyst who becomes too clever and who interprets too quickly, or who does not base the interpretation on the material of the session but, rather, on a vast storehouse of prior knowledge, may, as a result, inflict distress upon the patient, even if the interpretation might, technically, be correct: "The analyst may appear to be very clever, and the patient may express admiration, but in the end the correct interpretation is a trauma, which the patient has to reject, because it is not his" (Winnicott, 1960a, p. 592). And not long thereafter, in 1962, in his paper on "The Aims of Psycho-Analytical Treatment", Winnicott (1962, p. 167) counselled his colleagues in the British Psycho-Analytical Society that, "My interpretations are economical" and that, "One interpretation per session satisfies me" (Winnicott, 1962, p. 167). He underscored that, "I never use long sentences unless I am very tired" (Winnicott, 1962, p. 167).

So, in view of these aforementioned remarks, how might we come to regard the clinical interpretation? Does it constitute an essential component of the psychotherapeutic treatment process that can, if deployed with intelligence, sensitivity, and dexterity, result in profound psychic change, or does it become a vehicle for abuse, resulting in bitterness and destruction?

The act of interpretation raises many other questions. For those of us who *do* utilise interpretations, should we make long ones or short ones? Ought we to interpret in the transference (i.e., reflect upon the nature of the patient–analyst interaction) or would we benefit more greatly from interpreting the so-called "genetic" material (i.e., aspects of the patient's early childhood)—or, indeed, both? Do we interpret early on in the session, or only towards the end? Do we interpret in the opening stages of treatment or, perhaps, only after we have come to know the patient much better? (Glover and Brierley, 1940). The art of interpretation has vexed, and continues to vex, clinical practitioners since the very inception of the psychotherapeutic craft.

While most commentators have focused on questions such as whether one formulates a patient-centred interpretation or an analyst-centred interpretation, or whether one interprets superficially or deeply, or even partially or comprehensively, very few authors have examined what I have come to consider the "tonal elements" inherent in the rendering of an interpretation—namely, the vocal quality of the clinician, the musicality of the voice, the expression on the analyst's face, and so much more (e.g., Kahr, 2005; cf. Rothstein, 1983). After all, just as two comedians might relate the very same joke and yet elicit very different reactions from an audience depending upon their comic timing, so, too, might different clinicians interpret the very same material to the patient, each evoking rather divergent reactions: some favourable, if not transformative, and others quite detrimental.

In an effort to differentiate how and when interpretations might be helpful or might be harmful, I propose to turn *not* to the many contemporary psychoanalytic theoreticians of the interpretation, valuable though those reflections may be, but, rather, to the early history of our profession, in an effort to explore some of the more successful instances—both published and unpublished—from which we might continue to learn. In fact, I have often wondered whether the profession of psychoanalysis should boast a "Top Ten" list of the "Greatest Interpretations", which might serve as role models of inspiration. Could we, perhaps, identity ten truly remarkable interpretations, from which we might extract key curative ingredients that could guide our thinking about interventions and could well help to improve our clinical technique?

Choosing the ten best interpretations in the history of psychoanalysis might be construed as a most ridiculous undertaking. After all, I estimate that there must be some 5,000 psychoanalytically orientated psychotherapists in Great Britain alone, as well as some 10,000 psychodynamically orientated counsellors. If each of these 15,000 colleagues worked with, on average, eight patients per day and rendered, perhaps, two or three or four interpretations per session, one might conclude that on any given day British mental health professionals formulate, collectively, somewhere between 200,000 and 400,000 interpretations. All of these interpretations might well be brilliant and should, perhaps, qualify as candidates on a top-ten list. I therefore apologise in advance for my rather partisan and idiosyncratic choice of "winners". I have selected ten to serve merely as exemplars of what an interpretation could, perhaps, achieve, hopeful that I might also demonstrate a range of ways in which interpretations facilitate the psychotherapeutic process.

Let us now examine the "Top Ten".

The ten greatest interpretations
in the history of psychoanalysis

Lucy Freeman and the cathartic cure

During the 1940s, Miss Lucy Greenbaum, a young American jour-
nalist—intelligent, educated, kind-hearted, and privileged—suffered,
nevertheless, from a host of psychosomatic symptoms. Writing about
her hellish bodily state, she recalled:

> Standard routine reeled off by doctor after doctor had not eased
> agony.
>   "Get plenty of sleep and eat regular meals."
>   Trouble is, I can't sleep.
>   "Here are some pills, then."
>   How can I eat when everything upsets my stomach?
>   "Take these pills."
>   What about the splitting headaches?
>   "More pills."
> Or:
>   "It's the war, this dreadful war. Get away from your work for
> a few weeks. Relax."
>   One day war ended, World War II, that is. Another illness
> struck and again doctors could not help.
>   Then came a point in pain where I either had to accept suf-
> fering and give up all else or try to find a different way to stop
> torment.
>   Psychoanalysis was my way." [Freeman, 1951, p. xiii]

Lucy Greenbaum, cousin to the eminent New York City psychoanalyst Dr Lawrence Kubie, soon embarked upon treatment with a
young colleague, Dr John Thurrock, who proved to be a most compassionate and sensitive man. Shortly after the commencement of her
analysis, Miss Greenbaum recalled a long-forgotten event:

> Suddenly a scene flashed into memory, forgotten for twenty-one
> years. I stood alone in the street outside that school. January's ice-
> wind snapped in from the water. I waited for Mother to pick me
> up, as she usually did, to drive me home for lunch.
>   I was still there, long after lunch hour, my face blood-red from
> the cold.
>   A teacher walked by, asked why I stood in the street.
>   "My mother's forgotten me", I told her, teeth clattering.
>   She led me indoors. She found out Mother had telephoned,

asking that I eat at school as she was unable to call for me. The switchboard girl had neglected to tell me. As apology the school fed me a mammoth meal including double dessert.

But that could not remove the hurt in my heart. I was convinced Mother had finally forsaken me. She liked my brother and sister much better. She never would have left either of them standing alone in the street. [Freeman, 1951, p. 44]

After regaling Dr Thurrock with this childhood memory, Lucy Greenbaum suddenly began to sob and simply could not stop.

Greenbaum daubed her face with tissues and blew her nose; then, she apologised to her analyst for having embarrassed herself in this fashion and for having articulated such hateful feelings towards her mother. She lamented, "I'm sorry . . . I didn't mean to cry", whereupon Dr Thurrock replied, "Maybe it's time you cried . . . Maybe you have wanted to cry all these years and couldn't" (quoted in Freeman, 1951, p. 45).

Although one suspects that Dr Thurrock's comment would hardly win kudos from senior psychoanalysts in the twenty-first century, his very simple statement—neither a question, nor a comment, nor a recommendation, but, rather, an interpretation of a previously unarticulated feeling state—allowed Miss Greenbaum to continue crying in unrestricted fashion. To her utter amazement, she suddenly stood up and exclaimed that for the first time in years she could actually breathe and no longer found herself tormented by chronic nasal congestion. Miss Greenbaum asked her analyst, "Where's my sinus?", to which Dr Thurrock replied, "Perhaps it cleared up as your tears came out" (quoted in Freeman, 1951, p. 46).

Although seemingly quite simple and perhaps even a bit "old hat" from a modern perspective, one must remember that, during the early years of psychoanalysis, such extremely basic interpretative comments could often exert a profound cathartic impact upon individuals who had enjoyed few instances of emotional literacy whatsoever during their early developmental years. Dr Thurrock's interpretation that Miss Greenbaum's sinus symptom had resulted from an inhibition of tears proved so dramatic that the patient experienced a complete cure, in spite of the fact that numerous physicians had failed to help her up until that point.

Greenbaum found herself quite moved and relieved, not only by the content of Dr Thurrock's interpretation, but also by its vocal style. As she explained, "It was not what he said so much as how he said it.

His voice was always even, compassionate, rich with wisdom—truly an invitation to trust" (Freeman, 1951, p. xiv).

Dr Thurrock did not offer a transference interpretation at all; but one suspects that the young Miss Greenbaum, then a lonely single woman, may also have formed a parental transference and, perhaps, even an erotic transference, which afforded greater potency to Dr Thurrock's simple pronouncement. At any rate, this interchange resulted in relief from a lifetime of psychosomatic illness. Indeed, the previously grief-stricken Miss Greenbaum persevered with her psychoanalytic treatment for many years thereafter; eventually, she became a woman of remarkable creativity and productivity, known by her professional name Lucy Freeman, and would in time come to author numerous books on psychoanalysis, including the best-selling *Fight Against Fears* (Freeman, 1951), the first full-length memoir written by a patient about the experience of undergoing psychoanalysis. This book proved a landmark in American culture, and as a result of this positive portrayal of the psychoanalytic process innumerable people entered into treatment (Kahr, 1986, 1999a, 1999b).

Bertram Karon and the man who spoke in Latin

Many years ago, Dr Bertram Karon, an American psychoanalytic psychologist, worked with a hospital inpatient who suffered from schizophrenia. This particular man exhibited many of the classical symptoms of psychosis, including terrifying hallucinations of snakes coming out of his mouth. Apparently, Bertram Karon, then a young clinician, attempted to engage in conversation with this tormented person in an effort to provide psychological assistance. The patient had a history of being violent on the hospital ward and would often sneak up on other male patients from behind and choke them viciously. Throughout the course of psychotherapy, Dr Karon came to learn that this gentleman did not engage in such violent behaviour by accident, but, rather, that during his childhood his own mother used to tie a cloth around his neck and choke him as a punishment whenever he had misbehaved. Thus, the adult symptom proved to have very identifiable childhood roots. Karon also discovered that the patient's father—an alcoholic—had sodomised the boy during his eighth year. Regrettably, none of this important biographical information had ever appeared in the patient's case notes, as psychiatrists at that time had little, if any, interest in real, historical family events.

At one point during a psychotherapy session, this schizophrenic man started to stutter, and then, quite unexpectedly, he began to spew forth some words in Latin. Karon found this very intriguing, if not perplexing, in view of the fact that his patient hailed from Detroit, Michigan, and had only had a very rudimentary education. Unlike British schools of this period, virtually no American schools would have offered such classical instruction. With stunning and quick intuition, Karon suspected that this poorly educated man could only have learned Latin in church. When Karon enquired whether he had ever served as an altar boy, the patient's stuttering became even more feverish and he exclaimed, "You swallow a snake, and then you stutter; you mustn't let anyone know about it" (Karon and VandenBos, 1981, p. 38).

With great intelligence and with deep expertise in the art of thinking symbolically—something that Freud had taught us all decades previously—Dr Karon began to contemplate the meaning of snakes coming out of the mouth. Of course, one could dismiss a snake hallucination as little more than proof of the man's madness. But Karon desperately wished to understand why his patient should have this particular hallucination as opposed to any other, and whether the snake might serve as a symbol for something else: something dangerous and jutting and slithering that might have gone into, or come out of, the patient's mouth.

With tremendous insight and empathy, Karon spoke to the schizophrenic man and told him that he wondered whether, during his time as an altar boy, the priest had forced him to perform fellatio. Although mental health professionals must be careful that we do not put words into patients' mouths, Karon had already developed a very strong suspicion that an abusive adult had once inserted something horrible into his orifice during childhood. After Karon had made this observation—or interpretation—to the patient, the stuttering and the swearing in Latin ceased completely. The patient felt himself to be believed and understood, and he began to improve without the aid of medication.

Having, as a young trainee, read Karon's case report and the many others in his remarkable textbook, I soon began to apply this sort of symbolically orientated psychoanalytic thinking to my own very rudimentary work in psychiatric hospitals, often with great success.

I encountered one man who told me that the "Sinep" of the "Senoj" wished to hurt him and kill him. I found myself very troubled as I had never heard of a "Sinep" or a "Senoj", and I asked the psychiatrist and the psychiatric nurses for help. They threw up their hands in confusion and told me that many hospitalised psychotic patients create their own private language of madness—one that has no particular meaning whatsoever.

But having immersed myself in the not inconsiderable psychotherapeutic literature on schizophrenia, I continued in my fledgling efforts to understand this ostensibly private language of madness, and I persevered in my attempts to decipher the meaning of the "Sinep" of the "Senoj". Whenever I asked the schizophrenic patient directly, he refused to answer and became silent, clearly unimpressed that I had no clue as to the symbolism of his thoughts.

Nevertheless, I persevered with my work, and one day, while writing up my case notes to present to the Consultant Psychiatrist, it suddenly dawned on me. "Sinep" and "Senoj"—funny words in their own right—become far less amusing when one reverses the order of the letters. What would happen if one spelled "Sinep" backwards? . . . it would read "Penis" . . . and "Senoj", likewise, would read "Jones". Suddenly, the "Sinep" of the "Senoj" became the penis of Mr Jones!

With a certain degree of trepidation, I shared this observation with my patient, painfully aware that I had come up with this literary twist on my own and that the patient did not point me in this direction, at least not overtly. To my great surprise, the schizophrenic man—viewed by all the staff as crazy—began to speak in the most honest, ordinary, straightforward, and sane manner imaginable, and he told me that I had, indeed, "cracked the code", and that during his boyhood a next-door neighbour called "Mr Jones" had molested him with his penis.

Uwe Henrik Peters and the German neurology patient

In 1984, I had the privilege of speaking to the distinguished German neurologist and psychoanalytic psychiatrist, Professor Dr med. Uwe Henrik Peters (personal communication, 15 October 1984), who told me that, many years previously, during the 1960s, he had interviewed a patient afflicted by a very troubling symptom. This gentleman, whom I shall call "Johann Goldmann"—a baker living in a little village outside Köln—kept fainting. He seemed to be in reasonably good health for a man in his late thirties, except for these constant fainting spells. Over time, the symptom intensified, and on one occasion Herr Goldmann actually fell down while crossing a road; he nearly died, having narrowly avoided a head-on collision with a car. This scary episode prompted this gentleman to seek medical help.

Several of Germany's most distinguished neurologists examined him; but in spite of a multitude of medical work-ups, these physicians could find no abnormalities whatsoever; in desperation, they referred Herr Goldmann to Professor Peters, a psychiatrist. During the course of the consultation, Peters questioned Herr Goldmann about his private life—something the neurologists had neglected to do. Goldmann talked about his loving wife, his beautiful children, and his career as a baker and confectioner. He spoke glowingly about his situation, and Peters could detect no obvious areas of distress. And yet, Goldmann kept fainting ...

After two or three meetings, Professor Peters turned to his patient and mused, "If I am not mistaken, Goldmann is a Jewish name, is it not?" Herr Goldmann confirmed that he had, indeed, grown up Jewish; at this point Peters knew instantly that this 30-something-year-old man must have lived through the Second World War, and that he might well have lost relatives during the Holocaust. And so Professor Peters asked, "What happened to you and your family during the *Weltkrieg*?" Herr Goldmann gaped in amazement and replied, "I have seen many doctors in this hospital, but you are the very first to ask me if I am Jewish. Of course I have a story to tell."

It seems that one day in 1944, when Goldmann was living in a remote corner of Eastern Europe, a lorry full of German soldiers, armed with rifles and shot guns, stormed into his village, rounded up hundreds of Jews and transported them to a nearby forest. The Nazis forced Goldmann, then only a teenager, and his entire family, as well as many friends and neighbours, to remove their clothing and to stand trembling at the edge of a ditch. Within seconds, several officers began to fire their machine guns, perched on tripods; then they executed the entire village. One by one, the bodies fell into the pit below.

Apparently, just seconds before the hail of bullets would have hit him in the back, the young Goldmann fainted and collapsed into the pit. Several other bodies soon tumbled on top of him and, consequently, hid him from the soldiers who had to check for any survivors. Later that night, after the Nazis had departed, Goldmann awoke from his faint and managed to extract himself from under a heap of dead, bleeding bodies, and he fled to safety.

Fortunately, Professor Peters, an enlightened psychodynamic psychiatrist, had a much greater capacity than his neurological colleagues to speak to patients about difficult matters. He engaged Herr Goldmann in an ongoing series of conversations in which the patient could talk, for the first time in some twenty years, about the unbearable traumas and losses that he had experienced. After several psychotherapeutic sessions, Herr Goldmann began to weep as he recounted how he watched his mother, his father, his sister, and his brother die, and how he, too, came within moments of being killed. Previously he had never had the strength to articulate this traumatic tale, and whenever his own young children asked him about his background, Goldmann always dismissed them and refused to speak. Professor Uwe Peters, in true psychotherapeutic fashion, helped Herr Goldmann to put his story into words and to achieve a good old-fashioned Freudian catharsis in the process. Thereafter, Herr Goldmann stopped fainting for the first time in some twenty years.

Although we do not know the exact words of interpretation that Peters gave to the patient because he told me about this case in a private conversation, he did confirm that he hypothesised to Herr Goldmann that the fainting symptom might have resulted from the patient's attempts to master his unbearable traumatic experience. As Peters (personal communication, 15 October 1984) explained, "When the Nazis shot him, he fainted. But even though he survived the scene of execution, he still lived in fear that someone would shoot him again and make him fall dead to the ground. So, in order to 'master' this trauma . . . in order to *triumph* over this trauma . . . he developed the capacity to make himself faint, thus taking control of the situation. Of course, all of this thinking takes place in the unconscious mind, and so the patient does not realise what is happening."[1]

The three abovementioned examples of interpretation—Dr John Thurrock's comment to Lucy Greenbaum about the interconnection between her nasal symptom and her suppressed tears; Dr Bertram Karon's explanation about the way in which the schizophrenic patient's hallucination of snakes in his mouth could be traced to an earlier fellatio trauma; and Professor Uwe Henrik Peters's detective work about Johann Goldmann's fainting symptom as an attempt to master the horrific trauma of his near-death experience at the hands of the Nazis—all provide powerful evidence of the impact of Freud's fundamental cathartic model, allowing patients to transform affects and memories into words. In each case, the psychoanalytic interpretation inaugurated a process in which very dramatic symptoms began to reduce in intensity and, ultimately, disappear. Lucy Greenbaum (later Lucy Freeman) no longer suffered from psychosomatic nasal congestion; the schizophrenic patient ceased hallucinating about snakes in his mouth; and the baker, Johann Goldmann, stopped fainting. In each of these three instances, the psychoanalytic clinicians succeeded in offering help through listening and through interpretation of the material, whereas many previous physicians had failed to provide any relief whatsoever.

Interestingly, although all three of these interpretations unfolded in the context of kindly, attentive, and thoughtful therapeutic interviews, as demonstrated by the clinician's understanding and by the patients' willingness to confess, none of these interpretative comments evoked the transference in a direct fashion. We might refer to such comments as "extra-transference interpretations".

For many clinicians, especially contemporary British psychoanalytic practitioners, one cannot formulate an effective interpretation without engaging explicitly with the transference: in other words, that very particular relationship between the patient and the analyst at the current moment in time. The emphasis on the exclusivity of the transference interpretation has captivated many practitioners quite profoundly. For instance, according to the noted psychoanalyst Hanna Segal,

> A full transference interpretation should include the current external relationship in the patient's life, the patient's relationship to the analyst, and the relation between these and the relationships with the parents in the past. It should also aim at establishing a link between the internal figures and the external ones. Of course such an interpretation would have to be long and is seldom made fully, but for a transference interpretation to be complete at some point or other those elements should be brought together. [1973, pp. 120–121]

By contrast, the American psychoanalyst, Dr Harold Blum (1983, p. 615), cautioned that, "A 'transference only' position is theoretically untenable and could lead to an artificial reduction of all associations and interpretations into a transference mold and to an idealized *folie-à-deux*."

Bearing in mind the potential benefits as well as the potential risks of the transferential approach to clinical conversation, let us now consider several interpretations that engage explicitly with this dimension—much as I had done with my aforementioned patient "Montgomery", who feared unconsciously that I would become a murderous "Kahr" and that I would, therefore, run him over.

Hanna Segal and the clever supervisee

Hanna Segal, the distinguished follower of Melanie Klein, reported that one of her supervisees had treated a homosexual man who had had a psychotic breakdown prior to the start of his psychoanalysis. At the very first session, the patient spied the couch in the consulting room and exclaimed, "I will not lie down for you. I lay down and submitted to men often enough." Clearly, the patient had become frightened about his safety in this very new situation with a very new person. Dr Segal's supervisee responded to the patient with an immediate interpretation, "You are afraid that I shall not be able to distinguish between psychoanalytic treatment and buggery" (quoted in Segal, 1994, p. 21). Apparently this very focused, laser-like concentration on the specificity of the terrifying transference at this moment proved to be most effective: in consequence, according to Segal (1994, p. 21), "This communication made the patient relax almost immediately, and the psychoanalytic process had started."

Ronald Britton's "fucking thinking"

In similar vein, Dr Ronald Britton, the Kleinian psychoanalyst, utilised a more subtle form of transference interpretation in his work with a patient known as "Miss A", who had experienced a psychotic breakdown. According to Britton, this woman became deeply pained—and often violent—whenever another person dropped her from mind. In fact, if Dr Britton remained quiet during a psychoanalytic session, attempting to make sense of the patient's material in his mind, Miss A became enraged: indeed, on one occasion she shouted, "Stop that fucking thinking!" Reflecting on this experience, Britton explained, "I came to realize that these efforts of mine to consult my analytic self were detected by her and experienced as a form of internal intercourse of mine, which corresponded to parental intercourse. This she felt threatened her existence" (Britton, 1989, p. 88). In other words, when Britton maintained silence and did not engage directly with the patient, she fantasised that he had begun to have intercourse with *himself*, rather than with *her*. Britton's sagacious interpretation helped to reorientate the patient, and eventually he discovered that, bit by bit, the patient could at last begin to think and to recover the mind that had become so overwhelmed by the primitive oedipal constellation and by the feelings of profound exclusion.

Patrick Casement
and the refusal to hold the patient's hand

Some time ago, the British psychoanalyst Patrick Casement (1982) worked with an adult patient who had, as a baby of eleven months, scalded herself with boiling water, necessitating a surgical procedure some six months later. During the operation, the patient's mother had held her daughter's hand, but at one point she had fainted, thus severing physical contact between herself and her young daughter. In later years, the patient developed a profound fear of falling forever; and, when reliving the memory of this early childhood trauma, she asked her analyst Casement to comfort her by holding her hand.

Classically trained, Casement knew only too well that physical contact between a patient and an analyst could be provocative, if not unhelpful, and would certainly be regarded by colleagues as a violation of the basic psychoanalytic rule of abstinence. However, as an open-minded man, Casement endeavoured to approach his patient's request in a non-dogmatic way, and he agreed to think about the meaning of the wish for hand-holding, instead of dismissing it forthwith as a breach of good technique. Casement certainly realised that if he refused his hand, the patient might become furious or feel abandoned; and he revealed that the patient had even threatened to leave the analysis if he failed to accede to her request. However, Casement also recognised that if he held the patient's hand, as the mother had done, he would run the risk of becoming confused with the terrified mother who had fainted years previously.

After careful and prolonged thought, Patrick Casement did not, in the end, clasp this woman's hand. Scrutinising his countertransference, he interpreted,

> You are making me experience in myself the sense of despair, and the impossibility of going on, that you are feeling. I am aware of being in what feels to me like a total paradox. In one sense I am feeling that it is impossible to reach you just now, and yet in another sense I feel that my telling you this may be the only way I can reach you. [Casement, 1982, p. 283]

Casement further underscored,

> Similarly I feel as if it could be impossible to go on, and yet I feel that the only way I can help you through this is by my being prepared to tolerate what you are making me feel, and going on. [p. 283]

In other words, Casement had succeeded in finding a form of words, based on the experience in the transference, in which he articulated very clearly the wish and the necessity to tolerate the patient's anxiety rather than faint, as the mother had done, by arriving at a quick, enacted solution. As a result of his verbal interpretation, the patient responded, "For the first time I can believe you, that you *are* in touch with what I have been feeling, and what is so amazing is that you can bear it" (p. 283), and that, "You would have become a collapsed analyst. I could not realize it at the time but I can now see that you would then have become the same as my mother who fainted. I am so glad you didn't let that happen" (p. 283).

Donald Winnicott and the little thief

Thus far, we have explored some examples of ordinarily cathartic non-transferential interpretations, as well as more targeted transferential interpretations, each of which seems to have provided some relief and, possibly, some ongoing benefit for the patients under consideration. But interpretations need not be either cathartic or specifically transferential in nature in order to exert an impact.

Dr Donald Winnicott, one of the world's most famous and creative psychoanalysts, developed a particular style of interpretation in his work with parents of troubled children. Winnicott often rendered an interpretation *not* to the child but, rather, to the parent; and he did so in order to promote parental insight, which could help to contain and ameliorate the child's symptoms.

In his landmark paper on "The Antisocial Tendency", first presented to the British Psycho-Analytical Society in 1956 under the title "Study of the Antisocial Tendency", Winnicott (1956c, p. 307) described the case of a little boy whom he simply could not treat directly, because the child's father "objects to psychology on religious grounds". However, the mother, a friend of Winnicott's, decided to consult the great child psychiatrist nonetheless, explaining that her son "John" had begun to steal compulsively both from shops and from his own home. Winnicott actually spoke to the mother over the course of a meal in a restaurant, during which time he adumbrated his theory of stealing as an unconscious effort to compensate for early experiences of deprivation.

After listening to the mother describe her son's activities, Dr Winnicott (1956c, p. 307) decided that the mother "should find a good moment in her relationship with the boy and make an interpretation to him". As Winnicott suggested, "Why not tell him that you know that when he steals he is not wanting the things that he steals but he is looking for something that he has a right to; that he is making a claim on his mother and father because he feels deprived of their love" (Winnicott, 1956c, p. 307). Some time later, the mother wrote to Winnicott, explaining that she had followed his interpretative advice and noted that,

> I told him that what he really wanted when he stole money and food and things was his mum; and I must say I didn't really expect him to understand, but he did seem to. I asked him if he thought we didn't love him because he was so naughty sometimes, and he said right out that he didn't think we did, much. Poor little scrap! I felt so awful, I can't tell you. So I told him never, never to doubt it again. [Winnicott, 1956c, p. 307]

Eventually, John ceased his symptomatic stealing entirely.

Donald Winnicott and the constipated child

Dr Joyce McDougall (2003), a New Zealander who became one of the most distinguished members of the Société Psychanalytique de Paris [Paris Psycho-Analytical Society], recalled one of Donald Winnicott's memorable child psychiatric cases. According to McDougall, a

Cockney mother had consulted Winnicott, explaining that her young son "Bobbie" had become constipated and could not evacuate his bowels. Winnicott interviewed the mother, who spoke liberally about her family; and in the midst of her recitation Winnicott interrupted this Cockney woman and asked, "Tell me, how many weeks pregnant are you?" (quoted in McDougall, 2003, p. 20). The woman looked at Winnicott in utter amazement, as she had not spoken of her pregnancy to Winnicott and certainly not to any of the members of her family, apart, perhaps, from her husband. Winnicott hypothesised that Bobbie, the constipated son, had become unconsciously aware of his mother's pregnancy, and that he had developed a psychosomatic constipation as a means of keeping something tightly secured inside his own tummy, just like mummy! Winnicott recommended that the mother might discuss her pregnancy with her son, and he invited her to return for a follow-up appointment one week later. The mother did, indeed, reveal her pregnancy to Bobbie, and then, she exclaimed to Winnicott, "Oh, Doctor, he shits and shits and shits! It's a down-right miracle!" (quoted in McDougall, 2003, p. 21).

Here again Winnicott's interpretation broke new ground, because he made his observation *not* to the identified patient, Bobbie, but, rather, to the mother, just as he had done in the aforementioned case of John, the little boy who stole. Upon hearing of the story of Bobbie in a seminar, McDougall (2003, p. 21) reminisced, "It was lovely. We also were convinced that Winnicott was something of a miracle-worker."

Susie Orbach and the Vampire Casanova

Some years ago, Dr Susie Orbach (1999), the London-based psychoanalyst, wrote a groundbreaking book entitled *The Impossibility of Sex*. Well known for her public career, broadcasting on radio and television, and for her newspaper articles, Orbach wanted to avoid writing about her own case histories, as that would excite too much curiosity about who her patients might be. Instead, she preserved confidentiality by constructing a series of imaginary case histories and then "treating" them exactly as she would do if they had actually come to her consulting room. In a memorable chapter, Orbach described her work with "Adam", a vampiric Casanova figure who bedded innumerable women in compulsive fashion.

As a specialist in relational psychoanalysis, Orbach knew instantly that Adam must have suffered from some painful early experiences, resulting in a deep loneliness, which prevented him from forging intimate attachments. Consequently, as she observed, "My mind rushed to interpret" (Orbach, 1999, p. 20). However, in spite of her eagerness to render an interpretation straight away, she restrained herself and remained silent, exploring her countertransferential responses in exquisite and honest detail. As Orbach (1999, p. 4) explained,

> Today's analyses consist not of the earth-shattering realization, insight or interpretation, but of the slow building up of conditions in which it is possible for the patient to understand herself afresh and to construct a meaningful relationship with the therapist in which she feels more fully accepted and understood.

Instead of rushing to render the earth-shattering interpretation so prevalent in the history of psychoanalysis, Orbach (1999, p. 22) decided to offer what she described, instead, as "silent interpretations"—which she kept to herself, and which continued to inform her work with the patient Adam. By refraining from the wish to show off her psychoanalytic insightfulness, she allowed Adam's erotic transference towards her to unfold and develop fully and thus become better available for analysis. This approach also permitted Adam to know that the full ferocity of his symptom could become manifest in the consulting room, and that his psychoanalyst would not simply dismiss his erotic strivings with a quick-fire interpretation.

Orbach's slow and steady focus on the "silent interpretations" contains much merit and wisdom. It saddens me that more psychoanalysts do not make silent interpretations on a regular basis; many simply evacuate those of a gruff and unhelpful nature.

Some years ago, a male patient consulted me. He wished to embark upon intensive treatment, but he had many reservations, not least that he had only recently spent three months in analysis with a hyper-interpretative Kleinian psychoanalyst, who made him feel quite humiliated. During an early session with this colleague, the patient reported a dream in which he and the female analyst began to kiss on a beautiful windswept mountainside. The patient found the dream very exciting and very romantic, and he thought that it would be helpful to share this with the new analyst. Apparently, the Kleinian practitioner huffed, "I can see that you are already trying to destroy your psychoanalysis by attacking my role as your doctor, turning me into your lover." While this interpretation might contain an element of truth, the phrasing made the patient enraged, and he immediately broke off the treatment.

Clearly, Susie Orbach's notion of the "silent interpretation" deserves infinitely greater consideration. Her work serves as a powerful reminder that sometimes our best interpretations might be those that we do not articulate out loud at the first available opportunity!

Valerie Sinason at the Tavistock Clinic lift

Dr Valerie Sinason, for many years a Consultant Child and Adolescent Psychotherapist at the Tavistock Clinic in London, pioneered psychoanalytic work with patients burdened by severe and profound mental and physical handicaps (e.g., Sinason, 1992, 2010). Some years ago, Sinason had the opportunity to work with an adolescent called "Eve", who suffered from Goldenhar Syndrome: a rare congenital condition of unknown aetiology. As Sinason (1991a, p. 17) explained, "This means she has no outer ear, a curved deformed spine and thin wasted paralysed legs. She has no speech but a few makaton signs and a few grunts and cries. She was referred for eye-poking, wailing, bottom-poking and smearing." Indeed, Sinason (1991a, p. 17) described Eve as "the most handicapped patient" that she had ever seen at that point in her career.

On the day of Eve's first appointment at the Tavistock Clinic, Sinason stood by the entrance to the lift, awaiting Eve's arrival in a wheelchair, escorted by a care worker. As the doors of the lift opened, Sinason experienced a horrific shock; she reported that,

> She was looking at me through one curled hand. I knew she had seen my shock. My first thought was cowardice and corruption. How could I cover up my initial response? Then intelligence returned.

After catching her breath, Sinason (1991a, p. 18) spoke her first words to Eve:

> I said, "Hello, I am Mrs Sinason and you are Miss E, and perhaps you have got one arm covering your eyes because you know that when people first see you they get a shock at how handicapped you are." She put her hand down and looked at me with great intelligence and we were in business. [1991a, pp. 17–18]

With utter brilliance, Sinason had scrutinised her countertransference, noted her own sense of embarrassment and shame at having demonstrated shock in front of her patient, and then came to realise that this might represent Eve's lifelong experience of humiliation as a result of looking so very tragically deformed. Sinason found a style of language that allowed the patient to feel immediately recognised and understood. Thereafter Eve benefited from the tremendous compassion and experience for which Valerie Sinason has become known worldwide within the mental health profession, and consequently the patient enjoyed a most successful course of psychotherapy.

Interpretation and its opportunities

In the preceding pages I identified ten interpretations from the many thousands published in the psychoanalytic literature over the last century. These interpretations represent only an infinitesimally tiny percentage of the many wise interpretative comments rendered hourly by psychoanalytically orientated clinical practitioners in the course of an ordinary working day. I have identified these ten—and one could choose many others—merely as a paedagogical strategy for underscoring how, in an era dominated by pharmacology and cognitive-behavioural therapy, the nuanced language and understanding of psychoanalytic approaches still has much to offer. These ten interpretative comments emblematise, to me at least, the ways in which our colleagues have engaged boldly and sensitively with such ugly subjects as fellatio trauma and Nazi executions, as well as with more ordinary topics such as nasal congestion, humiliation, shame, and compulsive sexuality—always in a compassionate, intelligent fashion—helping patients to find language for that which cannot easily be spoken.

All of the abovementioned "top ten" interpretations provide very compelling evidence of the capacity of the clinical practitioner to connect seemingly unrelated pieces of data. A bruised head examined in a neurological clinic does not immediately imply Holocaust trauma; a child with constipation does not provide automatic proof of a pregnant mother; and a woman with sinusitis does not necessarily suggest a history of blocked tears. And yet, in each case, the establishment of a possible link between such seemingly random chunks of biography can often prove to be immensely therapeutic. As the American psychoanalyst Dr Jacob Arlow noted with prescience, "Interpretation is a hypothesis. It serves to transform observations that are unconnected into data that are related" (quoted in Rothstein, 1983, p. 238).

In my experience as a teacher of students of psychology, psycho-therapy, and counselling, I have come to discover that very many of these young practitioners—all sensitive, thoughtful, and warm-hearted people—often fail their patients by responding in rather hackneyed and uninteresting ways. They will frequently ask their patient to clarify statements: "When you say that you are 'depressed', what *exactly* do you mean by that?" These practitioners ask questions, press for more information, propose "strategies" and "techniques" for managing anxiety, and so forth. Rarely do those without a psycho-analytic training offer a more in-depth comment that risks making the unconscious conscious or dares to verbalise that which might be known at some level but cannot be formulated by the patient with ease.

Those practitioners who fail to render interpretations to their patients miss out on a great opportunity to formulate important com-ments that might become transformational. But similarly, those who interpret in a clumsy or insensitive fashion run the risk of damaging the patient.

In a sensitive paper on "Interpretation: Fresh Insight or Cliché?", the psychoanalyst Patrick Casement (1986, p. 93) described the work of a certain Latin American colleague who interpreted her patients' material with both a penetrative ferocity and with a "quite unu-sual sureness". This hyper-interpretative style prompted one patient to dream about having his head "squashed by someone sitting on my face" (quoted in Casement, 1986, p. 93). Upon hearing such a dream, a sensitive psychoanalyst might have seized the opportunity to reflect upon whether he or she had become overly interpretative, but this Latin American clinician simply attacked the patient further with a very punitive comment, to wit, exclaiming, "Because of your envy, you are unable to take in the good milk of my interpretations. Instead you take in my words as poisonous faeces" (p. 93). In a help-ful commentary, Casement hypothesised that this "stereotyped and repetitive" (p. 90) or, indeed, "cliché" (p. 90) approach to interpreta-tion might derive from the clinician's own insecurity over how to understand the patient's material in a fresh manner.

Casement's observations about the potential use of interpretation in the service of insensitivity or, even, cruelty remain a vital reminder that one can never interpret lightly. Indeed, back in 1941, the Vien-nese-born psychoanalyst Dr Richard Sterba (1941, p. 10), the author of an important but, alas, unremembered essay on "The Abuse of Interpretation", underscored that, "interpretation in analysis has the effect and, indeed, the purpose of awakening in the patient a mistrust of himself". Thus, in view of the sheer power of the interpretation to stir up unconscious material, the dedicated clinician must undertake any interventions with delicacy and thoughtfulness.

Psychoanalysis has suffered greatly over the last one hundred years or more from a monastic tendency. Many psychoanalysts have, for instance, failed to cooperate or to collaborate with practitioners from other branches of the mental health field; consequently, many humanistic and integrative psychotherapists detest psychoanalysis for its seeming ghetto-like mentality and, consequently, deride its contributions, not least the gruff, stereotypical interpretation. This results in a loss not only for psychoanalytic workers who remain further isolated, but also for those who practice in different psychotherapeutic accents and who, as a result, fail to grapple with all that psychoanalysis might perhaps provide.

As the historically minded American psychoanalyst Dr Joseph Coltrera (1981) remarked in a little-known book chapter entitled "On the Nature of Interpretation: Epistemology as Practice", Freud did not invent the interpretation. In fact, the art of interpreting meaning in material can be found in the resonances of untold numbers of philosophers, ranging from Aristotle, Roger Bacon, and William of Ockham, to Ludwig Feuerbach, Wilhelm Dilthey, Friedrich Nietzsche, Ferdinand de Saussure, Edmund Husserl, Ludwig Wittgenstein, Martin Heidegger, and others too numerous to mention.

But interpretation has become the caricature of psychoanalysis: I shall never forget a memorable lunch with the brilliant American psychoanalyst, Dr Robert Langs (personal communication, 15 May 1992), who told me that when he trained in New York in the 1960s, his teachers explained to him that psychoanalysis can be summarised, quite simply, in the following maxim: patients project and analysts interpret! He later wrote that he believed that his training had prepared him solely to become a "psychoanalytic interpreting machine" (Langs, 2002, p. 16). In fact, psychoanalysts must not only render interpretations: they must interpret in the transference. Langs's classmate at the Downstate Psychoanalytic Institute, in Brooklyn, New York, Dr Harold Blum (2016, p. 419), recalled, similarly, that, "Extra-transference interpretation, including genetic interpretation and reconstruction were considered subordinate to transference interpretation."

Indeed, Professor Robert Wallerstein (2015, p. 542), former President of both the American Psychoanalytic Association and the International Psycho-Analytical Association, who had trained during the

1940s, confirmed that, for decades, "the central and only curative agent of psychoanalytic technique was the persistent making of veridical interpretations, leading to working through, insight, and cure".

This stereotype of the psychoanalytic process in no way represented Freud's own views about interpretation. Indeed, Freud once underscored to his American pupil Dr Joseph Wortis that, "All interpretations are tentative" (quoted in Wortis, 1940, p. 847; cf. Wortis, 1934, p. 83).

Psychoanalysts who refrain from rendering stereotyped interpretations or cruel interpretations or incessant interpretations have the opportunity to help patients feel met, feel seen, and feel understood in a truly profound manner. But interpretations must be offered compassionately, intelligently, and judiciously, and, moreover, they must be verbalised in a musical manner, so that the tone of voice and the speed of delivery match the brilliance of the cognitive observations conveyed.

Although the psychoanalytic literature is replete with worthy tomes and articles about the nature of interpretation (e.g., Glover, 1931; Strachey, 1934; Heimann, 1956; Klauber, 1961, 1966, 1971a, 1971b, 1972, 1980; Bion, 1970; French, 1970; Brody, 1974; Pao, 1977; Segal, 1979; Malcolm, 1986; Rosenfeld, 1987), we still have much to learn about what we interpret, when we interpret, how we interpret, to whom we interpret, and even *where* we interpret, as far too many of our colleagues share their interpretative knowledge of someone else's unconscious mind at dinner parties all round North London and elsewhere.

But even when conveyed superbly well, an interpretation may not be the only curative ingredient in psychoanalytic or psychotherapeutic work. Interpretations must sit alongside such non-interpretative features as reliability, relationability, reasonableness, and any number of other components of treatment, which might include the practitioner who possesses a great memory for detail or who boasts a sensitive capacity for humour or who might have a warm smile and a pleasant handshake (e.g., Meissner, 1991; Oremland, 1991; Stern et al., 1998; Kahr, 2006b)!

I remember that, years ago, as a young trainee, one of my supervisors told me that I did not interpret enough with a particular patient. Another supervisor, to whom I later presented the same case, cautioned me against interpreting too much. This conundrum—very much a stylistic one—has dogged clinical practitioners for nearly a century. In 1934, the British psychoanalyst and Freud scholar James Strachey wrote that,

> We are told that if we interpret too soon or too rashly, we run the risk of losing a patient; that unless we interpret promptly and deeply we run the risk of losing a patient; that interpretation may give rise to intolerable and unmanageable outbreaks of anxiety by 'liberating' it; that interpretation is the only way of enabling a patient to cope with an unmanageable outbreak of anxiety by 'resolving' it; that interpretations must always refer to material on the very point of emerging into consciousness; that the most useful ones are really deep ones; 'Be cautious with your interpretations!' says once voice; 'When in doubt, interpret!' says another. [1934, pp. 141–142]

In the 1890s, Sigmund Freud not only preserved the very best of Dr Josef Breuer's cathartic technique but also developed his own approach through the development of the art of interpretation (e.g., Freud, 1895, 1909a). Unlike Breuer, who simply let his patients speak, Freud spoke *back*, in interpretative form. And this rich conversation has permitted a two-way interchange about the patient's mind and life that often proves surprisingly healing.

Freud did not, however, always interpret effectively. The American physician Dr Adolph Stern underwent not quite three months of psychoanalysis with Freud in Vienna, Austria, commencing in either late September 1920, or early October 1920. As Stern recalled, "There were so many interpretations—I don't remember—that he gave me that he didn't strike home" (quoted in Eissler, 1952, p. 4). Stern further lamented, "I left very much, as far as therapy went, as I came into the thing" (p. 4). In similar vein, the British scientist Professor Arthur Tansley (later Professor Sir Arthur Tansley), who began analysis with Freud in 1922, recalled that he found some of Freud's interpretations to be "far-fetched" (quoted in Eissler, 1953, p. 8).

But Freud's earliest disciples derived much inspiration from his prescience and from his capacity to interpret unconscious meanings of symptoms. In 1925 Dr Richard Sterba, then a young Viennese psychoanalyst, began to treat a 20-year-old male patient who suffered from an incapacity to obtain a penile erection. This young Jewish man also maintained the belief that the hair on his head stood on end, which observers would notice, producing such anxiety that he kept rushing into the toilet to mat his hair with a wet comb. Sterba (1982, p. 38), though inexperienced at the time, made an interpretation that exerted a "magical effect". He concluded, quite simply, that the patient had unconsciously displaced his absent erection onto his hair. At that point, the fear of the erect hair disappeared! Although Sterba's interpretation cured the patient of one of his symptoms, it did not eradicate the other—that is, the impotence—an important reminder that although interpretations can be magical, they do not always function omnipotently! After several years of further analysis, Sterba helped his patient to work through various conflicts; at this point the young man did become sufficiently potent; he managed to marry a woman and to father two children. Tragically, he, like so many other Jews, died, years later, at the hands of the Nazis (Sterba, 1982).

Whether we interpret childhood material or present-day material, whether or not we interpret the transference; whether we interpret dreams; whether we interpret the individual or the couple or the family or the group; whether we render long interpretations or short ones; whether we do so early in the session or late; whether we interpret defences before instinctual drives; whether we make accurate interpretations or inaccurate ones; and so on, the interpretation remains a vital ingredient of our conversations with patients. It must never be the sole component, but it must not be overlooked, something that might, I believe, be a threat in this era of conversational and relational approaches to psychotherapeutic work. Interpretations must never be over-fetishised, resulting in a *"furor interpretandis"* (Bloch, 1990, p. 114); but, similarly, they must not be underemployed.

Furthermore, interpretations should never be used as an opportunity to boast about our cleverness. As early as 1931, Dr Sándor Ferenczi (1931, p. 471) cautioned against rendering "learned, scientific interpretations". Indeed, the wise American psychoanalyst Professor Karl Menninger (1958, p. 129) underscored that young practitioners, in particular, "need to be reminded that they are not oracles, not wizards, not linguists, not detectives, not great wise men who, like Joseph and David, 'interpret' dreams—but quiet observers, listeners, and occasionally commentators." But just as we must not use interpretations for our own self-aggrandisement, so, too, must we share our intelligence liberally, when appropriate, and not prevent the patient benefiting from being in conversation with someone whose mind might be working well.

The art of interpretation raises many more critical questions. First of all, simply because the psychoanalyst or psychotherapist renders an excellent interpretation—one that, all colleagues might agree, contains traces of brilliance—does that mean that the analyst has actually succeeded in making a great interpretation? Perhaps the interpretation deserves to be celebrated only if the patient actually feels understood by it. Second of all, do we fetishise the interpretation and the "eureka" moments that can come in their wake? Might there be other, better ways of speaking with the patient? And might the interpretation be too masculine or too phallic an activity, inserting something pointed into the patient's mind? Do women interpret in the same way as men do, and might we have something to learn about the merits and demerits of masculine modes of interpretation as opposed to feminine modes?

We may also wish to consider whether patients reject our best interpretations unfairly, either through resistance or through envy of the fact that our minds might, at times, function more efficiently and more symbolically. We must also ask whether psychoanalysts work too hard on behalf of their patients, taking charge of the interpretative procedure rather than working with analysands more closely in order to ensure that interpretations will be co-constructed. While some practitioners endeavour to render interpretations collaboratively, others insist that the patient suffers from too much madness and must, therefore, be offered the interpretation fully formed, rather than co-constructed.

These and other questions deserve longer, fuller, richer answers. Thankfully, our profession does grapple with the complexities of interpretation all of the time, and I, for one, look forward to future publications on this topic.

But whatever our ultimate viewpoint, few would deny the seminal role of interpretation in our clinical work with those in distress.

One need not be a genius to render an efficacious interpretation. One need have only a bit of brains and a bit of heart to recognise that for many of our patients, we—the practitioners—might be the only people to whom they can turn for moments of sustenance in the bleak landscape of their lives.

Bertha

"Bertha", a lonely spinster with absolutely no family members or friends, used to spend hours of her life googling me, desperate for a connection. But after many years of analysis, Bertha ceased her googling activities, especially after I had interpreted that she had begun to lead *my* life rather than *hers*.

Ten years after the start of her analysis, Bertha developed a form of cancer and had to endure extensive and exhausting radiotherapy treatment which, thankfully, proved successful. During this time, her compulsive googling resurfaced.

On one occasion, she came to her session and confessed that she had found a photograph of me on the internet—a full-length photograph, in fact, in which she could see my shoes. She told me that she had spent the evening staring in fascination at my shoes, even though I wore only the most ordinary black dress shoes, just as I do every single day at the office. She explained that she could not understand quite why she found my undistinguished work shoes so fascinating, but she found herself drawn to them, and she stared at them on her computer screen all night.

I could, of course, have commented on the intrusiveness of Bertha's googling, as I had done in the past. I could have noted the repetitive and neurotic nature of her activities, as I had done in the past. I could have pontificated about a whole range of possible meanings of the resurfacing of Bertha's earlier symptom. But after some reflection, I rendered a very simple interpretation; and in a soft voice, I observed, "Well, in view of what you have just been through, with this tremendously challenging and painful course of radiotherapy, it hardly surprises me that you would want to be in my shoes." Bertha began to sob. I became slightly teary-eyed myself, which Bertha could not observe from her position on the couch. Although I could not remove the cancer, I believe that through a very ordinary interpretation—a transference interpretation, if you will—I helped, at least, to provide a moment of quiet in this woman's otherwise tormented and lonely life.

* * *

In his classic paper on "Primitive Emotional Development", published some three quarters of a century ago, Dr Donald Winnicott (1945a, p. 138) postulated that, "good interpretations are expressions of love, and symbolical of good food and care". Although the interpretation has become the hallmark of the stodgy, orthodox, old-fashioned approach to psychoanalysis, I wish to champion this essential ingredient as a true expression of the clinician's love through a deep and very intimate and uniquely personalised understanding.

In view of the many bombs thrown at clinical practitioners quite regularly in our consulting-room settings, the old-fashioned interpretation may prove to be one of our greatest sources of defence, and also of enhancement.

Note

1. I very much regret that I did not tape-record this memorable conversation with Professor Dr med. Uwe Henrik Peters. Consequently, I have taken the liberty of reconstructing his precise words to the best of my ability. The quotations attributed to Professor Peters in this vignette must be treated as approximations rather than as exactitudes; however, I do remember the essence of the case quite clearly, not least because of its impact and potency.

Conclusion

Durate, et vosmet rebus
    ſervate ſecundis.
[Endure the hardſhips of your present ſtate,
Live, and reſerve yourſelves for better fate.]

Publius Vergilius Maro [Virgil], Aeneidos, 29 B.C.E. to 19 B.C.E.,
Liber Primus, line 207 (Translation by John Dryden, 1772)

I began the "Introduction" to this collection of essays with a wonderful statement made by Enid Eichholz (1944, p. 92), the future Enid Balint, during the Second World War—namely, that, "When the flying bombs first began to fall most of us disliked them considerably."

Needless to say, no sane person enjoys bombs and the shrapnel that ensues. But as practising mental health professionals, we must inevitably deal with such difficult explosions, whether we wish to do so or not. Somehow we must mobilise our internal resources, seek collegial support, neutralise our "hate in the counter-transference", and allow ourselves to formulate sufficiently intelligent and heartfelt interpretative interventions that will allow us to make sense of the bombs with which our patients have lived for a lifetime.

I wish to conclude this account of some of my investigations from clinical practice, and also from the history of psychoanalytic work, by calling once again upon the wisdom of Enid Eichholz Balint, who, during the war, had coordinated a team of Citizens Advice Bureaux (CAB) staff. In that same essay on "Londoners and the Flying Bomb: (From the Point of View of the C.A.B. Worker)", she wrote,

> Londoners are experiencing such difficulty and hardship now. They are facing a stiff ordeal, which for some of them is hard to bear. It is good to know that the CAB worker is able to play a small part in helping them, and in doing something to improve the arrangements made for their care; it is good to know that the CAB worker has taken in his stride the considerable extra strain this work has put on him. We can only hope that it will be his privilege, when the war is over at last, to help in the rebuilding of what is being destroyed. [Eichholz, 1944, p. 95]

Just like the Londoners of the Second World War, who had to endure bombs, our twenty-first century psychotherapy patients have often had to do so as well. And just like the Citizens Advice Bureaux workers from the 1940s who had to bear the extra "strain", so, too, do we, as modern mental health clinicians, have not only the burden but also the privilege of sticking it through, and of persevering. And when we do so, we may, perhaps, from time to time, enjoy our capacity to save the lives of those who live in terrible distress. In this way, like Eichholz's team of CAB workers, we, too, can engage in the task of "the rebuilding of what is being destroyed".

ACKNOWLEDGEMENTS

I owe an immense amount of thanks to the many teachers, supervisors, colleagues, and friends who have supported and facilitated my clinical work over a very long period of time.

I could not have undertaken the work with "Alfonso", the juvenile sex offender, without the tremendously generous support of Dr Eileen Vizard, CBE, and her team at the Tavistock Clinic in London, or without the supervision from the late Dr Susanna Isaacs Elmhirst. I must also express my gratitude to the members of the New Resource Group of the Squiggle Foundation in London; and to the staff at Hear and Now of the North East London Mental Health Trust in Ilford, Essex; as well as to all the members of the Discussion Group on "Sexual Deviations: Theory and Therapy" at the American Psychoanalytic Association, for permitting me opportunities to present earlier drafts of this chapter. I should also like to thank my students on the "One Year Intermediate Course on Psychodynamic Work in Learning Disability", offered by the Tavistock Clinic, for having listened to various incarnations of this case history on many occasions.

Likewise, I owe huge thanks to all the members of the Mental Handicap Team and the Mental Handicap Workshop at the Tavistock Clinic, most particularly Dr Valerie Sinason and Mrs Judith Usiskin, for their warm encouragement of my work with "Albertina", the compulsive spitter. Mr Donald Campbell, my esteemed teacher at the Portman Clinic, offered helpful thoughts on this case, as did the late Dr Susanna Isaacs Elmhirst, as well as the members of the International Association for Forensic Psychotherapy. I must also convey my warm thanks to the members of the Academic Faculty of the Anna Freud National Centre for Children and Families, associated with University College London in the University of London, chaired by Professor Joan Raphael-Leff, who kindly afforded me an opportunity to discuss this case in great detail. I wish to extend particular thanks not only to Professor Raphael-Leff for her gracious invitation but also to all the participants and, most especially, to Mrs Jackie Gerrard, Dr Earl Hopper, Professor Julian Leff, Ms Ann Scott, Dr Valerie Sinason, Dr Judit Szekacs, and Dr Sarah Wynick. The late Dr Alan Corbett encouraged me to write up this complex case for publication, and through the goodly facilitation of Ms Ann Scott, editor of the *British Journal of Psychotherapy*, arranged for an earlier version of this chapter to appear in a special edition of essays on disability psychotherapy, published shortly after Dr Corbett's untimely death (Kahr, 2017a).

I have lectured on the "intra-marital affair", the "erotic tumour", the "conjugal aneurysm" and related topics to a number of different organisations, including The Bowlby Centre in London; the North London Branch of the British Association for Counselling and Psychotherapy in Finchley, London; the Oxford Psychotherapy Society in Oxford; the Society of Couple Psychoanalytic Psychotherapists in London; the Taunton Association for Psychodynamics in Monkton Heathfield, Taunton, Somerset; as well as at the Tavistock Centre for Couple Relationships in London; the Wessex Psychotherapy Society in Southampton, Hampshire; the West Midlands Institute of Psychotherapy in Birmingham, West Midlands; the Wimbledon Guild in London; and also to colleagues at the American Association of Sexuality Educators, Counselors, and Therapists, at their Annual Conference in Phoenix, Arizona, and in the Psychoanalytic Studies Program at the Graduate Institute of Liberal Arts in the Laney School of Graduate Studies and the Graduate School of Arts and Sciences at Emory University in Atlanta, Georgia. I owe particular thanks to all the colleagues who organised and attended these events, including, most especially, Professor Sander Gilman for his kind mentorship.

As for my work on sexual cruelty in the marital bed, I owe special thanks to my colleague Dr Amita Sehgal for her helpful remarks and for her interest.

With regard to the chapter on "non-forensic" patients who commit crimes, I take pleasure in extending my appreciation to Dr Sandra Grant, the late Professor Gill McGauley, Dr Carine Minne, and Dr Estela Welldon for their insightful remarks and support on the occasion of our shared conference on "Why Are We Murderous?: The Psychodynamic Treatment of the Forensic Patient", sponsored jointly by Confer and by the International Association for Forensic Psychotherapy, held at the Tavistock Centre in London. And through the kind offices of Ms Claudia Nielsen and Ms Josefine Speyer, I also had the opportunity to discuss this work with colleagues at the Hampstead Psychotherapy Club in Hampstead, London.

I owe an immense debt to my former student, and then, ultimately, my dear colleague and friend, Ms Jane Ryan, the Director of the Confer—the United Kingdom's leading mental health conference organisation—for having kindly invited me to present a number of these papers in earlier versions, not only in London but also in Dublin. I remain but one of the many hundreds of clinical practitioners and writers indebted to Jane for generous opportunities to share our work with colleagues and to receive extremely helpful feedback and engagement.

For the historical papers, I must thank, above all, Professor Sander Gilman, Dr Bruce Rudisch, and Professor Peter Rudnytsky, as well as the staff at Emory University in Atlanta, Georgia, and the members of the Atlanta Psychoanalytic Society in the Department of Psychiatry and Behavioral Sciences at the Emory University Medical School, for providing me with the very first outing of my work on Donald Winnicott's "anni horribiles" in its current form. Peter Rudnytsky then published an early version in the journal *American Imago: Psychoanalysis and the Human Sciences* (Kahr, 2011a), while Dr Margaret Boyle Spelman and Professor Frances Thomson-Salo published a further incarnation in their collection of essays on *The Winnicott Tradition: Lines of Development—Evolution of Theory and Practice Over the Decades*—an invitation kindly facilitated by Professor Joan Raphael-Leff (Kahr, 2015a). I also benefited from having presented earlier editions of this work to the Squiggle Foundation in London, and to the Philadelphia Society for Psychoanalytic Psychology, part of Division 39 of the American Psychological Association, in Philadelphia, Pennsylvania, where I received a warm welcome from Dr Denis Debiak,

Dr Linda Hopkins, and the late and much-missed Dr Elisabeth Young-Bruehl. A fuller treatment of this material will be published in due course in book form under the title *Winnicott's* Anni Horribiles: *The Creation of "Hate in the Counter-Transference"* (Kahr, 2020).

I wish to express my heartfelt gratitude to the staff at the Archives of Psychiatry in The Oskar Diethelm Library at the DeWitt Wallace Institute for the History of Psychiatry in the Department of Psychiatry at the Joan and Sanford I. Weill Medical College, Cornell University, at The New York Presbyterian Hospital, in New York, New York, and, also, to the staff at the Archives and Manuscripts division of the Wellcome Library in London, and, to everyone at the Winnicott Trust in London, for permission to quote from unpublished letters and typescripts by Dr. Donald Winnicott.

I could not possibly have completed chapter 7, on Enid Eichholz Balint and the creation of couple psychoanalysis, without warm assistance from a veritable village of colleagues. First and foremost, I wish to express my very deep gratitude to Ms Susanna Abse who, as Chief Executive Officer and Consultant Couple Psychotherapist of the Tavistock Centre for Couple Relationships in London, very kindly invited me to present the Twenty-First Enid Balint Lecture, in 2016, and who has warmly encouraged my research on the history of couple psychoanalysis. Likewise, I wish to extend my profound appreciation to Dr Nicholas Pearce and to the trustees of the Tavistock Institute of Medical Psychology for awarding me the post of Senior Fellow. I owe a particular debt of thanks to Dr Christopher Clulow, former Director of the Tavistock Centre for Couple Relationships, and also a Senior Fellow, for years of unstinting professional support and generosity. Additionally, I owe everlasting thanks to the staff in the Rare Materials Room in the Wellcome Library, London, where I had the privilege of studying the unpublished archives of the Tavistock Centre for Couple Relationships. Without the gracious facilitation of the Wellcome Library's archival staff, especially Dr Lesley Hall and Dr Jennifer Haynes, and also Ms Zoe Fullard, Ms Amelia Walker, and Ms Natalie Walters, I certainly could not have undertaken this investigation. Many colleagues offered interviews or reminiscences about some of the key personalities described in this paper, and many spoke in illuminating detail about both Enid Balint and Michael Balint. For memories of Enid Balint, I must thank, *inter alia*, Professor Arnon Bentovim, Mr Patrick Casement, Mrs Barbara Clark, Dr Christopher Clulow, Mrs Judy Cooper, the late Mrs Barbara Dearnley, Ms Katy Dearnley, Dr Andrew Elder, Dr Ernst Falzeder,

Dr Anthony Hazzard, Dr Juliet Hopkins, Dr Jennifer Johns, Mrs Ruth Brook Klauber, Dr David Lawlor, Mrs Susan Lawlor, the late Dr Isabel Menzies Lyth, Professor Juliet Mitchell, Mrs Elspeth Morley, Mr Paul Pengelly, Professor Peter Rudnytsky, the late Dr Charles Rycroft, Mr Christopher Vincent, Dr Estela Welldon, Dr Agnes Wilkinson, and Ms Frances Wilks. And for memories of Michael Balint, I wish to convey my gratitude to Dr Bernard Barnett, Professor Arnon Bentovim, Dr Reva Berstock, Mrs Mary Boston, Dr Stanford Bourne, Dr Abrahão Brafman, the late Dr Peter Bruggen, the late Dr Perry Calwell, Mrs Barbara Clark, Mrs Beta Copley, the late Dr Murray Cox, the late Professor Robert Dorn, Dr John Evans, the late Dr Peter Hildebrand, Professor Jeremy Holmes, the late Dr John Horder, OBE, CBE, the late Mrs Lydia James, Mrs Ann Jameson, the late Miss Pearl King, Mrs Ruth Brook Klauber, Mrs Susan Lawlor, Professor Julian Leff, the late Dr Isabel Menzies Lyth, the late Dr Joyce McDougall, Mrs Jane Shore Nicholas, OBE, Dr Malcolm Pines, the late Dr Eric Rayner, Dr Joel Shor, the late Count Andrew Skarbek, the late Professor Thomas Stapleton, Dr Estela Welldon, and Dr Agnes Wilkinson. Several generous colleagues offered interviews about Lily Pincus, especially Mr Patrick Casement, Mrs Barbara Clark, Mrs Elspeth Morley, Mrs Viveka Nyberg, and Dr Estela Welldon. And Sir Richard Bowlby kindly spoke about his father—the late Dr John Bowlby—and of his relationship to the pioneering social worker Noël Hunnybun, who proved such a support to Enid Eichholz (later Enid Balint) during the early days of the Family Discussion Bureau. Xenia, Lady Bowlby, and Mrs Barbara Clark shared their recollections of Dr Tommy Wilson. And the late Miss Pearl King, a generous facilitator of my research on the history of psychoanalysis over many years, provided copious and enlightening memories of Dr John Rickman. Furthermore, I must thank Dr Rosemary Stephens for her childhood recollections of Dr Hugh Crichton Miller, the first Medical Director of the Tavistock Clinic; and also I wish to acknowledge Dr Katharine Rees, niece of Dr John Rawlings Rees, the second Medical Director of the Tavistock Clinic, for her reminiscences. I thank all of these generous interviewees for sharing their precious anecdotes and reflections. I also had the privilege of learning a great deal about the Tavistock Clinic and the Tavistock Institute of Human Relations, as well as the Family Discussion Bureau, from more than fifty former staff members and trainees who had worked in these institutions prior to 1970, some of whom had begun their association with these organisations as early as 1935, and many of whom served as teachers of my own. For recollections, anecdotes, and for transmitting the ethos of the Tavistock culture, I wish to thank the following persons: Dr Anne Alvarez, the late Mrs Enid Balint, Ms Lynn Barnett, Mrs Mary Boston, Dr Stanford Bourne, the late Dr John Bowlby, CBE, the late Dr Peter Bruggen, the late Dr Perry Calwell, Mrs Beta Copley, Dr Christopher Dare, Mrs Dilys Daws, the late Mrs Barbara Dearnley, the late Mr Geoffrey Elkan, Mrs Judith Elkan, Dr John Evans, the late Dr Michael Fordham, the late Dr Thomas Freeman, the late Dr Robert Gosling, Mr Herbert Hahn, Dr Victoria Hamilton, the late Dr Peter Hildebrand, Dr Hyla Holden, Dr Juliet Hopkins, the late Mrs Shirley Hoxter, Dr Judith Issroff, the late Professor Elliott Jaques, the late Miss Pearl King, the late Dr Ronald D. Laing, the late Dr Margaret Little, the late Mrs Frederica Low-Beer, the late Dr Dora Lush, the late Dr Isabel Menzies Lyth, Dr David Malan, Mrs Elspeth Morley, the late Dr Robert Morley, Mrs Edna O'Shaughnessy, Mrs Eileen Orford, the late Dr John Padel, Mrs Irma Brenman Pick, the late Dr Michael Pokorny, Mr Alexander Pollock, the late Dr Christopher Reeves, the late Dr Herbert Rosenfeld, the late Dr Charles Rycroft, the late Professor Joseph Sandler, the late Mr Raymond Shepherd, Mrs Antonia Shooter, Mrs Jane Temperley, the late Mrs Frances Tustin, Miss Janice Uphill, Mr Paul Upson, the late Dr Arthur Hyatt Williams, the late Miss Doris Wills, Mrs Isca Wittenberg, and the late Mr Douglas Woodhouse. Above all, I wish to convey my appreciation to the late Mrs Enid Balint, whom I had the privilege of meeting in 1993. Little did I know then that one day, more than twenty years hence, I would come to write her history; if only I had had the foresight to ask her so many more questions. I did, however, have the privilege of proposing her, successfully, for the post of Honorary Visiting Fellow in the School of Psychotherapy and Counselling at Regent's College in London (now the Regent's School of Psychotherapy and Psychology at Regent's University London), where I then taught (Kahr, 1995a). Her work and her style of leadership remain an inspiration to all who toil in the field of couple mental health and beyond.

I thank Mrs Molly Ludlam, the founding Editor of the journal *Couple and Family Psychoanalysis,* for her kindness in offering me a space in her periodical for a considerably shortened version this chapter (Kahr, 2017b).

For the chapter on the art of interpretation, I owe my greatest thanks once again to Jane Ryan, for having organised such a stimulating conference at the Tavistock Centre on "Interpretation or Intersubjective Communication?: What Makes a Good Intervention?", where

I had the good fortune to share a platform with Dr Aaron Balick and Mr Patrick Casement, each of whom taught me a great deal. And I thank my colleague Dr Susie Orbach for her close reading of this essay and for her kind enthusiasm. This material on the art of interpretation appears here in print for the very first time.

Mr Oliver Rathbone, the long-standing Publisher and Managing Director of Karnac Books, kindly commissioned this book, shortly before the sale of his company to Routledge / Taylor and Francis Group. I owe him immense thanks for his tremendously generous support of my writing over many long years. I also wish to thank his long-serving editorial team—Ms Cecily Blench, Ms Constance Govindin, and Dr Rod Tweedy—for their warm encouragement and assistance on so many matters. Since the transfer of the Karnac Books list to Routledge, I have had the deep privilege of working closely with the wonderful Mr Russell George and with his gracious assistant, Dr Elliott Morsia, two of the most gentlemanly people in publishing. I feel truly grateful to be able to collaborate with two such intelligent and reliable and convivial comrades. I also wish to express my thanks to Mr Tomas Furby and Ms Naomi Hill—the production managers—for their assistance. And I take great delight in thanking the remarkably gifted and patient copy-editors, Mr Eric King and Mrs Klara Majthényi King of Communication Crafts, with whom I have had the privilege of collaborating on six previous tomes. Any author who has worked with Communication Crafts must consider himself very lucky indeed.

Once again, I thank my family for their invaluable love.

REFERENCES

Abraham, Karl (1917). Über Ejaculatio praecox. *Internationale Zeitschrift für ärztliche Psychoanalyse*, *4*, 171–186.

Abraham, Karl (1919). Über eine besondere Form des neurotischen Widerstandes gegen die psychoanalytische Methodik. *Internationale Zeitschrift für ärztliche Psychoanalyse*, *5*, 173–180.

Ahrenfeldt, Robert H. (1958). *Psychiatry in the British Army in the Second World War*. London: Routledge & Kegan Paul.

Alexander, Franz G., and Selesnick, Sheldon T. (1966). *The History of Psychiatry: An Evaluation of Psychiatric Thought and Practice from Prehistoric Times to the Present*. New York: Harper & Row.

Almásy, Endre (1936). Zur Psychoanalyse amentia-ähnlicher Falle. *Internationale Zeitschrift für Psychoanalyse*, *22*, 72–96.

American Psychiatric Association (1994). *Diagnostic and Statistical Manual of Mental Disorders: Fourth Edition*. Washington, DC: American Psychiatric Association.

American Psychiatric Association (2013). *Diagnostic and Statistical Manual of Mental Disorders: Fifth Edition. DSM–5™*. Washington, DC: American Psychiatric Publishing.

Anderson, Robin (1997). Violent Defenses Against Depressive Anxiety. In Roy Schafer (Ed.), *The Contemporary Kleinians of London*, pp. 223–238. Madison, CT: International Universities Press.

Anonymous (1934). A "Harley Street" for the Anxious Poor: Treatment of "Frightening Illnesses". *Banffshire Advertiser*, 17 May, n.p. Box 1. Folder 1. Tavistock Clinic Archives. Tavistock Centre, Tavistock and Portman NHS Trust, London.

Anonymous (1941). Notes of the Quarter. *Social Work*, 2, 1–5.

Anonymous (1949). Problems of Treatment in Psychiatry. *Medical Echo*, 25, 40–44.

Anonymous (n.d.). Notes: The Institute of Marital Studies, Formerly the Family Discussion Bureau. The Development of a Non-Medical Path into Work with Marital and Related Family Problems. Unpublished manuscript. SA/TCC/A/1/11. Tavistock Centre for Couple Relationships. Archives and Manuscripts, Rare Materials Room, Wellcome Library, Wellcome Collection, The Wellcome Building, London.

Ansbacher, Heinz L. (1981). Discussion of Alfred Adler's Preface to *The Diary of Vaslav Nijinsky*. *Archives of General Psychiatry*, 38, 836–841.

Anthony, E. James (1957). An Experimental Approach to the Psychopathology of Childhood: Encopresis. *British Journal of Medical Psychology*, 30, 146–175.

Attlee, Clement R. (1920). *The Social Worker*. London: G. Bell and Sons.

Attlee, Clement R. (1954). *As It Happened*. London: William Heinemann.

Bagenal, Alison (1949a). Letter to Donald W. Winnicott, 24 April. PP/ DWW/B/D/21. Donald Woods Winnicott Collection. Archives and Manuscripts, Rare Materials Room, Wellcome Library, Wellcome Collection, The Wellcome Building, London.

Bagenal, Alison (1949b). Letter to Donald W. Winnicott, 27 July. PP/ DWW/B/D/21. Donald Woods Winnicott Collection. Archives and Manuscripts, Rare Materials Room, Wellcome Library, Wellcome Collection, The Wellcome Building, London.

Bagenal, Alison (n.d.). Letter to Donald W. Winnicott, 6 April. PP/ DWW/B/D/21. Donald Woods Winnicott Collection. Archives and Manuscripts, Rare Materials Room, Wellcome Library, Wellcome Collection, The Wellcome Building, London.

Balint, Enid (1974). Letter to Douglas Woodhouse, 27 June. SA/ TCC/B/3/1. Tavistock Centre for Couple Relationships. Archives and Manuscripts, Rare Materials Room, Wellcome Library, Wellcome Collection, The Wellcome Building, London.

Balint, Enid (n.d.). The Girl on the Roof, or Listening to Strangers (Unfinished and Unpublished). Cited in Jennifer Johns, The Enid Files. In Judit Szekacs-Weisz and Tom Keve (Eds.), *Ferenczi for Our Time: Theory and Practice*, pp. 91–99. London: Karnac Books, 2012.

Balint, Enid, and Balint, Michael (1953). Letter to Family Discussion Bureau, 17 January. SA/TCC/A/2/1. Tavistock Centre for Couple Relationships. Archives and Manuscripts, Rare Materials Room, Wellcome Library, Wellcome Collection, The Wellcome Building, London.

Balint, Michael (1948). On Genital Love. *International Journal of Psycho-Analysis, 29*, 34–40.

Bannister, Kathleen; Lyons, Alison; Pincus, Lily; Robb, James; Shooter, Antonia; and Stephens, Judith (1955). *Social Casework in Marital Problems: The Development of a Psychodynamic Approach. A Study by a Group of Caseworkers.* London: Tavistock Publications.

Barlow, Kenneth (1985). The Peckham Experiment. *Medical History, 29*, 264–271.

Barron, Ian G., and Topping, Keith J. (2011). Sexual Abuse Prevention Programme Fidelity: Video Analysis of Interactions. *Child Abuse Review, 20*, 134–151.

Barrows, Paul (1996). Soiling Children: The Oedipal Configuration. *Journal of Child Psychotherapy, 22*, 240–260.

Bathurst, Georgina; Brown, Sibyl Clement; Bowlby, John; Bullen, G.A.; Fairbairn, Nancy; Isaacs, Susan; Mercer, N.S.; Rooff, Madeline; and Thouless, Robert H. (1941). *The Cambridge Evacuation Survey: A Wartime Study in Social Welfare and Education.* Susan Isaacs, Sibyl Clement Brown, and Robert H. Thouless (Eds.). London: Methuen and Company.

Beckett, Francis (1997). *Clem Attlee.* London: Richard Cohen Books.

Bernstein, Isidor (1959). Book Review of Donald W. Winnicott, *Collected Papers: Through Paediatrics to Psycho-Analysis. Psychoanalytic Quarterly, 28*, 389–391.

Beveridge, William (1942). *Social Insurance and Allied Services.* London: His Majesty's Stationery Office.

Bew, John (2016). *Citizen Clem: A Biography of Attlee.* London: riverrun/ Quercus Editions, Hachette UK.

Bion, Wilfred R. (1948a). Experiences in Groups: I. *Human Relations, 1*, 314–320.

Bion, Wilfred R. (1948b). Experiences in Groups: II. *Human Relations, 1*, 487–496.

Bion, Wilfred R. (1949a). Experiences in Groups: III. *Human Relations, 2*, 13–22.

Bion, Wilfred R. (1949b). Experiences in Groups: IV. *Human Relations, 2*, 295–301.

Bion, Wilfred R. (1950a). Experiences in Groups: V. *Human Relations, 3*, 3–14.

Bion, Wilfred R. (1950b). Experiences in Groups: VI. *Human Relations, 3,* 395–402.

Bion, Wilfred R. (1951). Experiences in Groups: VII. *Human Relations, 4,* 221–227.

Bion, Wilfred R. (1961). *Experiences in Groups and Other Papers.* London: Tavistock Publications.

Bion, Wilfred R. (1970). *Attention and Interpretation: A Scientific Approach to Insight in Psycho-Analysis and Groups.* London: Tavistock Publications.

Blackman, Noëlle (2003). *Loss and Learning Disability.* London: Worth Publishing.

Bleuler, Eugen (1911). *Dementia Praecox oder Gruppe der Schizophrenien.* In Gustav Aschaffenburg (Ed.), *Handbuch der Psychiatrie: Spezieller Teil. 4. Abteilung, 1. Hälfte,* pp. vii–420. Vienna: Franz Deuticke.

Bloch, Donald A. (1990). Carl/a Auer: An Invention. In Gunthard Weber and Fritz B. Simon (Eds.), *Carl Auer: Geist oder Ghost,* pp. 112, 114, 116, 118, 120, 122. Heidelberg: Carl-Auer-Systeme Verlag und Verlagsbuchhandlung.

Bloch, R. Howard (1991). *Medieval Misogyny and the Invention of Western Romantic Love.* Chicago, Illinois: University of Chicago Press.

Blum, Harold P. (1983). The Position and Value of Extratransference Interpretation. *Journal of the American Psychoanalytic Association, 31,* 587–617.

Blum, Harold P. (2016). A Psychoanalytic Odyssey. *American Imago, 73,* 417–434.

Bolland, Helen (1952). Letter to Benjamin E. Astbury, 31 July. SA/TCC/B/2/1. Tavistock Centre for Couple Relationships. Archives and Manuscripts, Rare Materials Room, Wellcome Library, Wellcome Collection, The Wellcome Building, London.

Bollas, Christopher, and Sundelson, David (1995). *The New Informants: The Betrayal of Confidentiality in Psychoanalysis and Psychotherapy.* London: H. Karnac (Books).

Borch-Jacobsen, Mikkel (2011). *Les Patients de Freud: Destins.* Auxerre Cedex: Sciences Humaines Éditions.

Bosanquet, Helen (1914). *Social Work in London: 1869 to 1912. A History of the Charity Organisation Society.* London: John Murray.

Bourke, Joanna (2007). *Rape: A History from 1860 to the Present Day.* London: Virago.

Bowlby, John (1939). Hysteria in Children. In Ronald G. Gordon (Ed.), *A Survey of Child Psychiatry,* pp. 80–94. London: Humphrey Milford/Oxford University Press.

Bowlby, John (1940a). The Problem of the Young Child. In John Rickman (Ed.), *Children in War-Time: The Uprooted Child, the Problem of the Young Child, the Deprived Mother, Foster-Parents, Visiting, the Teacher's Problems, Homes for Difficult Children*, pp. 19–30. London: New Education Fellowship.

Bowlby, John (1940b). The Influence of Early Environment in the Development of Neurosis and Neurotic Character. *International Journal of Psycho-Analysis, 21,* 154–178.

Bowlby, John (1944a). Forty-Four Juvenile Thieves: Their Characters and Home-Life. *International Journal of Psycho-Analysis, 25,* 19–53.

Bowlby, John (1944b). Forty-Four Juvenile Thieves: Their Characters and Home-Life (II). *International Journal of Psycho-Analysis, 25,* 107–128.

Bowlby, John (1946). *Forty-Four Juvenile Thieves: Their Characters and Home-Life.* Covent Garden, London: Baillière, Tindall and Cox.

Bowlby, John (1949a). The Study and Reduction of Group Tensions in the Family. *Human Relations, 2,* 123–128.

Bowlby, John (1949b). Letter to Enid Eicholz [*sic*] [Enid Eichholz], 12 August. SA/TCC/A/2/2. Tavistock Centre for Couple Relationships. Archives and Manuscripts, Rare Materials Room, Wellcome Library, Wellcome Collection, The Wellcome Building, London.

Bowlby, John (1949c). Letter to Enid Eicholz [*sic*] [Enid Eichholz], 28 November. SA/TCC/A/2/2. Tavistock Centre for Couple Relationships. Archives and Manuscripts, Rare Materials Room, Wellcome Library, Wellcome Collection, The Wellcome Building, London.

Bowlby, John (1988). *A Secure Base: Clinical Applications of Attachment Theory.* London: Routledge.

Bowlby, John; Miller, Emanuel; and Winnicott, Donald W. (1939). Evacuation of Small Children. *British Medical Journal,* 16 December, pp. 1202–1203.

Brennan, Brenda (1944). Letter to Donald W. Winnicott, 23 July. PP/DWW/B/D/21. Donald Woods Winnicott Collection. Archives and Manuscripts, Rare Materials Room, Wellcome Library, Wellcome Collection, The Wellcome Building, London.

Breuer, Josef (1895). Beobachtung I. Frl. Anna O . . . In Josef Breuer and Sigmund Freud, *Studien über Hysterie*, pp. 15–37. Vienna: Franz Deuticke.

Bridger, Harold (1985). Northfield Revisited. In Malcolm Pines (Ed.), *Bion and Group Psychotherapy*, pp. 87–107. London: Routledge & Kegan Paul.

Britton, Clare (1943a). Letter to Donald W. Winnicott, 4 January. PP/ DWW/L.4. Donald Woods Winnicott Collection. Archives and Manuscripts, Rare Materials Room, Wellcome Library, Wellcome Collection, The Wellcome Building, London.

Britton, Clare (1943b). Letter to Donald W. Winnicott, 5 April. PP/ DWW/L.4. Donald Woods Winnicott Collection. Archives and Manuscripts, Rare Materials Room, Wellcome Library, Wellcome Collection, The Wellcome Building, London.

Britton, Clare (1943c). Letter to Donald W. Winnicott, 12 July. PP/ DWW/L.4. Donald Woods Winnicott Collection. Archives and Manuscripts, Rare Materials Room, Wellcome Library, Wellcome Collection, The Wellcome Building, London.

Britton, Clare (1943d). Letter to Donald W. Winnicott, 25 October. PP/ DWW/L.4. Donald Woods Winnicott Collection. Archives and Manuscripts, Rare Materials Room, Wellcome Library, Wellcome Collection, The Wellcome Building, London.

Britton, Ronald (1989). The Missing Link: Parental Sexuality in the Oedipus Complex. In Ronald Britton, Michael Feldman, and Edna O'Shaughnessy, *The Oedipus Complex Today: Clinical Implications*, John Steiner (Ed.), pp. 83–101. London: H. Karnac (Books).

Brody, Morris W. (1974). Interpretation in Psychoanalysis: Some Clinical Considerations. *International Journal of Psychoanalytic Psychotherapy, 3,* 204–216.

Brooks, Lilian (1971). Letter to Clare Winnicott, 16 March. PP/DWW/G/6 /1. Folder 2. Donald Woods Winnicott Collection. Archives and Manuscripts, Rare Materials Room, Wellcome Library, Wellcome Collection, The Wellcome Building, London.

Buckle, Richard (1971). *Nijinsky*. London: Weidenfeld and Nicolson.

Burn, Gordon (1984). *Somebody's Husband, Somebody's Son: The Story of Peter Sutcliffe*. London: Heinemann/William Heinemann.

Burridge, Trevor (1985). *Clement Attlee: A Political Biography*. London: Jonathan Cape.

Butler, Sara M. (2007). *The Language of Abuse: Marital Violence in Later Medieval England*. Leiden: Brill/Koninklijke Brill.

Caine, Osmund (1949). Letter to Donald W. Winnicott, 12 February. PP/ DWW/B/D/15. Donald Woods Winnicott Collection. Archives and Manuscripts, Rare Materials Room, Wellcome Library, Wellcome Collection, The Wellcome Building, London.

Casement, Patrick J. (1982). Some Pressures on the Analyst for Physical Contact During the Re-Living of an Early Trauma. *International Review of Psycho-Analysis, 9,* 279–286.

Casement, Patrick (1986). Interpretation: Fresh Insight or Cliché? *Free Associations*, *5*, 90–104.

Celenza, Andrea, and Gabbard, Glen O. (2003). Analysts Who Commit Sexual Boundary Violations: A Lost Cause? *Journal of the American Psychoanalytic Association*, *51*, 617–636.

Chidester, Leona, and Menninger, Karl A. (1936). The Application of Psychoanalytic Methods to the Study of Mental Retardation. *American Journal of Orthopsychiatry*, *6*, 616–625.

Clark, Leon Pierce; Uniker, Thomas E.; Cushing, W. K.; Rourke, Ethel L.; and Cairns, Margaret C. (1933). *The Nature and Treatment of Amentia: Psychoanalysis and Mental Arrest in Relation to the Science of Intelligence.* Baltimore, MD: William Wood and Company.

Clulow, Christopher (1990). Introduction. In Christopher Clulow (Ed.), *Marriage: Disillusion and Hope. Papers Celebrating Forty Years of the Tavistock Institute of Marital Studies*, pp. 1–4. London: H. Karnac (Books).

Clulow, Christopher (2001a). Introduction. In Christopher Clulow (Ed.), *Adult Attachment and Couple Psychotherapy: The "Secure Base" in Practice and Research*, pp. 1–11. Hove, East Sussex: Routledge.

Clulow, Christopher (2001b). Attachment, Narcissism and the Violent Couple. In Christopher Clulow (Ed.), *Adult Attachment and Couple Psychotherapy: The "Secure Base" in Practice and Research*, pp. 132–151. Hove, East Sussex: Routledge.

Cohen, Deborah (2013). *Family Secrets: Living with Shame from the Victorians to the Present Day.* London: Viking/Penguin Books, Penguin Group.

Cole, Robert H. (1913). *Mental Diseases: A Text-Book of Psychiatry for Medical Students and Practitioners.* London: University of London Press.

Coles, Joyce (1971). The P.L. Loses a Friend. *Plan: Monthly Journal of the Progressive League*, *41* (4), 8–9.

Coltrera, Joseph T. (1981). On the Nature of Interpretation: Epistemology as Practice. In Shelley Orgel and Bernard D. Fine (Eds.), *Clinical Psychoanalysis: Volume III. Downstate Psychoanalytic Institute. Twenty-Fifth Anniversary Series*, pp. 83–127. New York: Jason Aronson.

Cooper, Duff (1945). Diary Entry, 6 March. In *The Duff Cooper Diaries: 1915–1951*, John Julius Norwich (Ed.), pp. 356–357. London: Weidenfeld and Nicolson, 2005.

Corbett, Alan (2014). *Disabling Perversions: Forensic Psychotherapy with People with Intellectual Disabilities.* London: Karnac Books.

Cosens, Marjorie (1940). Evacuation: A Social Revolution. *Social Work*, *1*, 165–182.

Cottis, Tamsin (Ed.) (2009a). *Intellectual Disability, Trauma and Psychotherapy*. London: Routledge / Taylor and Francis Group, and Hove, East Sussex: Routledge / Taylor and Francis Group.

Cottis, Tamsin (2009b). Life Support or Intensive Care? Endings and Outcomes in Psychotherapy for People with Intellectual Disabilities. In Tamsin Cottis (Ed.), *Intellectual Disability, Trauma and Psychotherapy*, pp. 189–204. London: Routledge / Taylor and Francis Group, and Hove, East Sussex: Routledge / Taylor and Francis Group.

Coward, Noël (1945). Diary Entry, 29 April. In Graham Payn and Sheridan Morley (Eds.), *The Noel Coward Diaries*, p. 26. London: Weidenfeld and Nicolson/George Weidenfeld and Nicolson, 1982.

Crichton Miller, Hugh (1921). *The New Psychology and the Teacher*. London: Jarrolds.

Crichton Miller, Hugh (1922). The Outlook for Analytical Psychology in Medicine. *Medical Press and Circular*, 14 June, pp. 409–411.

Culpin, Millais (1924). *The Nervous Patient*. London: H.K. Lewis.

Culpin, Millais (1927). *Medicine: And the Man*. London: Kegan Paul, Trench, Trubner and Company.

Darley, Gillian (1990). *Octavia Hill*. London: Constable.

Davies, Daniel T., and Wilson, A. Thomson M. (1937). Observations on the Life-History of Chronic Peptic Ulcer. *The Lancet*, 11 December, pp. 1353–1360.

Dax, Eric Cunningham (1949). Physical Methods of Treatment. In John R. Rees (Ed.), *Modern Practice in Psychological Medicine 1949*, pp. 357–380. London: Butterworth and Company.

de Maré, Patrick B. (1985). Major Bion. In Malcolm Pines (Ed.), *Bion and Group Psychotherapy*, pp. 108–113. London: Routledge & Kegan Paul.

de Salies, Alexandre (1874). *Histoire de Foulques-Nerra: Comte d'Anjou. D'Après les chartres contemporaines et les anciennes chroniques. Suivie de l'office du Saint-Sépulcre de l'abbaye de Beaulieu dont les leçons forment une chronique inédite. Avec 12 planches et une grande carte*. Paris: J.-B. Dumoulin, Libraire, and Angers: E. Barassé, Imprimerie-Libraire.

Dicks, Henry V. (1970). *Fifty Years of the Tavistock Clinic*. London: Routledge & Kegan Paul.

Donoho, Carrie J.; Crimmins, Eileen M.; and Seeman, Teresa E. (2013). Marital Quality, Gender, and Markers of Inflammation in the MIDUS Cohort. *Journal of Marriage and Family*, 75, 127–141.

Double, Duncan B. (2006). Historical Perspectives on Anti-psychiatry. In Duncan B. Double (Ed.), *Critical Psychiatry: The Limits of Madness*, pp. 19–39. Houndmills, Basingstoke, Hampshire: Palgrave Macmillan.

Dragstedt, Naome Rader (1998). Creative Illusions: The Theoretical and Clinical Work of Marion Milner. *Journal of Melanie Klein and Object Relations, 16,* 425–536.

Duval, Jules (1867). *Gheel ou une colonie des aliénés vivant en famille et en liberté: Étude sur le patronage familial appliqué au traitement des maladies mentales. Avec une carte de la commune de Gheel.* Paris: Hachette et Compagnie, Libraires-Éditeurs.

Eichholz, Enid (1944). Londoners and the Flying Bomb: (From the Point of View of the C.A.B. Worker.). *Social Work, 3,* 91–95.

Eichholz, Enid (1948a). Draft Letter to Medical Officer of Health, Middlesex County Council. n.d. SA/TCC/A/2/2. Tavistock Centre for Couple Relationships. Archives and Manuscripts, Rare Materials Room, Wellcome Library, Wellcome Collection, The Wellcome Building, London.

Eichholz, Enid (1948b). Letter to John Bowlby, 19 July. SA/TCC/A/2/2. Tavistock Centre for Couple Relationships. Archives and Manuscripts, Rare Materials Room, Wellcome Library, Wellcome Collection, The Wellcome Building, London.

Eichholz, Enid (1948c). Letter to P.S. [*sic*] Main [Thomas Main], 21 July. SA/TCC/A/2/3. Tavistock Centre for Couple Relationships. Archives and Manuscripts, Rare Materials Room, Wellcome Library, Wellcome Collection, The Wellcome Building, London.

Eichholz, Enid (1948d). Letter to William Morison McIntyre, 15 September. SA/TCC/A/2/3. Tavistock Centre for Couple Relationships. Archives and Manuscripts, Rare Materials Room, Wellcome Library, Wellcome Collection, The Wellcome Building, London.

Eichholz, Enid (1948e). Letter to John Sutherland, 26 October. SA/TCC/A/2/8. Tavistock Centre for Couple Relationships. Archives and Manuscripts, Rare Materials Room, Wellcome Library, Wellcome Collection, The Wellcome Building, London.

Eichholz, Enid (1949a). Research Project into the Social Structure and Social Needs of Communities. Unpublished manuscript notes. SA/TCC/A/2/9. Tavistock Centre for Couple Relationships. Archives and Manuscripts, Rare Materials Room, Wellcome Library, Wellcome Collection, The Wellcome Building, London.

Eichholz, Enid (1949b). Staffing Plans. Unpublished memorandum. SA/TCC/A/2/1. Tavistock Centre for Couple Relationships. Archives and Manuscripts, Rare Materials Room, Wellcome Library, Wellcome Collection, The Wellcome Building, London.

Eichholz, Enid (1949c). Note. n.d. SA/TCC/A/2/1. Tavistock Centre for Couple Relationships. Archives and Manuscripts, Rare Materials

Room, Wellcome Library, Wellcome Collection, The Wellcome Building, London.

Eichholz, Enid (1949d). Letter to Doreen Widdell [*sic*] [Doreen Weddell], 14 January. SA/TCC/A/2/3. Tavistock Centre for Couple Relationships. Archives and Manuscripts, Rare Materials Room, Wellcome Library, Wellcome Collection, The Wellcome Building, London.

Eichholz, Enid (1949e). Letter to Doreen Weddell, 24 February. SA/TCC/A/2/3. Tavistock Centre for Couple Relationships. Archives and Manuscripts, Rare Materials Room, Wellcome Library, Wellcome Collection, The Wellcome Building, London.

Eichholz, Enid (1949f). Letter to Michael Balint, 25 March. SA/TCC/A/2/1. Tavistock Centre for Couple Relationships. Archives and Manuscripts, Rare Materials Room, Wellcome Library, Wellcome Collection, The Wellcome Building, London.

Eichholz, Enid (1949g). Letter to Michael Balint, 18 July. SA/TCC/A/2/1. Tavistock Centre for Couple Relationships. Archives and Manuscripts, Rare Materials Room, Wellcome Library, Wellcome Collection, The Wellcome Building, London.

Eichholz, Enid (1949h). Letter to Michael Balint, 9 August. SA/TCC/A/2/1. Tavistock Centre for Couple Relationships. Archives and Manuscripts, Rare Materials Room, Wellcome Library, Wellcome Collection, The Wellcome Building, London.

Eichholz, Enid (1949i). Letter to John Bowlby, 9 August. SA/TCC/A/2/2. Tavistock Centre for Couple Relationships. Archives and Manuscripts, Rare Materials Room, Wellcome Library, Wellcome Collection, The Wellcome Building, London.

Eichholz, Enid (1949j). Letter to John Bowlby, 29 August. SA/TCC/A/2/2. Tavistock Centre for Couple Relationships. Archives and Manuscripts, Rare Materials Room, Wellcome Library, Wellcome Collection, The Wellcome Building, London.

Eichholz, Enid (1950a). Visit by Mrs Eichholz. Unpublished note. SA/TCC/A/2/3. Tavistock Centre for Couple Relationships. Archives and Manuscripts, Rare Materials Room, Wellcome Library, Wellcome Collection, The Wellcome Building, London.

Eichholz, Enid (1950b). Letter to A. Thomson M. Wilson, 5 January. SA/TCC/A/2/9. Tavistock Centre for Couple Relationships. Archives and Manuscripts, Rare Materials Room, Wellcome Library, Wellcome Collection, The Wellcome Building, London.

Eichholz, Enid (1950c). Letter to Noël Hunnybun, 8 February. SA/TCC/A/2/5. Tavistock Centre for Couple Relationships. Archives and Manuscripts, Rare Materials Room, Wellcome Library, Wellcome Collection, The Wellcome Building, London.

Eichholz, Enid (1950d). Letter to Millicent Dewar, 27 February. SA/ TCC/A/2/4. Tavistock Centre for Couple Relationships. Archives and Manuscripts, Rare Materials Room, Wellcome Library, Wellcome Collection, The Wellcome Building, London.

Eichholz, Enid (1952a). Memorandum on the Work of the Family Discussion Bureaux for the Period April 1951 to March 1952. Unpublished manuscript. SA/TCC/B/1/3/2. Tavistock Centre for Couple Relationships. Archives and Manuscripts, Rare Materials Room, Wellcome Library, Wellcome Collection, The Wellcome Building, London.

Eichholz, Enid (1952b). Letter to Noël K. Hunnybun, 7 March. SA/ TCC/A/2/5. Tavistock Centre for Couple Relationships. Archives and Manuscripts, Rare Materials Room, Wellcome Library, Wellcome Collection, The Wellcome Building, London.

Eissler, Kurt R. (1952). *Interview with Dr Adolph Stern: November 13, 1952*. Unpublished transcript. Box 122. Folder 10. Sigmund Freud Papers. Sigmund Freud Collection, Manuscript Reading Room, Room 101, Manuscript Division, James Madison Memorial Building, Library of Congress, Washington, DC.

Eissler, Kurt R. (1953). *Sonoband No. 17: Sir Arthur Tansley. Summer 1953*. Unpublished transcript. Box 122. Folder 12. Sigmund Freud Papers. Sigmund Freud Collection, Manuscript Reading Room, Room 101, Manuscript Division, James Madison Memorial Building, Library of Congress, Washington, DC.

Epstein, Lawrence (1977). The Therapeutic Function of Hate in the Countertransference. *Contemporary Psychoanalysis*, *13*, 442–461.

Family Discussion Bureau (n.d.). Estimate of Expenditure for the Period 1 April 1952–31 March 1953. Unpublished memorandum. SA/ TCC/B/1/3/2. Tavistock Centre for Couple Relationships. Archives and Manuscripts, Rare Materials Room, Wellcome Library, Wellcome Collection, The Wellcome Building, London.

Farber, Stephen, and Green, Marc (1993). *Hollywood on the Couch: A Candid Look at the Overheated Love Affair between Psychiatrists and Moviemakers*. New York: William Morrow and Company.

Farrell, Nicholas (2003). *Mussolini: A New Life*. London: Weidenfeld and Nicolson/Orion Publishing Group.

Fenichel, Otto (1942). Book Review of Edward Glover and Marjorie Brierley, *An Investigation of the Technique of Psycho-Analysis*. *Psychoanalytic Quarterly*, *11*, 230–234.

Ferenczi, Sándor (1931). Child-Analysis in the Analysis of Adults. *International Journal of Psycho-Analysis*, *12*, 468–482.

Finkelhor, David, and Yllo, Kersti (1985). *License to Rape: Sexual Abuse of Wives*. New York: Holt, Rinehart and Winston.

Fliess, Robert (1949). Silence and Verbalization: A Supplement to the Theory of the "Analytic Rule". *International Journal of Psycho-Analysis*, *30*, 21–30.

Flynn, Denis (1987). Internal Conflict and Growth in a Child Preparing to Start School. *Journal of Child Psychotherapy*, *13* (1), 77–91.

Forth, Mary J. (1992). The Little-Girl Lost: Psychotherapy with an Anal-Retentive and Soiling Four Year Old. *Journal of Child Psychotherapy*, *18* (2), 63–85.

Fraher, Amy L. (2004). *A History of Group Study and Psychodynamic Organizations*. London: Free Association Books.

Frankish, Patricia (2016). *Disability Psychotherapy: An Innovative Approach to Trauma-Informed Care*. London: Karnac Books.

Frederickson, Jon (1990). Hate in the Countertransference as an Empathic Position. *Contemporary Psychoanalysis*, *26*, 479–496.

Freeman, Lucy (1951). *Fight Against Fears*. New York: Crown Publishers.

Freeman, Michael D. A. (1979). The Law and Sexual Deviation. In Ismond Rosen (Ed.), *Sexual Deviation: Second Edition*, pp. 376–440. Oxford: Oxford University Press.

French, Thomas M. (1970). *Psychoanalytic Interpretations: The Selected Papers of Thomas M. French, M.D.* Chicago, Illinois: Quadrangle Books.

Freud, Anna (1963). The Concept of Developmental Lines. *Psychoanalytic Study of the Child*, *18*, 245–265. New York: International Universities Press.

Freud, Anna (1967). About Losing and Being Lost. *Psychoanalytic Study of the Child*, *22*, 9–19. New York: International Universities Press.

Freud, Sigmund (1895). Fräulein Elisabeth v. R … In Josef Breuer and Sigmund Freud, *Studien über Hysterie*, pp. 116–160. Vienna: Franz Deuticke.

Freud, Sigmund (1898a). Letter to Wilhelm Fliess, 7 July. In Sigmund Freud, *Briefe an Wilhelm Fliess 1887–1904: Ungekürzte Ausgabe*, Jeffrey Moussaieff Masson and Michael Schröter (Eds.), pp. 348–350. Frankfurt am Main: S. Fischer/S. Fischer Verlag, 1986.

Freud, Sigmund (1898b). Letter to Wilhelm Fliess, 7 July. In Sigmund Freud, *The Complete Letters of Sigmund Freud to Wilhelm Fliess: 1887–1904*, Jeffrey Moussaieff Masson (Ed.), Lottie Newman, Marianne Loring, and Jeffrey Moussaieff Masson (Transls.), pp. 319–320. Cambridge, MA: Belknap Press of Harvard University Press, 1985.

Freud, Sigmund (1900). *Die Traumdeutung*. Vienna: Franz Deuticke.

Freud, Sigmund (1901a). Zur Psychopathologie des Alltagslebens: (Vergessen, Versprechen, Vergreifen) nebst Bemerkungen über eine Wurzel des Aberglaubens. [Part One]. *Monatsschrift für Psychiatrie und Neurologie, 10,* 1–32.

Freud, Sigmund (1901b). Zur Psychopathologie des Alltagslebens: (Vergessen, Versprechen, Vergreifen) nebst Bemerkungen über eine Wurzel des Aberglaubens. [Part Two]. *Monatsschrift für Psychiatrie und Neurologie, 10,* 95–143.

Freud, Sigmund (1904a). *Zur Psychopathologie des Alltagslebens: (Über Vergessen, Versprechen, Vergreifen, Aberglaube und Irrtum)*. Berlin: Verlag von S. Karger.

Freud, Sigmund (1904b). Die Freud'sche psychoanalytische Methode. In Leopold Loewenfeld, *Die psychischen Zwangserscheinungen: Auf klinischer Grundlage dargestellt*, pp. 545–551. Wiesbaden: Verlag von J.F. Bergmann.

Freud, Sigmund (1904c). Freud's Psycho-Analytic Procedure. Judith Bernays and James Strachey (Transls.). In *The Standard Edition of the Complete Psychological Works of Sigmund Freud: Volume VII (1901–1905). A Case of Hysteria. Three Essays on Sexuality and Other Works*, James Strachey, Anna Freud, Alix Strachey, and Alan Tyson (Eds. and Transls.), pp. 249–254. London: Hogarth Press and the Institute of Psycho-Analysis, 1953.

Freud, Sigmund (1905). *Drei Abhandlungen zur Sexualtheorie*. Vienna: Franz Deuticke.

Freud, Sigmund (1906). Letter to Carl Gustav Jung, 27 October. In Sigmund Freud and Carl Gustav Jung, *Briefwechsel*, William McGuire and Wolfgang Sauerländer (Eds.), pp. 8–9. Frankfurt am Main: S. Fischer/S. Fischer Verlag, 1974.

Freud, Sigmund (1907). Letter to Carl Gustav Jung, 14 April. In Sigmund Freud and Carl Gustav Jung, *Briefwechsel*, William McGuire and Wolfgang Sauerländer (Eds.), pp. 35–38. Frankfurt am Main: S. Fischer/S. Fischer Verlag, 1974.

Freud, Sigmund (1909a). Bemerkungen über einen Fall von Zwangsneurose. *Jahrbuch für psychoanalytische und psychopathologische Forschungen, 1,* 357–421.

Freud, Sigmund (1909b). Notes Upon a Case of Obsessional Neurosis. Alix Strachey and James Strachey (Transls.). In *The Standard Edition of the Complete Psychological Works of Sigmund Freud: Volume X. (1909). Two Case Histories ("Little Hans" and the "Rat Man")*, James Strachey, Anna Freud, Alix Strachey, and Alan Tyson (Eds. and Transls.), pp.

155–249. London: Hogarth Press and the Institute of Psycho-Analysis, 1955.

Freud, Sigmund (1910). Beiträge zur Psychologie des Liebeslebens: I. Über einen besonderen Typus der Objektwahl beim Manne. *Jahrbuch für psychoanalytische und psychopathologische Forschungen*, 2, 389–397.

Freud, Sigmund (1912). Beiträge zur Psychologie des Liebeslebens: II. Über die allgemeinste Erniedrigung des Liebeslebens. *Jahrbuch für psychoanalytische und psychopathologische Forschungen*, 4, 40–50.

Freud, Sigmund (1914). Weitere Ratschläge zur Technik der Psychoanalyse: II. Erinnern, Wiederholen und Durcharbeiten. *Internationale Zeitschrift für ärztliche Psychoanalyse*, 2, 485–491.

Freud, Sigmund (1916). Einige Charaktertypen aus der psychoanalytischen Arbeit. *Imago*, 4, 317–336.

Freud, Sigmund (1918). Beiträge zur Psychologie des Liebeslebens: III. Das Tabu der Virginität. In *Sammlung kleiner Schriften zur Neurosenlehre: Vierte Folge*, pp. 229–251. Vienna: Hugo Heller und Compagnie.

Freud, Sigmund (1919). "Ein Kind wird geschlagen": Beitrag zur Kenntnis der Entstehung sexueller Perversionen. *Internationale Zeitschrift für ärztliche Psychoanalyse*, 5, 151–172.

Freud, Sigmund (1923a). Bemerkungen zur Theorie und Praxis der Traumdeutung. *Internationale Zeitschrift für Psychoanalyse*, 9, 1–11.

Freud, Sigmund (1923b). Remarks on the Theory and Practice of Dream-Interpretation. In *The Standard Edition of the Complete Psychological Works of Sigmund Freud: Volume XIX. (1923–1925). The Ego and the Id and Other Works*, James Strachey, Anna Freud, Alix Strachey, and Alan Tyson (Eds. and Transls.), pp. 109–121. London: Hogarth Press and the Institute of Psycho-Analysis, 1961.

Freud, Sigmund (1928a). Letter to István Hollós, 10 April. Box 15. Freud Museum London, London.

Freud, Sigmund (1928b). Letter to István Hollós, 10 April. Peter Gay (Transl.). Cited in Peter Gay. *Freud: A Life for Our Time*, p. 537. New York: W.W. Norton and Company, 1988.

Freud, Sigmund (1928c). Letter to "Herr Präsident und lieber Bruder", Vereins B'nai B'rith, Vienna, Austria, 22 April. In Walter Boehlich (Ed.), *Jugendbriefe an Eduard Silberstein: 1871–1881*, p. 214. Frankfurt am Main: S. Fischer/S. Fischer Verlag, 1989.

Friedman, Leonard J. (1962). *Virgin Wives: A Study of Unconsummated Marriages*. London: Tavistock Publications, and Springfield, Illinois: Charles C Thomas.

Gabbard, Glen O., and Lester, Eva P. (1995). *Boundaries and Boundary Violations in Psychoanalysis*. New York: Basic Books.

General Secretary (1948). Letter to P.S. Maine [*sic*] [Thomas Main], 3 June 1948. SA/TCC/A/2/3. Tavistock Centre for Couple Relationships. Archives and Manuscripts, Rare Materials Room, Wellcome Library, Wellcome Collection, The Wellcome Building, London.

Gilbert, Martin (2006). *Kristallnacht: Prelude to Destruction*. London: HarperCollins.

Giroud, Françoise (1981). *Une Femme honorable*. Paris: Fayard/Librairie Arthème Fayard.

Glass, Shirley P., and Wright, Thomas L. (1977). The Relationship of Extramarital Sex, Length of Marriage, and Sex Differences on Marital Satisfaction and Romanticism: Athanasiou's Data Reanalyzed. *Journal of Marriage and the Family*, *39*, 691–703.

Glover, Edward (1931). The Therapeutic Effect of Inexact Interpretation: A Contribution to the Theory of Suggestion. *International Journal of Psycho-Analysis*, *12*, 397–411.

Glover, Edward, and Brierley, Marjorie (Eds.) (1940). *An Investigation of the Technique of Psycho-Analysis*. London: Baillière, Tindall and Cox.

Godley, Wynne (2001a). Saving Masud Khan. *London Review of Books*, 22 February, pp. 3, 5–7.

Godley, Wynne (2001b). My Lost Hours on the Couch. *The Times*, 23 February, Section 2, pp. 2–5.

Goldberg, Jeremy (2008). *Communal Discord, Child Abduction, and Rape in the Later Middle Ages*. New York: Palgrave Macmillan/St. Martin's Press.

Gonçalves, Camila Salles (1996). Ódio e medo na contratransferência. *Percurso: Revista de psicanálise*, *9* (17), 35–40.

Gorer, Geoffrey, and Rickman, John (1949). *The People of Great Russia: A Psychological Study*. London: Cresset Press.

Gray, Sidney G. (1970). The Tavistock Institute of Human Relations. In Henry V. Dicks, *Fifty Years of the Tavistock Clinic*, pp. 206–227. London: Routledge & Kegan Paul.

Grier, Francis (2001). No Sex Couples, Catastrophic Change and the Primal Scene. *British Journal of Psychotherapy*, *17*, 474–488.

Griffith, Edward F. (1981). *The Pioneer Spirit*. Upton Grey, Basingstoke, Hampshire: Green Leaves Press.

Grosskurth, Phyllis (1981). Interview with Clare Winnicott, 18 September. In *Melanie Klein: Her World and Her Work*. New York: Alfred A. Knopf, 1986.

Guillot, Olivier (1972). *Le Comte d'Anjou et son entourage au XIᵉ siècle: Tome I. Étude et appendices*. Paris: Éditions A. et J. Picard.

Guntrip, Harry (1971). Letter to Clare Winnicott, 19 March. PP/

DWW/G/6/1. Folder 2. Donald Woods Winnicott Collection. Archives and Manuscripts, Rare Materials Room, Wellcome Library, Wellcome Collection, The Wellcome Building, London.

Guntrip, Harry (1975). My Experience of Analysis with Fairbairn and Winnicott: (How Complete a Result Does Psycho-Analytic Therapy Achieve?). *International Review of Psycho-Analysis*, 2, 145–156.

Haggett, Ali (2012). *Desperate Housewives, Neuroses and the Domestic Environment, 1945–1970*. London: Pickering and Chatto / Pickering and Chatto (Publishers).

Haggett, Ali (2015). *A History of Male Psychological Disorders in Britain, 1945–1980*. Houndmills, Basingstoke, Hampshire: Palgrave Macmillan.

Hamilton, Alan (1992). Sad Queen Dubs 1992 Her 'Annus Horribilis'. *The Times*, 25 November, pp. 1, 3.

Hancock, W. K. (1951). *Statistical Digest of the War: Prepared in the Central Statistical Office*. London: His Majesty's Stationery Office/Longmans Green and Company.

Harder, Susanne (2014). Attachment in Schizophrenia: Implications for Research, Prevention, and Treatment. *Schizophrenia Bulletin*, 40, 1189–1193.

Harrington, William, and Young, Peter (1978). *The 1945 Revolution*. London: Davis-Poynter.

Harris, Alana (2015). Love Divine and Love Sublime: The Catholic Marriage Advisory Council, the Marriage Guidance Movement and the State. In Alana Harris and Timothy Willem Jones (Eds.), *Love and Romance in Britain, 1918–1970*, pp. 188–224. Houndmills, Basingstoke, Hampshire: Palgrave Macmillan.

Harris, Kenneth (1982). *Attlee*. London: Weidenfeld and Nicolson.

Harrison, Tom (2000). *Bion, Rickman, Foulkes and the Northfield Experiments: Advancing on a Different Front*. London: Jessica Kingsley Publishers.

Heaton, John M. (2006). From Anti-psychiatry to Critical Psychiatry. In Duncan B. Double (Ed.), *Critical Psychiatry: The Limits of Madness*, pp. 41–59. Houndmills, Basingstoke, Hampshire: Palgrave Macmillan.

Heimann, Paula (1956). Dynamics of Transference Interpretations. *International Journal of Psycho-Analysis*, 37, 303–310.

Hill, William Thomson (1956). *Octavia Hill: Pioneer of the National Trust and Housing Reformer*. London: Hutchinson.

Hinshelwood, Robert D. (1994). *Clinical Klein*. London: Free Association Books.

Hodgkinson, Ruth G. (1967). *The Origins of the National Health Service: The*

Medical Services of the New Poor Law, 1834–1871. London: Wellcome Historical Medical Library.

Hollins, Sheila (1990a). Group Analytic Therapy with People with Mental Handicap. In Anton Došen, Adriaan van Gennep, and Gosewijn J. Zwanikken (Eds.), *Treatment of Mental Illness and Behavioral Disorder in the Mentally Retarded: Proceedings of the International Congress. May 3–4, 1990. Amsterdam, The Netherlands*, pp. 81–89. Leiden: Logon Publications.

Hollins, Sheila (1990b). Grief Therapy for People with Mental Handicap. In Anton Došen, Adriaan van Gennep, and Gosewijn J. Zwanikken (Eds.), *Treatment of Mental Illness and Behavioral Disorder in the Mentally Retarded: Proceedings of the International Congress. May 3—4, 1990, Amsterdam, The Netherlands*, pp. 139–142. Leiden: Logon Publications.

Hollins, Sheila (1997). Counselling and Psychotherapy. In Oliver Russell (Ed.), *Seminars in the Psychiatry of Learning Disabilities*, pp. 245–258. London: Gaskell/Royal College of Psychiatrists.

Hollins, Sheila, and Sinason, Valerie (2000). Psychotherapy, Learning Disabilities and Trauma: New Perspectives. *British Journal of Psychiatry*, 176, 32–36.

Hopkins, Linda (2006). *False Self: The Life of Masud Khan*. New York: Other Press.

Hopkins, Philip (2004). Balint, Michael Maurice [*formerly* Mihaly Bergsmann] (1896–1970). In H. Colin G. Matthew and Brian Harrison (Eds.), *Oxford Dictionary of National Biography: In Association with the British Academy. From the Earliest Times to the Year 2000. Volume 3. Avranches-Barnewall*, pp. 550–553. Oxford: Oxford University Press.

Hughes, Judith (1989). *Reshaping the Psychoanalytic Domain: The Work of Melanie Klein, W.R.D. Fairbairn, and D.W. Winnicott*. Berkeley, CA: University of California Press.

Hunnybun, Noël K. (1949). Letter to Enid Eicholz [*sic*] [Enid Eichholz], 11 August. SA/TCC/A/2/5. Tavistock Centre for Couple Relationships. Archives and Manuscripts, Rare Materials Room, Wellcome Library, Wellcome Collection, The Wellcome Building, London.

Hunnybun, Noël K. (1950a). Letter to Enid Eichholz, 10 February. SA/TCC/A/2/5. Tavistock Centre for Couple Relationships. Archives and Manuscripts, Rare Materials Room, Wellcome Library, Wellcome Collection, The Wellcome Building, London.

Hunnybun, Noël K. (1950b). Letter to Enid Eichholz, 21 August. SA/TCC/A/2/5. Tavistock Centre for Couple Relationships. Archives and Manuscripts, Rare Materials Room, Wellcome Library, Wellcome Collection, The Wellcome Building, London.

Hunnybun, Noël K. (1951). Letter to Enid Eichholz, 24 August. SA/ TCC/A/2/5. Tavistock Centre for Couple Relationships. Archives and Manuscripts, Rare Materials Room, Wellcome Library, Wellcome Collection, The Wellcome Building, London.

Inventory of Furniture at 4 Chandos Street, Cavendish Square, W.1.: 2nd & 3rd Floors. November 16th 1951 (1951). Unpublished memorandum. SA/TCC/B/2/1. Tavistock Centre for Couple Relationships. Archives and Manuscripts, Rare Materials Room, Wellcome Library, Wellcome Collection, The Wellcome Building, London.

James, D. Colin (1991). On Winnicott's "Fear of Breakdown". Lecture to Conference on "Contributions of Donald Winnicott". The British Psycho-Analytical Society, London, at the Cavendish Conference Centre, London, 2 March.

Johns, Jennifer (2009). How Do You Get Where You Want to Be When You Don't Know Where You Want to Be? *Psychoanalytic Inquiry*, *29*, 223–235.

Jones, Ernest (1922). Letter to Sigmund Freud, 22 January. In Sigmund Freud and Ernest Jones, *The Complete Correspondence of Sigmund Freud and Ernest Jones: 1908–1939*, R. Andrew Paskauskas (Ed.), pp. 453–454. Cambridge, MA: Belknap Press of Harvard University Press, 1993.

Jung, Carl Gustav (1907a). Letter to Sigmund Freud, 17 April. In Sigmund Freud and Carl Gustav Jung, *Briefwechsel*, William McGuire and Wolfgang Sauerländer (Eds.), pp. 39–41. Frankfurt am Main: S. Fischer/S. Fischer Verlag, 1974.

Jung, Carl Gustav (1907b). Letter to Sigmund Freud, 13 May. In Sigmund Freud and Carl Gustav Jung, *Briefwechsel*, William McGuire and Wolfgang Sauerländer (Eds.), pp. 47–50. Frankfurt am Main: S. Fischer/S. Fischer Verlag, 1974.

Jung, Carl Gustav (1907c). Letter to Sigmund Freud, 12 June. In Sigmund Freud and Carl Gustav Jung, *Briefwechsel*, William McGuire and Wolfgang Sauerländer (Eds.), pp. 68–70. Frankfurt am Main: S. Fischer/S. Fischer Verlag, 1974.

Kahr, Brett (1986). *Is There Life After Analysis?* Television Interview with Lucy Freeman. *Fifty Minutes: Psychological Analysis of Current Events*. New York: Manhattan Cable Television. Producer: Steven Borns. Director: Steven Borns. [Date of Recording: 1 February 1986. Date of Broadcast: 1 April 1986].

Kahr, Brett (1987). Nijinsky's Madness: A Psychoanalytic Study. Lecture to the Discussion Group on "The Nature of the Creative Process", Fall Meeting, American Psychoanalytic Association, New York, New York, 18 December.

Kahr, Brett (1993). Ancient Infanticide and Modern Schizophrenia: The Clinical Uses of Psychohistorical Research. *Journal of Psychohistory*, 20, 267–273.

Kahr, Brett (1995a). Enid Balint: A Memorial Tribute. *Newsletter. School of Psychotherapy and Counselling*, Autumn Term, pp. 15–18.

Kahr, Brett (1995b). Mucus, Saliva, Urine, Faeces, Semen, Menstrual Blood, Flatus, Vomitus, and Phlegm: On Patients Who Evacuate Bodily Fluids in Psychotherapy. Lecture to the Tavistock Clinic Mental Handicap Workshop, Child and Family Department, Tavistock Clinic, Tavistock Centre, Tavistock and Portman NHS Trust, London, 16 June.

Kahr, Brett (1995c). Breaches of Confidentiality in the History of Psycho-Analysis. Lecture to the Conference on "Celebrating One Hundred Year of Psychoanalysis and Learning from Our Mistakes", European Society for Communicative Psychotherapy. Regent's College, Inner Circle, Regent's Park, London, 3 June.

Kahr, Brett (1996a). *D.W. Winnicott: A Biographical Portrait*. London: H. Karnac (Books).

Kahr, Brett (1996b). Donald Winnicott and the Foundations of Child Psychotherapy. *Journal of Child Psychotherapy*, 22, 327–342.

Kahr, Brett (1997). Patients Who Evacuate Bodily Fluids During Psychotherapy. Lecture to the Tavistock Clinic Mental Handicap Workshop, Child and Family Department, Tavistock Clinic, Tavistock Centre, Tavistock and Portman NHS Trust, London, 10 November.

Kahr, Brett (1999a). The Adventures of a Psychotherapist: Lucy Freeman and Her Fight Against Fear. *Psychotherapy Review*, 1, 199.

Kahr, Brett (1999b). The Adventures of a Psychotherapist: Lucy Freeman's Pioneering Contributions to the Study of Mental Health Journalism. *Psychotherapy Review*, 1, 244–248.

Kahr, Brett (1999c). Book Review of Paul Roazen, *How Freud Worked: First-Hand Accounts of Patients. Psychoanalysis and History*, 1, 273–281.

Kahr, Brett (2000a). "A Harley Street for the Anxious Poor": The Tavistock Clinic in the 1930s. *Psychotherapy Review*, 2, 397–399.

Kahr, Brett (2000b). Towards the Creation of Disability Psychotherapists. *Psychotherapy Review*, 2, 420–423.

Kahr, Brett (2000c). The Institute of Psychotherapy and Disability. *The Psychotherapist*, 14, 18, 21.

Kahr, Brett (2003). Masud Khan's Analysis with Donald Winnicott: On the Hazards of Befriending a Patient. *Free Associations*, 10, 190–222.

Kahr, Brett (2004). Juvenile Paedophilia: The Psychodynamics of an Adolescent. In Charles W. Socarides and Loretta R. Loeb (Eds.), *The Mind of the Paedophile: Psychoanalytic Perspectives*, pp. 95–119. London: H. Karnac (Books).

Kahr, Brett (2005). The Fifteen Key Ingredients of Good Psychotherapy. In Jane Ryan (Ed.), *How Does Psychotherapy Work?*, pp. 1–14. London: H. Karnac (Books).

Kahr, Brett (2006a). Winnicott's Experiments with Physical Contact: Creative Innovation or Chaotic Impingement? In Graeme Galton (Ed.), *Touch Papers: Dialogues on Touch in the Psychoanalytic Space*, pp. 1–14. London: Karnac Books.

Kahr, Brett (2006b). The Handshake. *American Imago, 63*, 359–369.

Kahr, Brett (2007a). *Sex and the Psyche*. London: Allen Lane/Penguin Books, Penguin Group.

Kahr, Brett (2007b). The Infanticidal Attachment. *Attachment: New Directions in Psychotherapy and Relational Psychoanalysis, 1*, 117–132.

Kahr, Brett (2007c). The Infanticidal Attachment in Schizophrenia and Dissociative Identity Disorder. *Attachment: New Directions in Psychotherapy and Relational Psychoanalysis, 1*, 305–309.

Kahr, Brett (2009a). Psychoanalysis and Sexpertise. In Christopher Clulow (Ed.), *Sex, Attachment, and Couple Psychotherapy: Psychoanalytic Perspectives*, pp. 1–23. London: Karnac Books.

Kahr, Brett (2011a). Winnicott's "*Anni Horribiles*": The Biographical Roots of "Hate in the Counter-Transference". *American Imago, 68*, 173–211.

Kahr, Brett (2011b). The Holes in Winnicott's Trousers: The Brilliance and the Failure of a Psychoanalytical Genius. (Object Lessons for Twenty-First Century Clinicians). The Michael Jacobs Annual Lecture, Vaughan Psychotherapy Seminars, Institute of Lifelong Learning, Vaughan College, University of Leicester, Leicester, 12 February.

Kahr, Brett (2012a). The Infanticidal Origins of Psychosis: The Role of Trauma in Schizophrenia. In Judy Yellin and Kate White (Eds.), *Shattered States: Disorganised Attachment and its Repair. The John Bowlby Memorial Conference Monograph 2007*, pp. 7–126. London: Karnac Books.

Kahr, Brett (2012b). Foreword. In Andrew Balfour, Mary Morgan, and Christopher Vincent (Eds.), *How Couple Relationships Shape Our World: Clinical Practice, Research, and Policy Perspectives*, pp. xvii–xxi. London: Karnac Books.

Kahr, Brett (2014a). Series Editor's Foreword: Towards Forensic Disability Psychotherapy. In Alan Corbett, *Disabling Perversions: Forensic Psychotherapy with People with Intellectual Disabilities*, pp. xiii–xxii. London: Karnac Books.

Kahr, Brett (2014b). The Intra-Marital Affair: From Erotic Tumour to Conjugal Aneurysm. Lecture to the Conference on "The Couple in the Room, the Couple in Mind: Reflections from an Attachment Perspective", the 21st John Bowlby Memorial Conference 2014, The Bowlby Centre, Highbury East, London, at The Kennedy Lecture Theatre, Wellcome Trust Building, Institute of Child Health, University College London, University of London, London, 4 April.

Kahr, Brett (2015a). Winnicott's *Anni Horribiles*: The Biographical Roots of "Hate in the Counter-Transference". In Margaret Boyle Spelman and Frances Thomson-Salo (Eds.), *The Winnicott Tradition: Lines of Development—Evolution of Theory and Practice Over the Decades*, pp. 69–84. London: Karnac Books.

Kahr, Brett (2015b). "Led Astray by Their Half-Baked Pseudo-Scientific Rubbish": John Bowlby and the Paradigm Shift in Child Psychiatry. *Attachment: New Directions in Psychotherapy and Relational Psychoanalysis, 9*, 297–317.

Kahr, Brett (2017a). From the Treatment of a Compulsive Spitter: A Psychoanalytical Approach to Profound Disability. *British Journal of Psychotherapy, 33*, 31–47.

Kahr, Brett (2017b). "How to Cure Family Disturbance": Enid Balint and the Creation of Couple Psychoanalysis. Twenty-first Enid Balint Memorial Lecture 2016. *Couple and Family Psychoanalysis, 7*, 1–25.

Kahr, Brett (2018a). Committing Crimes without Breaking the Law: Unconscious Sadism in the "Non-Forensic" Patient. In Brett Kahr (Ed.), *New Horizons in Forensic Psychotherapy: Exploring the Work of Estela V. Welldon*, pp. 239–261. London: Routledge / Taylor and Francis Group, and Abingdon, Oxfordshire: Routledge / Taylor and Francis Group.

Kahr, Brett (2018b). Sexual Cruelty in the Marital Bed: Unconscious Sadism in Non-Forensic Couples. In Amita Sehgal (Ed.), *Sadism: Psychoanalytic Developmental Perspectives*. London: Routledge / Taylor and Francis Group, and Abingdon, Oxfordshire: Routledge / Taylor and Francis Group.

Kahr, Brett (2020). *Winnicott's* Anni Horribiles: *The Creation of "Hate in the Counter-Transference"*. London: Routledge / Taylor and Francis Group, and Abingdon, Oxfordshire: Routledge / Taylor and Francis Group.

Kanter, Joel (2004). Clare Winnicott: Her Life and Legacy. In Clare Winnicott, *Face to Face with Children: The Life and Work of Clare Winnicott*, Joel Kanter (Ed.), pp. 1–94. London: H. Karnac (Books).

Karon, Bertram P., and VandenBos, Gary R. (1981). *Psychotherapy of Schiz-ophrenia: The Treatment of Choice*. New York: Jason Aronson.

Khan, M. Masud R. (1963). Silence as Communication. *Bulletin of the Men-ninger Clinic, 27*, 300–313.

Khan, Masud (1987). Foreword. In Anne Clancier and Jeannine Kalmano-vitch (Eds.), *Winnicott and Paradox: From Birth to Creation*, Alan Sheri-dan (Transl.), pp. xvi–xvii. London: Tavistock Publications.

Khan, M. Masud R. (1988). *When Spring Comes: Awakenings in Clinical Psy-choanalysis*. London: Chatto & Windus.

Kiecolt-Glaser, Janice K.; Loving, Timothy J.; Stowell, Jeffrey R.; Malar-key, William B.; Lemeshow, Stanley; Dickinson, Stephanie L.; and Glaser, Ronald (2005). Hostile Marital Interactions, Proinflammatory Cytokine Production, and Wound Healing. *Archives of General Psy-chiatry, 62*, 1377–1384.

Kiernan, Kathleen (1991). Changing Marriage Patterns. *Journal of Social Work Practice, 5*, 123–131.

King, Pearl (Ed.) (2003a). *No Ordinary Psychoanalyst: The Exceptional Con-tributions of John Rickman*. London: H. Karnac (Books).

King, Pearl (2003b). Introduction: The Rediscovery of John Rickman and His Work. In Pearl King (Ed.), *No Ordinary Psychoanalyst: The Exceptional Contributions of John Rickman*, pp. 1–68. London: H. Karnac (Books).

Klauber, John (1961). The Structure of the Session as a Guide to Interpre-tation. In *Difficulties in the Analytic Encounter*, pp. 77–90. New York: Jason Aronson, 1981.

Klauber, John (1966). Die Struktur der psychoanalytischen Sitzung als Leitlinie für die Deutungsarbeit. *Psyche, 20*, 29–39.

Klauber, John (1971a). Übertragung und Deutung in der psychoana-lytischen Therapie, Jeannette Friedeberg (Transl.). In Hans-Joachim Bannach and Gerhard Maetze (Eds.), *Psychoanalyse in Berlin: Beiträge zur Geschichte, Theorie und Praxis. 50-Jahr-Gedenkfeier des Berliner Psy-choanalytischen Instituts (Karl Abraham-Institut)*, pp. 153–162. Meisen-heim: Verlag Anton Hain.

Klauber, John (1971b). On the Relationship of Transference and Interpre-tation in Psychoanalytic Therapy. *Scientific Bulletin: The British Psycho-Analytical Society and the Institute of Psycho-Analysis, 46*, 8–17.

Klauber, John (1972). On the Relationship of Transference and Interpreta-tion in Psychoanalytic Therapy. *International Journal of Psycho-Analy-sis, 53*, 385–391.

Klauber, John (1980). Formulating Interpretations in Clinical Psychoa-nalysis. *International Journal of Psycho-Analysis, 61*, 195–201.

Klein, Melanie (1927a). The Psychological Principles of Infant Analysis. *International Journal of Psycho-Analysis*, *8*, 25–37.

Klein, Melanie (1927b). Symposium on Child-Analysis. *International Journal of Psycho-Analysis*, *8*, 339–370.

Klein, Melanie (1932). *Die Psychoanalyse des Kindes*. Vienna: Internationaler Psychoanalytischer Verlag.

Klein, Melanie (1946). Notes on Some Schizoid Mechanisms. *International Journal of Psycho-Analysis*, *27*, 99–110.

Langland, William (c. 1362–1399). Will's Visions of Piers Plowman, Do-Well, Do-Better and Do-Best. In George Kane and E. Talbot Donaldson (Eds.), *Piers Plowman: The B Version. Will's Visions of Piers Plowman, Do-Well, Do-Better and Do-Best. An Edition in the Form of Trinity College Cambridge MS B.15.17, Corrected and Restored from the Known Evidence, with Variant Readings*, pp. 227–681. London: University of London/Athlone Press, 1975.

Langs, Robert (2002). D.W. Winnicott: The Transitional Thinker. In Brett Kahr (Ed.), *The Legacy of Winnicott: Essays on Infant and Child Mental Health*, pp. 13–22. London: H. Karnac (Books)/Other Press.

Lewin, Bertram D. (1930). Kotschmieren, Menses und weibliches Über-Ich. *Internationale Zeitschrift für Psychoanalyse*, *16*, 43–56.

Lewis, Jane (1991). *Women and Social Action in Victorian and Edwardian England*. Aldershot, Hampshire: Edward Elgar.

Little, Margaret (1971). Letter to Clare Winnicott, 26 January. PP/DWW/G/6/1. Folder 1. Donald Woods Winnicott Collection. Archives and Manuscripts, Rare Materials Room, Wellcome Library, Wellcome Collection, The Wellcome Building, London.

Little, Margaret I. (1985). Winnicott Working in Areas Where Psychotic Anxieties Predominate: A Personal Record. *Free Associations*, No. 3, 9–42.

Lynch, Joseph H. (1992). *The Medieval Church: A Brief History*. London: Longman, and Harlow, Essex: Longman Group UK.

Lyth, Isabel Menzies; Scott, Ann; and Young, Robert M. (1988). Reflections on My Work: Isabel Menzies Lyth in Conversation with Ann Scott and Robert M. Young. In Isabel Menzies Lyth, *Containing Anxiety in Institutions: Selected Essays, Volume I*, pp. 1–42. London: Free Association Books.

Mackintosh, James M. (1944). *The War and Mental Health in England*. New York: Commonwealth Fund, and London: Humphrey Milford/Oxford University Press.

Mahony, Patrick J. (1997a). An Introduction to Clifford Scott: His Theory, Technique, Manner of Thinking and Self-Expression. In Michel

Grignon (Ed.), *Psychoanalysis and the Zest for Living: Reflections and Psychoanalytic Writings in Memory of W.C.M. Scott*, pp. 89–129. Binghamton, New York: Esf Publishers.

Mahony, Patrick J. (1997b). W.C.M. Scott and Otherness. In Michel Grignon (Ed.), *Psychoanalysis and the Zest for Living: Reflections and Psychoanalytic Writings in Memory of W.C.M. Scott*, pp. 81–85. Binghamton, New York: Esf Publishers, 1997.

Malcolm, Ruth Riesenberg (1986). Interpretation: The Past in the Present. *International Review of Psycho-Analysis, 13*, 433–443.

Mannin, Ethel (1971). *Young in the Twenties: A Chapter of Autobiography.* London: Hutchinson of London/Hutchinson and Company (Publishers).

Mannoni, Maud (1964). *L'Enfant arriéré et sa mère: Étude psychanalytique.* Paris: Éditions du Seuil.

Mannoni, Maud (1967). *L'Enfant, sa "maladie" et les autres: Le Symptôme et la parole.* Paris: Éditions du Seuil.

Mannoni, Maud (1999). Words of Greeting: Psychoanalysis and Handicap. In Johan De Groef and Evelyn Heinemann (Eds.), *Psychoanalysis and Mental Handicap*, Andrew Weller (Transl.), pp. 1–6. London: Free Association Books.

Marr, Andrew (2007). *A History of Modern Britain.* London: Macmillan/Pan Macmillan.

Marriage Guidance Centres Committee (1946). Meeting, Monday, 9 December. Minutes. In *Marriage Guidance Centres: Agenda and Minutes. From: 22.1.46* (1946–1956). SA/TCC/A/3/1/7. Tavistock Centre for Couple Relationships. Archives and Manuscripts, Rare Materials Room, Wellcome Library, Wellcome Collection, The Wellcome Building, London.

Marriage Welfare Centres Committee (1948). Meeting, Monday, 31 May at 10.30 a.m. Minutes. In *Marriage Guidance Centres: Agenda and Minutes. From: 22.1.46* (1946–1956). SA/TCC/A/3/1/7. Tavistock Centre for Couple Relationships. Archives and Manuscripts, Rare Materials Room, Wellcome Library, Wellcome Collection, The Wellcome Building, London.

Marriage Welfare Committee (1948). Meeting Held at the Tavistock Institute of Human Relations on Monday 14 June at 10 o'clock. Minutes. In *Marriage Guidance Centres: Agenda and Minutes. From: 22.1.46* (1946–1956). SA/TCC/A/3/1/7. Tavistock Centre for Couple Relationships. Archives and Manuscripts, Rare Materials Room, Wellcome Library, Wellcome Collection, The Wellcome Building, London.

Marwick, Arthur (1982). *British Society Since 1945*. London: Allen Lane/ Penguin Books.

McDougall, Joyce (2003). Donald Winnicott the Man: Reflections and Recollections. In *Donald Winnicott. The Man: Reflections and Recollections*, pp. 17–37. London: Karnac (Books), and Ruislip, Middlesex: Winnicott Clinic of Psychotherapy.

Meier, Richard (2011). *Briefing Paper 1*. London: Tavistock Centre for Couple Relationships, Tavistock Institute of Medical Psychology.

Meissner, William W. (1991). *What Is Effective in Psychoanalytic Therapy: The Move from Interpretation to Relation*. Northvale, NJ: Jason Aronson.

Memorandum on Visit to the Cassel Hospital on Monday, 28th June 1948, by Mr. Astbury, Miss Menzies and Mrs Eichholz (1948). Unpublished Memorandum. SA/TCC/A/2/3. Tavistock Centre for Couple Relationships. Archives and Manuscripts, Rare Materials Room, Wellcome Library, Wellcome Collection, The Wellcome Building, London.

Menaker, Esther (1989). *Appointment in Vienna: An American Psychoanalyst Recalls Her Student Days in Pre-War Austria*. New York: St. Martin's Press.

Menninger, Karl (1958). *Theory of Psychoanalytic Technique*. New York: Basic Books.

Menzies, Isabel E. P. (1949). Factors Affecting Family Breakdown in Urban Communities: A Preliminary Study Leading to the Establishment of Two Pilot Family Discussion Bureaux. *Human Relations*, 2, 363–373.

Milner, Marion (1969). *The Hands of the Living God: An Account of a Psychoanalytic Treatment*. London: Hogarth Press and the Institute of Psycho-Analysis.

Milner, Marion (2012). *Bothered by Alligators*. London: Routledge / Taylor and Francis Group, and Hove, East Sussex: Routledge / Taylor and Francis Group.

Mostofsky, Elizabeth; Penner, Elizabeth Anne; and Mittleman, Murray A. (2014). Outbursts of Anger as a Trigger of Acute Cardiovascular Events: A Systematic Review and Meta-Analysis. *European Heart Journal*, 35, 1404–1410.

Motz, Anna (2014). *Toxic Couples: The Psychology of Domestic Violence*. London: Routledge / Taylor and Francis Group, and Hove, East Sussex: Routledge / Taylor and Francis Group.

Mowat, Charles Loch (1961). *The Charity Organisation Society: 1869–1913. Its Ideas and Work*. London: Methuen and Company.

Muirhead, Campbell (1987). *The Diary of a Bomb Aimer*. Speldhurst, Tunbridge Wells, Kent: Spellmount.

Nijinsky, Romola (1933). *Nijinsky*. London: Victor Gollancz.

Nijinsky, Tamara (1991). *Nijinsky and Romola*. London: Bachman and Turner/United Arts Publishers.

O'Driscoll, David (1999). A Short History of People with Learning Difficulties. Unpublished manuscript.

O'Driscoll, David (2000). *"The Need for a Better Understanding of the Emotional Life of the Feebleminded": Two Pioneers of Psychoanalytic Psychotherapy with People with Learning Difficulties*. MA dissertation in Psychotherapy and Counselling, City University, London, at School of Psychotherapy and Counselling, Regent's College, Inner Circle, Regent's Park, London.

O'Driscoll, David (2009). Psychotherapy and Intellectual Disability: A Historical View. In Tamsin Cottis (Ed.), *Intellectual Disability, Trauma and Psychotherapy*, pp. 9–28. London: Routledge / Taylor and Francis Group, and Hove, East Sussex: Routledge / Taylor and Francis Group.

Orbach, Susie (1999). *The Impossibility of Sex*. London: Allen Lane/Penguin Press, Penguin Books, Penguin Group.

Oremland, Jerome D. (1991). *Interpretation and Interaction: Psychoanalysis or Psychotherapy?* Hillsdale, NJ: Analytic Press.

Ortmann, David M., and Sprott, Richard A. (2013). *Sexual Outsiders: Understanding BDSM Sexualities and Communities*. Lanham, MD: Rowman and Littlefield.

Ostwald, Peter (1991). *Vaslav Nijinsky: A Leap into Madness*. New York: Lyle Stuart.

Pao, Ping-Nie (1977). The Experience at Chestnut Lodge on Long-Term Treatment of Psychotic States, with Particular Reference to Inexact Interpretations. In Colette Chiland and Paul Bequart (Eds.), *Long-Term Treatment of Psychotic States*, pp. 314–331. New York: Human Sciences Press.

Park, B. (1950). Letter to Enid Eichholz, 17 February. SA/TCC/A/2/5. Tavistock Centre for Couple Relationships. Archives and Manuscripts, Rare Materials Room, Wellcome Library, Wellcome Collection, The Wellcome Building, London.

Payn, Graham, and Morley, Sheridan (1982). 1947. In Noël Coward, *The Noel Coward Diaries*, Graham Payn and Sheridan Morley (Eds.), p. 75. London: George Weidenfeld and Nicolson.

Pearce, Robert (1994). *Attlee's Labour Governments: 1945–51*. London: Routledge.

Pearce, Robert (1997). *Attlee*. London: Longman, and Harlow, Essex: Addison Wesley Longman.

Pflaum, Rosalind (1989). *Grand Obsession: Madame Curie and Her World*. New York: Doubleday/Bantam Doubleday Dell Publishing Group.

Rankin-Esquer, Lynn A.; Deeter, Allison; and Taylor, Craig Barr (2000). Coronary Heart Disease and Couples. In Karen B. Schmaling and Tamara Goldman Sher (Eds.), *The Psychology of Couples and Illness: Theory, Research, and Practice*, pp. 43–70. Washington, DC: American Psychological Association.

Rees, John Rawlings (1945). *The Shaping of Psychiatry by War*. New York: W.W. Norton and Company.

Rickman, John (1926a). A Psychological Factor in the Aetiology of Descensus Uteri, Laceration of the Perineum and Vaginismus. *International Journal of Psycho-Analysis*, 7, 363–365.

Rickman, John (1926b). A Survey: The Development of the Psycho-Analytical Theory of the Psychoses. 1894–1926. [Part I]. *British Journal of Medical Psychology*, 6, 270–294.

Rickman, John (1927a). A Survey: The Development of the Psycho-Analytical Theory of the Psychoses. 1894–1926. [Part II]. *British Journal of Medical Psychology*, 7, 94–124.

Rickman, John (1927b). A Survey: The Development of the Psycho-Analytical Theory of the Psychoses. 1894–1926. [Part III]. *British Journal of Medical Psychology*, 7, 321–374.

Rickman, John (1928). *Index Psychoanalyticus: 1893–1926. Being an Authors' Index of Papers on Psycho-Analysis*. London: Leonard and Virginia Woolf at the Hogarth Press, and the Institute of Psycho-Analysis.

Rickman, John (1932). The Psychology of Crime: IV. *British Journal of Medical Psychology*, 12, 264–269.

Rickman, John (1939). The Medical Section of the British Psychological Society: 1901. In D'Arcy Power (Ed.), *British Medical Societies*, pp. 240–252. London: Medical Press and Circular.

Rickman, John (Ed.) (1940a). *Children in War-Time: The Uprooted Child, the Problem of the Young Child, the Deprived Mother, Foster-Parents, Visiting, the Teacher's Problems, Homes for Difficult Children*. London: New Education Fellowship.

Rickman, John (1940b). Introduction. In John Rickman (Ed.), *Children in War-Time: The Uprooted Child, the Problem of the Young Child, the Deprived Mother, Foster-Parents, Visiting, the Teacher's Problems, Homes for Difficult Children*, pp. 3–5. London: New Education Fellowship.

Rickman, John (1940c). On the Nature of Ugliness and the Creative Impulse: (Marginalia Psychoanalytica. II). *International Journal of Psycho-Analysis*, 21, 294–313.

Rickman, John (1943). The Psychiatric Interview in the Social Setting of a War Office Selection Board. In Pearl King (Ed.), *No Ordinary Psychoanalyst: The Exceptional Contributions of John Rickman*, pp. 132–139. London: H. Karnac (Books), 2003.

Rickman, John (1947). Psychology in Medical Education. *British Medical Journal*, 6 September, pp. 363–366.

Rickman, John (1948). The Application of Psychoanalytical Principles to Hospital In-Patients. *Journal of Mental Science*, 94, 764–766.

Roazen, Paul (1975). *Freud and His Followers*. New York: Alfred A. Knopf.

Roazen, Paul (1995). *How Freud Worked: First-Hand Accounts of Patients*. Northvale, NJ: Jason Aronson.

Rosenfeld, Herbert (1987). *Impasse and Interpretation: Therapeutic and Anti-Therapeutic Factors in the Psychoanalytic Treatment of Psychotic, Borderline, and Neurotic Patients*. London: Tavistock Publications.

Rosenfeld, Sara (1968). Choice of Symptom: Notes on a Case of Retention. *Journal of Child Psychotherapy*, 2 (2), 38–49.

Rothstein, Arnold (1983). Interpretation: Toward a Contemporary Understanding of the Term. *Journal of the American Psychoanalytic Association*, 31, 237–245.

Rudnytsky, Peter L. (2000). Enid Balint: The Broken Couch. In Peter L. Rudnystky (Ed.), *Psychoanalytic Conversations: Interviews with Clinicians, Commentators, and Critics*, pp. 1–25. Hillsdale, NJ: Analytic Press.

Rudnytsky, Peter L. (2011). *Rescuing Psychoanalysis from Freud and Other Essays in Re-vision*. London: Karnac Books.

Rushforth, Winifred (1984). *Ten Decades of Happenings*. London: Gateway Books.

Savage, N. G. (1952). Letter to Helen Bolland, 6 August. SA/TCC/B/2/1. Tavistock Centre for Couple Relationships. Archives and Manuscripts, Rare Materials Room, Wellcome Library, Wellcome Collection, The Wellcome Building, London.

Scott, W. Clifford M. (1948). Psychiatric Problems Amongst Evacuated Children: A Contribution to the Symposium on 'Lessons for Child Psychiatry'. Given at a Meeting of the Medical Section of the British Psychological Society on 27 February 1946. *British Journal of Medical Psychology*, 21, 171–174.

Segal, Hanna (1973). *Introduction to the Work of Melanie Klein: New, Enlarged Edition*. London: Hogarth Press and the Institute of Psycho-Analysis.

Segal, Hanna (1979). Postscript 1979: The Curative Factors in Psychoanalysis. In *The Work of Hanna Segal: A Kleinian Approach to Clinical Practice*, pp. 79–80. New York: Jason Aronson, 1981.

Segal, Hanna M. (1994). Paranoid Anxiety and Paranoia. In John M. Oldham and Stanley Bone (Eds.), *Paranoia: New Psychoanalytic Perspectives*, pp. 17–26. Madison, CT: International Universities Press.

Segal, Hanna (2006). Reflections on Truth, Tradition, and the Psychoanalytic Tradition of Truth. *American Imago*, *63*, 283–292.

Seward, Desmond (2014). *The Demon's Brood*. London: Constable.

Shane, Morton (1967). Encopresis in a Latency Boy: An Arrest Along a Developmental Line. *Psychoanalytic Study of the Child*, *22*, 296–314. New York: International Universities Press.

Simmel, Ernst (1940). Sigmund Freud: The Man and His Work. *Psychoanalytic Quarterly*, *9*, 163–176.

Simon, George (1949). Report on the Portable X-Ray Examination of the Chest, 15 February. PP/DWW/G.4. Donald Woods Winnicott Collection. Archives and Manuscripts, Rare Materials Room, Wellcome Library, Wellcome Collection, The Wellcome Building, London.

Sinason, Valerie (1986). Secondary Handicap and its Relationship to Trauma. *Psychoanalytic Psychotherapy*, *2*, 131–154.

Sinason, Valerie (1988). Smiling, Swallowing, Sickening and Stupefying: The Effect of Sexual Abuse on the Child. *Psychoanalytic Psychotherapy*, *3*, 97–111.

Sinason, Valerie (1990). Individual Psychoanalytical Psychotherapy with Severely and Profoundly Handicapped Patients. In Anton Došen, Adriaan van Gennep, and Gosewijn J. Zwanikken (Eds.), *Treatment of Mental Illness and Behavioral Disorder in the Mentally Retarded: Proceedings of the International Congress. May 3–4, 1990. Amsterdam, The Netherlands*, pp. 71–80. Leiden: Logon Publications.

Sinason, Valerie (1991a). Interpretations That Feel Horrible to Make and a Theoretical Unicorn. *Journal of Child Psychotherapy*, *17*, 11–24.

Sinason, Valerie (1991b). A Brief and Selective Look at the History of Disability. Unpublished manuscript.

Sinason, Valerie (1992). *Mental Handicap and the Human Condition: New Approaches from the Tavistock*. London: Free Association Books.

Sinason, Valerie (1999). Psychoanalysis and Mental Handicap: Experience from the Tavistock Clinic. In Johan De Groef and Evelyn Heinemann (Eds.), *Psychoanalysis and Mental Handicap*, Andrew Weller (Transl.), pp. 194–206. London: Free Association Books.

Sinason, Valerie (2010). *Mental Handicap and the Human Condition: An Analytic Approach to Intellectual Disability. Revised Edition*. London: Free Association Books.

Stansky, Peter (2007). *The First Day of the Blitz: September 7, 1940*. New Haven, CT: Yale University Press.

Stephen, Adrian (1940). Letter to Vanessa Bell, 24 June. Quoted in Jean

MacGibbon, *There's the Lighthouse: A Biography of Adrian Stephen*, p. 154. London: James and James (Publishers), 1997.

Sterba, Editha (1934). Aus der Analyse eines Zweijährigen. *Zeitschrift für psychoanalytische Pädagogik, 8*, 37–72.

Sterba, Richard (1941). The Abuse of Interpretation. *Psychiatry, 4*, 9–12.

Sterba, Richard F. (1982). *Reminiscences of a Viennese Psychoanalyst*. Detroit, MI: Wayne State University Press.

Stern, Daniel N.; Sander, Louis W.; Nahum, Jeremy P.; Harrison, Alexandra M.; Lyons-Ruth, Karlen; Morgan, Alec C.; Bruschweiler-Stern, Nadia; and Tronick, Edward Z. (1998). Non-Interpretive Mechanisms in Psychoanalytic Therapy: The "Something More" Than Interpretation. *International Journal of Psycho-Analysis, 79*, 903–921.

Strachey, Alix (1924). Letter to James Strachey, 29 December. In James Strachey and Alix Strachey, *Bloomsbury/Freud: The Letters of James and Alix Strachey, 1924–1925*, Perry Meisel and Walter Kendrick (Eds.), pp. 165–166. New York: Basic Books, 1985.

Strachey, Giles Lytton (1908). Letter to Virginia Stephen, 24 August. In Virginia Woolf and Lytton Strachey, *Letters*, Leonard Woolf and James Strachey (Eds.), pp. 15–17. London: Hogarth Press/Chatto and Windus, 1956.

Strachey, James (1934). The Nature of the Therapeutic Action of Psycho-Analysis. *International Journal of Psycho-Analysis, 15*, 127–159.

Sutherland, John D. (1955). Letter to Lily Pincus, 11 October. SA/TCC/A/2/8. Tavistock Centre for Couple Relationships. Archives and Manuscripts, Rare Materials Room, Wellcome Library, Wellcome Collection, The Wellcome Building, London.

Sutherland, John D. (1985). Bion Revisited: Group Dynamics and Group Psychotherapy. In Malcolm Pines (Ed.), *Bion and Group Psychotherapy*, pp. 47–86. London: Routledge & Kegan Paul.

Syllabus for the Advanced Course for Post Graduate Case Workers (1951). SA/TCC/A/2/5. Tavistock Centre for Couple Relationships. Archives and Manuscripts, Rare Materials Room, Wellcome Library, Wellcome Collection, The Wellcome Building, London.

Tavistock Centre for Couple Relationships (2015). *Annual Review: 2015*. London: Tavistock Centre for Couple Relationships.

Taylor, James (n.d.). Letter to Donald W. Winnicott. n.d. PP/DWW/B/A/8. Donald Woods Winnicott Collection. Archives and Manuscripts, Rare Materials Room, Wellcome Library, Wellcome Collection, The Wellcome Building, London.

Thomas-Symonds, Nicklaus (2010). *Attlee: A Life in Politics*. London: I.B. Tauris & Co.

Trist, Eric (1985). Working with Bion in the 1940s: The Group Decade. In Malcolm Pines (Ed.), *Bion and Group Psychotherapy*, pp. 1–46. London: Routledge & Kegan Paul.

U.N.E.S.C.O. (1945). The Constitution, United Nations Educational, Scientific and Cultural Organization. [http://www.unesco.org/new/en/unesco/about-us/who-we-are/history/constitution/; accessed on 15 July 2017].

Valenstein, Elliot S. (1986). *Great and Desperate Cures: The Rise and Decline of Psychosurgery and Other Radical Treatments for Mental Illness*. New York: Basic Books.

Vieyra, Rosita Braunstein (1989). Biographical Notes on Dr Eduard Silberstein, Compiled by his Granddaughter, Rosita Braunstein Vieyra. In Sigmund Freud, *Jugendbriefe an Eduard Silberstein: 1871–1881*, Walter Boehlich (Ed.), pp. 217–219. Frankfurt am Main: S. Fischer Verlag.

Walker, Evelyn, and Young, Perry Deane (1986). *A Killing Cure*. New York: Henry Holt & Co.

Wallerstein, Robert S. (2015). Psychoanalysis as I Have Known It: 1949–2013. *Psychoanalytic Dialogues, 25*, 536–556.

Ward, Mary Jane (1946). *The Snake Pit*. New York: Random House.

Webster, Charles (1988). *The Health Services Since the War: Volume I. Problems of Health Care. The National Health Service Before 1957*. London: Her Majesty's Stationery Office.

Weddell, Doreen (1949). Letter to Enid Eicholz [*sic*] [Enid Eichholz], 25 February. SA/TCC/A/2/3. Tavistock Centre for Couple Relationships. Archives and Manuscripts, Rare Materials Room, Wellcome Library, Wellcome Collection, The Wellcome Building, London.

Weitzman, Susan (2000). *"Not to People Like Us": Hidden Abuse in Upscale Marriages*. New York: Basic Books.

Welldon, Estela V. (1993). Forensic Psychotherapy and Group Analysis. *Group Analysis, 26*, 487–502.

Welldon, Estela V. (1994). Forensic Psychotherapy. In Petruska Clarkson and Michael Pokorny (Eds.), *The Handbook of Psychotherapy*, pp. 470–493. London: Routledge.

Welldon, Estela (2012). Couples Who Kill: The Malignant Bonding. In John Adlam, Anne Aiyegbusi, Pam Kleinot, Anna Motz, and Christopher Scanlon (Eds.), *The Therapeutic Milieu Under Fire: Security and Insecurity in Forensic Mental Health*, pp. 162–172. London: Jessica Kingsley Publishers.

Widom, Cathy Spatz (1977). A Methodology for Studying Noninstitutionalized Psychopaths. *Journal of Consulting and Clinical Psychology, 45*, 674–683.

Willis, Graham C. (1993). *Unspeakable Crimes: Prevention Work with Perpetrators of Child Sexual Abuse*. London: Children's Society.

Wilson, A. Thomson M. (1939). Psychological Observations on Haematemesis. *British Journal of Medical Psychology, 18,* 112–121.

Wilson, A. Thomson M. (1946). The Serviceman Comes Home. *Pilot Papers, 1,* 9–28.

Wilson, A. Thomson M. (1947). Evolution of Civil Resettlement [pp. 735–736]. In A. Thomson M. Wilson, Martin Doyle, and John Kelnar, Group Techniques in a Transitional Community. *The Lancet,* 31 May, pp. 735–738.

Wilson, A. Thomson M. (1949). Some Reflections and Suggestions on the Prevention and Treatment of Marital Problems. *Human Relations, 2,* 233–252.

Wilson, A. Thomson M.; Doyle, Martin; and Kelnar, John (1947). Group Techniques in a Transitional Community. *The Lancet,* 31 May, pp. 735–738.

Wilson, A. Thomson M.; Menzies, Isabel; and Eichholz, Enid (1949). The Marriage Welfare Sub-Committee of the Family Welfare Association. *Social Work, 6,* 258–262.

Wilson, Shula (2003). *Disability, Counselling and Psychotherapy: Challenges and Opportunities*. Houndmills, Basingstoke, Hampshire: Palgrave Macmillan.

Winnicott, Clare (1978). D.W.W.: A Reflection. In Simon A. Grolnick, Leonard Barkin, and Werner Muensterberger (Eds.), *Between Reality and Fantasy: Transitional Objects and Phenomena*, pp. 17–33. New York: Jason Aronson.

Winnicott, Donald W. (1938). Letter to W. Clifford M. Scott. 12 September. Cited in Patrick J. Mahony, W.C.M. Scott and Otherness. In Michel Grignon (Ed.), *Psychoanalysis and the Zest for Living: Reflections and Psychoanalytic Writings in Memory of W.C.M. Scott*, pp. 81–85. Binghamton, New York: Esf Publishers, 1997.

Winnicott, Donald W. (1939). Letter to W. Clifford M. Scott. 16 October. Cited in Patrick J. Mahony, W.C.M. Scott and Otherness. In Michel Grignon (Ed.), *Psychoanalysis and the Zest for Living: Reflections and Psychoanalytic Writings in Memory of W.C.M. Scott*, pp. 81–85. Binghamton, New York: Esf Publishers, 1997.

Winnicott, Donald W. (1941). The Observation of Infants in a Set Situation. In Donald W. Winnicott, *Collected Papers: Through Paediatrics to Psycho-Analysis*, pp. 52–69. New York: Basic Books, 1958.

Winnicott, Donald W. (1943a). Prefrontal Leucotomy. *The Lancet,* 10 April, p. 475.

Winnicott, Donald W. (1943b). Shock Treatment of Mental Disorder. *British Medical Journal*, 25 December, pp. 829–830.

Winnicott, Donald W. (1943c). Treatment of Mental Disease by Induction of Fits. In Donald W. Winnicott, *Psycho-Analytic Explorations*, Clare Winnicott, Ray Shepherd, and Madeleine Davis (Eds.), pp. 516–521. London: H. Karnac (Books), 1989.

Winnicott, Donald W. (1944a). Shock Therapy. *British Medical Journal*, 12 February, pp. 234–235.

Winnicott, Donald W. (1944b). Introduction to a Symposium on the Psycho-Analytic Contribution to the Theory of Shock Therapy. In Donald W. Winnicott, *Psycho-Analytic Explorations*, Clare Winnicott, Ray Shepherd, and Madeleine Davis (Eds.), pp. 525–528. London: H. Karnac (Books), 1989.

Winnicott, Donald W. (1944c). Kinds of Psychological Effect of Shock Therapy. In Donald W. Winnicott, *Psycho-Analytic Explorations*, Clare Winnicott, Ray Shepherd, and Madeleine Davis (Eds.), pp. 529–533. London: H. Karnac (Books), 1989.

Winnicott, Donald W. (1945a). Primitive Emotional Development. *International Journal of Psycho-Analysis*, 26, 137–143.

Winnicott, Donald W. (1945b). The Return of the Evacuated Child. In Donald W. Winnicott, *The Child and the Outside World: Studies in Developing Relationships*, Janet Hardenberg (Ed.), pp. 88–92. London: Tavistock Publications, 1957.

Winnicott, Donald W. (1945c). Physical Therapy in Mental Disorder. *British Medical Journal*, 22 December, pp. 901–902.

Winnicott, Donald W. (1946). Letter to William Beveridge, Lord Beveridge, 15 October. In Donald W. Winnicott, *The Spontaneous Gesture: Selected Letters of D.W. Winnicott*, F. Robert Rodman (Ed.), p. 8. Cambridge, MA: Harvard University Press, 1987.

Winnicott, Donald W. (1947a). Physical Therapy of Mental Disorder. *British Medical Journal*, 17 May, pp. 688–689.

Winnicott, Donald W. (1947b). Battle Neurosis Treated with Leucotomy. *British Medical Journal*, 13 December, p. 974.

Winnicott, Donald W. (1948). Children's Hostels in War and Peace: A Contribution to the Symposium on "Lessons for Child Psychiatry". Given at a Meeting of the Medical Section of the British Psychological Society, 27 February 1946. *British Journal of Medical Psychology*, 21, 175–180.

Winnicott, Donald W. (1949a). *The Ordinary Devoted Mother and Her Baby: Nine Broadcast Talks. (Autumn 1949)*. London: C.A. Brock and Company.

Winnicott, Donald W. (1949b). Hate in the Counter-Transference. *International Journal of Psycho-Analysis*, *30*, 69–74.

Winnicott, Donald W. (1949c). Hate in the Countertransference. In Donald W. Winnicott, *Collected Papers: Through Paediatrics to Psycho-Analysis*, pp. 194–203. New York: Basic Books, 1958.

Winnicott, Donald W. (1949d). Birth Memories, Birth Trauma, and Anxiety. In Donald W. Winnicott, *Collected Papers: Through Paediatrics to Psycho-Analysis*, pp. 174–193. London: Tavistock Publications, 1958.

Winnicott, Donald W. (1949e). Leucotomy. *British Medical Students' Journal*, *3* (2), 35–38.

Winnicott, Donald W. (1949f). Letter to Ronald MacKeith, 10 February. Joyce Coles Papers. Ealing, London.

Winnicott, Donald W. (1949g). Letter to John Rickman, 26 April. Joyce Coles Papers. Ealing, London.

Winnicott, Donald W. (1949h). Letter to The Editor, *The Medical Echo*, 18 August. Joyce Coles Papers. Ealing, London.

Winnicott, Donald W. (1949i). Report on Miss "Laetitia Ingleby". Aet 30. Unpublished manuscript. Joyce Coles Papers. Ealing, London.

Winnicott, Donald W. (1951a). Leucotomy in Psychosomatic Disorders. *The Lancet*, 18 August, pp. 314–315.

Winnicott, Donald W. (1951b). Ethics of Prefrontal Leucotomy. *British Medical Journal*, 25 August, pp. 496–497.

Winnicott, Donald W. (1951c). Notes on the General Implications of Leucotomy. In Donald W. Winnicott, *Psycho-Analytic Explorations*, Clare Winnicott, Ray Shepherd, and Madeleine Davis (Eds.), pp. 548–552. London: H. Karnac (Books), 1989.

Winnicott, Donald W. (1953). Transitional Objects and Transitional Phenomena: A Study of the First Not-Me Possession. *International Journal of Psycho-Analysis*, *34*, 89–97.

Winnicott, Donald W. (1956a). Primary Maternal Preoccupation. In Donald W. Winnicott, *Collected Papers: Through Paediatrics to Psycho-Analysis*, pp. 300–305. London: Tavistock Publications, 1958.

Winnicott, Donald W. (1956b). Primary Maternal Preoccupation. In Donald W. Winnicott, *Collected Papers: Through Paediatrics to Psycho-Analysis*, pp. 300–305. New York: Basic Books, 1958.

Winnicott, Donald W. (1956c). The Antisocial Tendency. In Donald W. Winnicott, *Collected Papers: Through Paediatrics to Psycho-Analysis*, pp. 306–315. London: Tavistock Publications, 1958.

Winnicott, Donald W. (1956d). The Antisocial Tendency. In Donald W. Winnicott, *Collected Papers: Through Paediatrics to Psycho-Analysis*, pp. 306–315. New York: Basic Books, 1958.

Winnicott, Donald W. (1956e). Prefrontal Leucotomy. *British Medical Journal*, 28 January, pp. 229–230.

Winnicott, Donald W. (1957). Letter to Thomas Main, 25 February. In Donald W. Winnicott, *The Spontaneous Gesture: Selected Letters of D.W. Winnicott*, F. Robert Rodman (Ed.), pp. 112–114. Cambridge, MA: Harvard University Press, 1987.

Winnicott, Donald W. (1958a). *Collected Papers: Through Paediatrics to Psycho-Analysis*. London: Tavistock Publications.

Winnicott, Donald W. (1958b). *Collected Papers: Through Paediatrics to Psycho-Analysis*. New York: Basic Books.

Winnicott, Donald W. (1959). Letter to Donald Meltzer, 21 May. In Donald W. Winnicott, *The Spontaneous Gesture: Selected Letters of D.W. Winnicott*, F. Robert Rodman (Ed.), pp. 124–125. Cambridge, MA: Harvard University Press, 1987.

Winnicott, Donald W. (1960a). The Theory of the Parent–Infant Relationship. *International Journal of Psycho-Analysis*, 41, 585–595.

Winnicott, Donald W. (1960b). String. *Journal of Child Psychology and Psychiatry and Allied Disciplines*, 1, 49–52.

Winnicott, Donald W. (1962). The Aims of Psycho-Analytical Treatment. In Donald W. Winnicott, *The Maturational Processes and the Facilitating Environment: Studies in the Theory of Emotional Development*, pp. 166–170. London: Hogarth Press and the Institute of Psycho-Analysis, 1965.

Winnicott, Donald W. (1963a). Psychiatric Disorder in Terms of Infantile Maturational Processes. In Donald W. Winnicott, *The Maturational Processes and the Facilitating Environment: Studies in the Theory of Emotional Development*, pp. 230–241. London: Hogarth Press and the Institute of Psycho-Analysis, 1965.

Winnicott, Donald W. (1963b). Two Notes on the Use of Silence. In Donald W. Winnicott, *Psycho-Analytic Explorations*, Clare Winnicott, Ray Shepherd, and Madeleine Davis (Eds.), pp. 81–86. London: H. Karnac (Books), 1989.

Winnicott, Donald W. (1964a). The Neonate and His Mother. *Acta Paediatrica Latina*, 17, *Supplement*, 747–758.

Winnicott, Donald W. (1964b). Letter to John Klauber, 9 November. Box 4. File 11. Donald W. Winnicott Papers. Archives of Psychiatry, The Oskar Diethelm Library, The DeWitt Wallace Institute for the History of Psychiatry, Department of Psychiatry, Joan and Sanford I. Weill Medical College, Cornell University, The New York Presbyterian Hospital, New York, New York.

Winnicott, Donald W. (1966). Letter to David Malan, 2 December. PP/

DWW/B/B/2/2. Donald Woods Winnicott Collection. Archives and Manuscripts, Rare Materials Room, Wellcome Library, Wellcome Collection, The Wellcome Building, London.

Winnicott, Donald W. (1967). Trips into Partisanship. Unpublished typescript. PP/DWW/A/A/37. Donald Woods Winnicott Collection. Archives and Manuscripts, Wellcome Library, Wellcome Collection, The Wellcome Building, London.

Winnicott, Donald W. (1969). The Use of an Object. *International Journal of Psycho-Analysis, 50,* 711–716.

Winnicott, Donald W. (1970). The Place of the Monarchy. In Donald W. Winnicott, *Home is Where We Start From: Essays by a Psychoanalyst,* Clare Winnicott, Ray Shepherd, and Madeleine Davis (Eds.), pp. 260–268. New York: W.W. Norton and Company, 1986.

Winnicott, Donald W. (1977). *The Piggle: An Account of the Psychoanalytic Treatment of a Little Girl,* Ishak Ramzy (Ed.). New York: International Universities Press.

Winnicott, Donald W., and Britton, Clare (1947). Residential Management as Treatment for Difficult Children: The Evolution of a Wartime Hostels Scheme. *Human Relations, 1,* 87–97.

Woodhouse, Douglas (1975). Letter to Enid Balint, 9 June. SA/TCC/B/3/1. Tavistock Centre for Couple Relationships. Archives and Manuscripts, Wellcome Library, Wellcome Collection, The Wellcome Building, London.

Woodhouse, Douglas (1990). The Tavistock Institute of Marital Studies: Evolution of a Marital Agency. In Christopher Clulow (Ed.), *Marriage: Disillusion and Hope. Papers Celebrating Forty Years of the Tavistock Institute of Marital Studies,* pp. 69–119. London: H. Karnac (Books).

Wortis, Joseph (1934). Diary Entry. 21 November. In Joseph Wortis, *Fragments of an Analysis with Freud,* pp. 82–84. New York: Simon & Schuster, 1954.

Wortis, Joseph (1940). Fragments of a Freudian Analysis. *American Journal of Orthopsychiatry, 10,* 843–849.

Wurtele, Sandy K.; Kvaternick, Mary; and Franklin, Corrina F. (1992). Sexual Abuse Prevention for Preschoolers: A Survey of Parents' Behaviors, Attitudes, and Beliefs. *Journal of Child Sexual Abuse, 1,* 113–128.

Zaretsky, Eli (2004). *Secrets of the Soul: A Social and Cultural History of Psychoanalysis.* New York: Alfred A. Knopf.

Zaretsky, Eli (2016). My Life and Psychoanalysis. *American Imago, 73,* 451–468.